THE LEGACY & THE GLORY

Greatest Moments in Kentucky Basketball History

Edited by
FRANCIS J. FITZGERALD

Published by

AdCraft

ACKNOWLEDGMENTS

Chapters 1, 6, 7, 7-sidebar, 8, 9, 10-sidebar, 11, 11-sidebar, 14, 14-sidebar, 26, 28, 29, 31, 33, 42, 43, 43-sidebar, 45 and 49 have been previously published in *The New York Times*. Copyright © 1935/46/47/48/50/66/75/76/78/84/85/89 by The New York Times Company. Reprinted by permission.

Chapters 2, 10, 12, 15, 16, 17, 18, 19, 20, 21, 22, 23, 24, 26-sidebar, 27, 30, 30-sidebar, 32, 34, 35, 36, 37, 38, 39, 40, 41, 44, 44-sidebar, 46, 46-sidebar, 47, 47-sidebar, 48, 48-sidebar, 50, 51, 53 and 54 have been previously published in *The Courier-Journal*, Louisville, Ky. Reprinted by permission of *The Courier-Journal*.

Chapters 3, 4 and 5 have previously published in *The Courier-Journal*. Reprinted by permission of The Associated Press.

Chapter 13 has been previously published in *The New York Times*. Reprinted by permission of The Associated Press.

The following article is reprinted courtesy of *Sports Illustrated* from the March 7, 1966 issue. Copyright © 1966, Time Inc.
"Bravo for the Baron" by Frank Deford.
All rights reserved.

The following article is reprinted courtesy of *Sports Illustrated* from the November 23, 1992 issue. Copyright © 1992, Time Inc.
"Bluegrass Revival" by Alexander Wolff.
All rights reserved.

Research Assistance: Russell Rice, Paul Willman, Brooks Downing, Joyce Baxter, Rena Vicini and the University of Kentucky Sports Information Office; David Coyle, Joanne Heumann, Sharon Bidwell, Tom Woods, Frank Stanger and the University of Kentucky Archives.

ISBN 1-887761-01-2

Cover Design by Chris Willis; Book Design by Shayne Bowman.
Typeface: Kis-Janson

PUBLISHED BY:
AdCraft Sports Marketing
Kaden Tower, 10th Floor
6100 Dutchmans Lane
Louisville, KY 40205
(502) 473-1124

"We feel that every boy who puts on a Kentucky uniform just plays a little better than he would in one of another color."
— Adolph Rupp

CONTENTS

Contents

INTRODUCTION

WHEN I CAME to the University of Kentucky in 1989, I knew the program had its back to the wall. Much of the talent had departed following the three-year probation which the N.C.A.A. had recently levied. In addition, the upcoming schedule would be too challenging for the talent at hand.

But I knew I had two things on my side — a grand tradition as well as the best fans in the nation. Still, I had to change one thing: the perception of the program. The program's problems had left many people in the state feeling depressed. It was my job to instill confidence back into the fans, while returning to them the winning tradition they had always cherished.

We first had to survey the recent history of the program. Kentucky had last been to a Final Four in 1984, and its last national title was in 1978. The year before my arrival, the Cats had suffered their first losing season since the 1920's, so who knew what the fans' expectations would be?

Yet, the players that made up my first UK team — "The Bombinos" — had the heart, the desire and the work ethic to make the Big Blue faithful proud. The 14-14 season of 1989-90 showed the college basketball world that Kentucky would be back, stronger than ever, and sooner than most expected.

Two years later, "The Unforgettables" — Richie Farmer, Deron Feldhaus, John Pelphrey and Sean Woods — along with Jamal Mashburn, were a picture of desire on the hardwood, leading the Cats to one of the most memorable games in the history of college basketball. Unfortunately, it was a 104-103 overtime win by Duke.

The following season, the unstoppable Mashburn returned to lead us to the 1993 Final Four, and, had he not fouled out in overtime in the semi-final game against Michigan, who knows what would have happened in the championship game?

It has now been seven years since I accepted the UK job. In the past six years the program has been to one Final Four, finished in the Elite Eight twice, won four consecutive S.E.C. tournament titles, and captured one league title. Our achievements signify that the program is back on the right track.

Today, the talent level has been increased ten-fold.

We now have four McDonald's all-Americans and seven players who were Mr. Basketball selections in their respective states. The feeling of confidence at UK has been restored, and hopes of the future are painted in Kentucky blue.

Yet, that's life in the Bluegrass State. In fact, probably my biggest surprise since my arrival at UK is how much this program means to the fans. It's one thing to support the team when we're playing in Rupp Arena. It's quite another to see the support this program garners on the road. The faithful fans are so dedicated, they're always looking to the future — and not just in recruiting. They plan their lives around the Wildcats' basketball schedule — weddings, vacations, even funerals; it doesn't matter.

But what else would be expected here in the capital of college basketball — the home of five national titles, the second winningest program in the country and the top program in the Southeastern Conference?

As everyone knows, the success of the program began with legendary Coach Adolph Rupp.

Rupp was just a high school coach before he took over the UK program in 1930. He made certain his players were fundamentally sound, and like so many of my teams, they loved to push it up and down the floor.

Forty-two years later, he had earned four national titles, an Olympic gold medal and retired as the winningest basketball coach of all-time. And he had some outstanding teams.

The Fabulous Five — Ralph Beard, Kenny Rollins, Alex Groza, Wah Wah Jones and Cliff Barker — were, at the time, the best collection of talent any college program had ever seen. That squad still ranks as one of the top college teams of all-time, having won the 1948 and 1949 N.C.A.A. Championships, as well as teaming with the Phillips 66ers to win the 1948 Olympic Gold Medal.

In the early 1950's, Cliff Hagan and Frank Ramsey were two of the most dominating players on one team. After winning the 1951 N.C.A.A. Tournament, both went on to become outstanding professional players.

Vernon Hatton and Johnny Cox helped UK to its fourth national crown in 10 years in 1958. And as The Baron entered his later years, he put together one of his most overachieving squads, affectionately known as "Rupp's Runts." The starting five, which included no player taller than 6-5, was made up of Pat Riley, Larry Conley, Louie Dampier, Thad Jaracz and Tommy Kron. It was one of the most celebrated teams in UK history and came within eight points of the school's fifth national title.

Before his retirement, Rupp had opponents backpedaling, trying to figure out how to stop the school's most prolific scorer of all-time, Dan Issel.

After Rupp's departure, Joe B. Hall then had the unenviable task of following in "The Great One's" footsteps. And what a great job he did. To most, the shadow of Rupp would have been too intimidating, but Hall set his sights on the national title. In his tenure he won one N.C.A.A. crown and nearly won three.

In 1975, his squad was beaten in the final by U.C.L.A. It was a game in which the Cats were favored, but the tables were turned by the emotional Bruins, who found out that legendary coach John Wooden was resigning after the championship game.

The loss was a hard pill for the UK squad to swallow. Freshmen like Jack Givens, Rick Robey and Mike Phillips would return, and return big. After winning the N.I.T. title in 1976, the trio, with the help of Truman Claytor and transfer Kyle Macy, became the most dominant team in college basketball during the 1977-78 season. They capped the year by leading the Wildcats to a 30-2 record and their first N.C.A.A. title in 20 years, a 94-88 victory over Duke.

Hall returned to the Final Four in 1984, with the Twin Towers of Sam Bowie and Melvin Turpin, but a cold-shooting night and a Patrick Ewing-led Georgetown squad ended the Cats' run in the semi-finals.

Eddie Sutton came to the Cats following Hall's retirement and in just his first season, led the Cats to The Elite Eight finish before they were victimized by L.S.U., a team UK had beaten three times during the season.

Looking back over the years, it doesn't matter whether it's 1945 or 1995, the hopes and ambitions at UK are the same.

This book, *The Legacy and The Glory: Greatest Moments in Kentucky Basketball History*, brings to life once again the 50 biggest games in UK basketball's past 65 years. It is a wonderful collection of the many never-to-be-forgotten tales, triumphs, heart-breaking losses and those legendary UK hardcourt heroes who have made the Wildcats' tradition a special one.

And as the UK story continues, I am confident there will be more great games ahead, more thrilling finishes and more spectacular plays. There will also be more all-Americans, more S.E.C. crowns and more national titles.

But most of all, there will be more young student-athletes who will experience the UK tradition, the fans and the glory, while also receiving an outstanding education. This one-of-a-kind experience, like so many former UK lettermen have enjoyed, will lead these student-athletes to the ultimate goal — a goal of being successful in life and contributing members of society.

After all, it's not just basketball. It's Kentucky basketball.

RICK PITINO
Lexington, Kentucky
October 30, 1995

The 1930-31 Wildcats — Adolph Rupp's first team — won 15 games and lost 3. It was the beginning of college basketball's greatest dynasty.

N.Y.U. Five Beats Kentucky by 23-22 as 16,500 Look On

By Arthur J. Daley
Special to The New York Times

New York, Jan. 5, 1935 — The ball teetered on the front edge of the rim with agonizing uncertainty and then toppled through the net to give the New York University quintet its twenty-second successive victory over a two-year span in Madison Square Garden last night.

That foul goal by Sidney Gross in the last minute of play gave the Violet a 23-22 triumph over the University of Kentucky, the powerhouse of the South, in the feature game of the college double-header before basketball's largest crowd in Eastern court history.

With the steel-girdered walls of the Garden resounding to the cheers of a gathering of 16,500, Gross stepped to the fifteen-foot line with total nonchalance, crouched for a split second and then straightened up as his swinging arms propelled the spheroid to its mark.

Up it went as the breath of the huge crowd caught in unison. Up it went to the front end of the rim, bounced straight in the air and came down to bound crazily on that slender cast-iron hoop before swishing through the cords to decide for the Violet one of its hardest-earned victories. Bedlam broke loose as the ball fell through.

With that dramatic finale, the second of a series of

In the 1934-35 season, Rupp's cagers posted a record of 19 wins and 2 losses.

six college double-headers came to a close and thus ended a fray that was so bitterly fought that the score was tied six times before the issue was decided.

It was a grand show that was put on for the amazing crowd; a gathering that had seen, earlier in the evening, one of those typical metropolitan college rivalries produce — a hammer-and-tong battle. In that game, a St. John's team which had led, 13-3, at one stage in the proceedings, capitulated before the second half rally of C.C.N.Y., 32-22.

As thrilling as was that first encounter, however, with its intense display of partnership, it could hardly compare with the class that concluded the evening's entertainment. This was a struggle between teams that exemplified two entirely distinct types of basketball.

The Violet displayed a brand of play that is indigenous to the East. It was one of the fast break, the quick-cut for the basket and a short flick in. Kentucky, on

THE LINE-UPS

KENTUCKY (22)

	FG	FT	Pts.
Tucker	2	2	6
Lawrence	3	0	6
Edwards	1	4	6
Lewis	0	0	0
Anderson	1	0	2
Donohue	1	0	2
Totals	**8**	**6**	**22**

N. Y. U. (23)

	FG	FT	Pts.
Gross	2	1	5
Maidman	2	0	4
Terjesen	0	1	1
Klein	2	0	4
Schulman	1	1	3
Rubenstein	2	2	6
Totals	**9**	**5**	**23**

the other hand, demonstrated something quite new to metropolitan court circles.

The Southerners, with a background of twenty-nine victories out of their last thirty games and seventy-six out of their last eighty-five, employ a slow, deliberate style of offense that is built around thirteen set plays.

It was so sharp a contrast that the spectators, used to the swift-moving panorama of metropolitan basketball, were inclined to be impatient with the other type. But it was highly effective.

It was so effective, in fact, that N.Y.U., coming from four points behind at 22-18 with four and one-half minutes of play left, took everybody by complete surprise. It was two of the infrequent long shots at the basket that set the stage. The rangy Colonels managed twice to break an 18-18 deadlock.

The timers' watches were moving quickly toward

the close and the highly partisan Violet crowd went into ecstasies of delight as Lenny Maidman, ball-hawk that he is, caromed the ball through the hoop when Red Klein's long shot misfired.

That cut the Kentucky margin in half and the New York adherents exhorted their favorites with intense fervor to tie the score at least. They did. There was a brisk scrimmage under the N.Y.U. backboard and Gross broke clear. Maidman snapped the ball to him and the Violet captain dribbled once and laid the ball up for the field goal that brought about the deadlock.

There was only a minute to play and the two teams battled energetically for the ball, eager to gain possession for one more fling at the nets. Kentucky pressed the fight, seized the ball on the tap and worked it up. The moving block that is the Colonels' stock in trade spelled their downfall. Ed Edwards was seen by Umpire Jack Murray perpetrating a block. He was accused of picking off and Gross got the try that was to decide the game.

Prior to that dramatic finale it was nip and tuck all the way. The score, never tied in the first half as N.Y.U. trailed at the intermission, 9-8, was tied in the second at 9-all, 11-all, 13-all, 15-all, 18-all, and then at 22-all.

As was the case a week ago when a crowd of 15,000 watched N.Y.U. turn back Notre Dame, there was no standout Violet hero. Honors were pretty well distributed among Gross, Willie Rubenstein, Maidman and Milt Schulman. Rubenstein, however, was the high scorer with 5 points.

Three Southerners matched this aggregate, Jack Tucker, Edwards and Dave Lawrence. It was Edwards in the pivot position who was the keyman for the Colonels and he was so closely guarded by Irving Terjesen that the latter went out on personal fouls in the first half. Klein finished the job quite adequately.

Dave Lawrence was a favorite among all-American voters following the 1934-35 season.

CHAPTER 2

Biggest Crowd Ever Watches Notre Dame Top Kentucky

BY BRUCE DUDLEY
Special to The Courier-Journal

LOUISVILLE, Jan. 5, 1937 — "Big Time" basketball for which Louisville long has hungered, was served to the city by Notre Dame and Kentucky last night at the Jefferson County Armory, and the feast was wildly relished by the greatest gathering ever to see a game in the State. The throng, of holiday spirit and Kentucky Derby enthusiasm, 6,352 strong and jubilant, thrilled to the skill of the Wildcats and the Ramblers as they wove with adroit zest and amazing smoothness their intricate patterns of play to fashion the score at Notre Dame 41, Kentucky 28.

But it was not the score, nor who won, that was of throbbing significance. The fascination of the game itself made the result of but little consequence to the host city, which considered itself flattered at the privilege of embracing with equal fondness the two teams as old friends that had stayed away too long.

Louisville had been famished for a dish of first-flight basketball, and it ate it up, clapped its hands, smacked its lips, and is shouting for more. It had a big time at the "Big Time" game, the first to take place here. None other has been comparable in interest here since Dr. James Naismith took a pair of peach baskets and established the sport in 1891.

And a game of no more appeal than the one of last night could have been arranged for the Louisville appetite. There was our own beloved University of Kentucky, which, since the coming of Adolph Rupp in 1930 always had a sparkling team, squared off against Notre Dame — and what magic there is in the name of Notre Dame!

The success of the game is expected to bring more big college tests to Louisville.

Making the event all the more savory and palatable was the presence of three Louisville boys — Warfield Donohue, Joe Hagan and Jim Goforth, and

Carey Spicer was Rupp's first all-American, in 1930.

Rupp's 1932-33 squad, with a record of 21 wins and 3 losses, was named National Champion by the Helms Foundation.

Tubby Thompson of Jeffersonville — on the Kentucky team. The attraction further was spiced by the presence of two all-Americans, John Moir and Paul Nowak, on the Notre Dame team, which Coach George Keogan guided to the national championship last season, flecking aside en route Kentucky by a 41-20 score.

But that was last year and on the Notre Dame floor, and the Wildcats had hoped to gain revenge on the neutral floor of the Armory. This floor, however, proved to be far worse in structure and no more favorable than the Notre Dame floor. The floor simply is not suited for basketball, which means that Louisville either is going to have to give the Armory a new floor or its citizens a municipal basketball palace.

Both coaches, however, were pleased with the test. Mr. Rupp said:

"The whole story can be boiled down to the fact that we were up against too much Nowak and Moir, the all-Americans. They are real all-Americans. Before the test, Coach Keogan told me he had a good team but it had not started to click. It clicked tonight, and I don't believe any team in the world is going to beat

it. Nowak tallied sixteen points in the first half, Moir contributed a total of twelve, and there were times when it seemed that they could have scored more."

Moir played in a rubber helmet, which protected a recently fractured jaw. Nowak recently recovered from an appendicitis operation.

The loss was Kentucky's first in six tests. The victory was Notre Dame's sixth in eight starts, Northwestern and Illinois having defeated the Ramblers. Nowak was not in those games.

"It was a great game, and I enjoyed it very much, and I also enjoyed the fine crowd. It is a pleasure to play before such a gathering," Mr. Keogan asserted as hundreds surged forward to congratulate him on the victory, and have a close up look at his talented basketeers.

Dick Bray, of Cincinnati, who officiated the game with Nick Kearns, of Chicago, said that the condition of the Armory floor had prevented the teams from appearing at their best, but they looked highly efficient to the vast majority of spectators.

"The ball was hard for the fellows to follow because of the dark floor," Bray explained, "and because of its slipperiness the fellows slid into each other, which made for a rougher game than usually is played by college boys."

Thirty-three fouls were committed.

A crowd larger in number had been expected, but this merely proves that the Armory will not hold with comfort for basketball a throng greater than 6,342, for this number jammed the place, and hundreds stood on the balcony. One of those who sat at the end of the court was Gov. A.B. (Happy) Chandler who elated the fans by appearing during intermission and tossing a foul shot with no more effort than is required for him to tip his hat.

S.A. Boles, the revered "Daddy" of University of Kentucky athletics, figured the attendance. He said that 8,180 tickets were printed and of these 2,030 remained unsold. The remaining tickets — 6,150 — were either sold or used as complementaries. In addition, 192 coupons were given to schools, which

Based on his phenomenal play in 1938-39, Bernie Opper was picked to lead several all-America teams.

placed the possible paid attendance at 6,342. The gate receipts are approximately $5,700.

Kentucky trailed at the half, 28-9, but got the score to 38-28 and then the tempo really quickened. Joe Hagan led Kentucky with eight points. Ralph Carlisle of Lawrenceburg followed with six.

Carlisle opened the scoring on a free throw at Earl Brown's expense. Moir deuced the count by connecting on Walter Hodge's foul. Hogan fouled Brown

while shooting and he made both free throws to give Notre Dame a 3-1 edge. Nowak fouled Thompson and he made one of two. Nowak flipped one in from the side and Tommy Jordan's crip brought the margin to 7-2 as Kentucky took time-out.

Nowak sank a long one from the side and followed in Carlisle's attempt from out on the floor for a tip-in and a 11-2 edge. Hodge brought Kentucky into the game with a short basket but Brown cashed in on

Hagan's infraction and Nowak followed with a bucket to boost the lead to 14-4.

Hagan later netted a clean one from the side for 18-8. Nowak's 2-pointers increased Notre Dame's advantage to 21-8. With Moir, he combined to give the Ramblers a 25-8 lead. Bernie Opper missed the first but caged the second of two free throws to bring the count to 28-9 as the half ended.

Shortly after the beginning of the second half Nowak hacked Thompson, who flipped in one attempt. Thompson then committed his third infraction and Nowak missed. Hogan dribbled in to place the score at 28-12. Brown missed on Carlisle's foul, but the persistent Moir followed in. Carlisle contributed a free-toss tally.

With fifteen minutes left, Notre Dame led, 30-14, but those leaning toward the Wildcats still had hope, for the Wildcats have performed many basketball miracles. Last night though, they could not perform the miracle of keeping the Ramblers from rambling on to victory.

Hagan — everybody could follow him because of his flaming red hair — zoomed in a long shot and was given a rest by Opper. Eddie Sadowski tallied and then Nowak was blown out on fouls. Carlisle added one point and so did James Goforth. As Hagan returned to the fray, with ten minutes remaining, Kentucky paused to reflect.

THE LINE-UPS

KENTUCKY (28)

	FG	FT	Pts.
Carlisle	1	4	6
Hagan	4	0	8
Thompson	1	2	4
Donohue	0	0	0
Hodge	1	0	2
Opper	1	2	4
Walker	0	1	1
Goforth	1	1	3
Totals	**9**	**10**	**28**

NOTRE DAME (41)

	FG	FT	Pts.
Moir	3	6	12
Meyer	0	1	1
Nowak	6	4	16
Jordan	1	1	3
Brown	0	4	4
Sadowski	1	0	2
Demots	1	0	2
Wukovits	0	1	1
Ducharme	0	0	0
Totals	**12**	**17**	**41**

Opper then got the ball at long range and hit and Goforth eased one in from the side to make the margin 34-22.

Opper agitated the net with a free shot granted by Sadowski but a moment later Tommy Wukovits did the same trick. Carlisle replaced Opper after he had suffered a hard fall. J.R. Walker fouled Moir, who added a pair of points, and then Goforth fouled Moir, who looped in another tally. When Donahue replaced Goforth, Hagan nestled in a soft one and Notre Dame took time-out. Four minutes remained.

After John Demots missed a free throw off Walker, Carlisle broke loose and cripped, bringing the score to 38-27.

Moir was then told by Coach Keogan that he could knock off for the remainder of the night, and as the all-American left the floor he was given an ovation of such spontaneity and vigor his Irish heart must have warmed considerably to Louisville.

Brown fouled Carlisle and he made him sorry. Jordan, who was aggrieved by Donahue, strung another point to the Notre Dame belt. Hagan then fouled Demots as he caged a crip. It was Red's fourth personal.

An instant later the game ended during a wild scramble in the middle of the floor with the score Notre Dame 41, Kentucky 28.

CHAPTER 3

(Left to right) Leroy Edwards, Garland Lewis and Courtland Bliss in 1935.

Kentucky Stuns Pittsburgh in Sugar Bowl Battle

By The Associated Press
The Courier-Journal

New Orleans, Dec. 29, 1937 — A fast and straight shooting Kentucky basketball team that exhibited an air-tight defense defeated Pittsburgh, 40-29, in the 4th annual Sugar Bowl basketball game here tonight.

Kentucky started fast and at the half led Pittsburgh, 28-13, mainly because of close defensive work, but shortly after the start of the 2d half, Pittsburgh, led by Edward Spotovich and Robert Johnson, brought the score up to 31-29, and it seemed for a moment as though they would overtake the Kentuckians.

Joe Hagan, the Kentucky forward, then stepped

THE LINE-UPS

KENTUCKY (40)	FG	FT	Pts.
Curtis	4	2	10
Hagan	4	1	9
Thompson	4	3	11
Opper	4	0	8
Rouse	1	0	2
Goodman	0	0	0
Walker	0	0	0
Cluggish	0	0	0
Totals	**17**	**6**	**40**

PITTSBURGH (29)	FG	FT	Pts.
Zeiegnik	0	0	0
R.E. Johnson	3	3	9
Garcia	4	1	9
Radvansky	1	1	3
Spotovich	4	0	8
Scott	0	0	0
R.W. Johnson	0	0	0
Scherer	0	0	0
Lawry	0	0	0
Weiburg	0	0	0
Totals	**12**	**5**	**29**

into the picture, and started tossing them in from all angles to increase his team's lead to a safe margin.

Pittsburgh led only once during the game, and that was immediately after it dropped in the first field goal. Kentucky came right back, and ran the score up to 10-2 before the Easterners could tally again.

Pittsburgh frequently worked the ball past midcourt in the first half but found their clockwise and counter-clockwise attack effectively bottled up, principally by a never-tiring dynamo, Bernie Opper, at guard.

The night's high scorer was Homer Thompson,

the Kentucky center. His teammate, Fred Curtis, posted 10 points. Hagan, of Kentucky, and Robert Johnson and Joe Garcia, both of Pitt, got 9 each.

Pittsburgh played in the Sugar Bowl game several years ago but Kentucky had never appeared in the game before. The teams met only once before, at Lexington, Ky., in 1935, when Kentucky won, 35-17.

Kentucky was presented the Sugar Bowl Trophy and Hagan, the Kentucky forward who led his team in the spirited 2d-half rally, was given the basketball used for the game. The individual players got medals.

Rupp's Wildcats defeated Pittsburgh, 40-29, to win the 1937 Sugar Bowl Tournament in New Orleans.

CHAPTER 4

Alumni Gym served as the Wildcats' home court from 1924 to 1950.

Hagan's Late Long Shot Defeats Marquette, 35-33

BY THE ASSOCIATED PRESS
The Courier-Journal

LEXINGTON, Feb. 14, 1938 — The University of Kentucky Wildcats fought their way to a spectacular 35-33 victory over the classy Marquette Hilltoppers here tonight.

With only 10 seconds to go and the score tied at 33-33 Kentucky took time-out. The Wildcats went to their knees in a huddle, then scampered to their feet — all but Joe Hagan, the hard-fighting forward, who remained a second or 2 longer, his hands clasped and his eyes closed. Then, he got to his feet and the time-out ended.

Kentucky then got the ball and the crowd of 4,000 screamed for a shot as the seconds ticked. The ball was passed to Joe Hagan, far back in the court and near the sideline. The red-headed Louisville boy heaved a mighty shot at the target and it went through without touching the rim. Hagan's long shot had won

the game from the team that beat Notre Dame and many other of the nation's best.

It was a battle from the start to the finish. Kentucky took a 7-0 lead before Dave Cofone, the Marquette guard, dropped in a left-handed 2-pointer. The Wildcats ran their margin to 13-3, then Bob Deneen, a guard, ran on a rampage and scored 9 points to put his team within a point of the Wildcats and George Hesak dropped one in to make it 14-13 for the visitors. A few seconds before the half ended Mickey Rouse, Kentucky's sophomore guard, dropped one in from the middle of the floor to tie the score at 18-18.

Marquette went into a 4-point lead at the beginning of the 2d half, but with 5 minutes left Hagan made 2 quick fielders to tie it up at 24. But again Marquette grabbed a 4-point advantage and held it until only 3 minutes were left, when Bernie Opper dropped one in to tie at 31. In the next minute Erwin Graf, the Marquette forward, got away for a crip but Opper threw one in from afar to make it 33-33. There was no more scoring until 10 seconds of the game remained.

Mickey Rouse led the Wildcats in scoring with 175 points during the 1939-40 season.

THE LINE-UPS

KENTUCKY (35)	FG	FT	Pts.	MARQUETTE (33)	FG	FT	Pts.
Hagan	5	1	11	Adams	1	0	2
Goodman	1	1	3	Graf	3	0	6
Walker	1	2	4	Sokody	2	1	5
Opper	4	0	8	Quabius	1	1	3
Rouse	3	0	6	Deneen	3	3	9
Combs	0	0	0	Cofone	1	0	2
Curtis	0	0	0	Hesak	2	2	6
Thompson	1	1	3	**Totals**	**13**	**7**	**33**
Totals	**15**	**5**	**35**				

CHAPTER 5

After winning its sixth S.E.C. title in 1942, the Wildcats defeated Illinois, 46-44, in the N.C.A.A. Tournament.

UK Tips Illinois, 46-44, in N.C.A.A. Tourney

BY THE ASSOCIATED PRESS
The Courier-Journal

NEW ORLEANS, March 20, 1942 — In two of the fastest and most thrilling basketball games ever seen here, Kentucky's Wildcats and the Dartmouth Indians won the right to meet each other tomorrow night for the National Collegiate Athletic Association's eastern championship. After Dartmouth beat Penn State, 44-39, in the opening game, Kentucky, arising to the occasion to outscore and outfight a mighty University of Illinois team, won a hair-lifting game, 46-44.

The Kentucky-Illinois game was so full of action that the crowd of 3,000 was kept in a constant uproar as the teams traded sensational shots and fought for every point.

At times the play became so scintillating that terrific contacts sent members of both teams headlong on the floor. Right near the end of the game Jim King of Kentucky crashed against the basket supports and for a time it was believed he was seriously hurt, as he was knocked out cold.

Illinois led, 22-20, at the end of the first half, but some magnificent goal shooting by Milton Ticco, Carl Staker and Marvin Akers brought the Wildcats into their own not long after the second half got under-

UK had an easy time defeating Tennessee, 37-28, in Alumni Gym.

way and King put the Kentuckians in front with a brilliant field goal, making the score 28-27.

Kentucky could not be stopped after that, with King following with another fine shot for two points and Ermal Allen giving his team a 6-point lead with still another.

Because Kentucky was the "home" team of the four participating, the crowd was with the Wildcats all the way. It cheered them when, in the waning moments of the game and with King still groggy on the sidelines, the Wildcats lasted to win in the face of a courageous and dangerous attack Illinois launched.

Desperate as the seconds of the last minute ticked away, Arthur Smiley of Illinois caged a brilliant shot from deep in the court to make the score 46-44 and it was mighty ticklish when Illinois got the ball again a few moments later and was charging down to Kentucky's basket as the game ended.

Ticco, with 13 points, 12 of which were made on field goals; Staker, with nine points; and Akers with eight starred for Kentucky. Jim Menke, with seven field goals and 15 points, and Smiley, with five field goals and three foul shots for a total of 13 points, stood out for Illinois.

For the first five minutes of play it was nip and tuck with the lead see-sawing as Akers and Staker got in a

Ermal Allen starred in football and basketball at UK.

Lee Huber, an all-American in 1940 and 1941, was widely known for his deadly aim.

couple of fancy field goals to offset some fine shooting by Henry Sachs and Andy Phillip of Illinois.

Smiley and Menke opened a lead for Illinois with a couple of beautiful field goals, but the Wildcats kept registering foul shots and were crowding Illinois when Victor Wukovits got a perfect crip with nobody near him and put Illinois in front, 22-18.

Then Akers scored a long field goal on a magnificent shot and, as the gong sounded the end of the half, he got another one from far out on the court, sending the Wildcats to the dressing rooms two points behind, 20-22.

Penn State and Illinois will meet in the first half of tomorrow night's double-header and Kentucky and Dartmouth will clash in the second half.

THE LINE-UPS

KENTUCKY (46)	FG	FT	Pts.	ILLINOIS (44)	FG	FT	Pts.
White	0	1	1	Menke	7	1	15
Allen	2	0	4	Hocking	0	0	0
Ticco	6	1	13	Smiley	5	3	13
Brewer	0	1	1	Fowler	0	0	0
King	2	2	6	Matsen	0	1	1
Staker	4	1	9	Wukovits	2	0	4
England	1	2	4	Phillip	2	2	6
Akers	4	0	8	Vance	0	0	0
Totals	**19**	**8**	**46**	Sachs	2	1	5
				Totals	**18**	**8**	**44**

CHAPTER 6

The Wildcats had a record of 28 wins and 2 losses in the 1945-46 season. They defeated Rhode Island, 46-45, to capture the N.I.T. title.

Wildcats Nip Rams of Rhode Island, 46-45

BY LOUIS EFFRAT
Special to The New York Times

NEW YORK, March 20, 1946 — To the Wildcats of Kentucky went top honors in the ninth annual National Invitation College Basketball Tournament, but the hearts of 18,475 fans, thrilled by the gallantry of courageous underdogs who refused to concede an inch, belonged to the Rams of Rhode Island State.

Battling to the end, Rhode Island finally succumbed, 46-45, to the experienced, taller Southerners in a nerve-tingling finale that left the experts in a state of bewilderment last night at Madison Square Garden.

If the experts were in such a condition, one is privileged to guess how Kentucky's players felt, struggling to convince the Rams they just were not supposed to make it that close. For here was a heavy favorite, rated superior by 11½ points, barely pulling the title out of the fire.

Kentucky was behind, 27-26, at the half, and two minutes before the finish, the Wildcats still found themselves a point in the red, 45-44.

This was not according to script. Rhode Island, under the tutelage of Frank Keaney, was not supposed to be equipped with the defense necessary to stop so smooth an aggregation as Kentucky. The helter-skelter, hipper-dipper New England attack, with its electrifying one-handers, had been subjected to ridicule and certainly did not compare with Kentucky's orthodox offense, revolving around the pivot man in the key hole.

In fact, everything pointed to a comfortable victory for Kentucky. However, it was the Wildcat coach, Adolph Rupp, who summed it all up in a nutshell a few minutes after he had accepted the N.I.T.'s Edward A. Kelleher Trophy from Mrs. Kelleher.

"Who," Rupp asked, "said Rhode Island State had no defense?"

"Who," he continued, "said Rhode Island State had no offense?"

The Rams had both. They had, also, Ernie Calverley, who, though limited to a mere 8 points by freshman Ralph Beard, Kentucky's standout offensively and defensively, clinched the most valuable player award in the tournament with another sparkling all-around exhibition. Calverley, feeding his teammates, intercepting passes and setting up numerous scoring plays, unquestionably merited the honor.

Still fortune frowned on the slim, 145-pound New Englander, who had amazed the basketball world with a 55-foot shot in the first round. Perhaps it was a miscarriage of justice that he was the cause of Kentucky's winning point, which came exactly 40 seconds before the final buzzer and sent Calverley out on personal fouls.

Perhaps it was, but none in the crowd — which helped set a tournament attendance record of 73,894 for four nights of competition — put the blame on the youngster. It was a heart-breaking windup

THE LINE-UPS

KENTUCKY (46)

	FG	FT	Pts.
Tingle	2	1	5
Holland	1	0	2
Schu	3	3	9
Jones	3	4	10
Campbell	0	2	2
Parkinson	1	0	2
Beard	5	3	13
Parker	1	1	3
Totals	**16**	**14**	**46**

RHODE ISLAND (45)

	FG	FT	Pts.
Hale	5	2	12
Nichols	5	1	11
Palmieri	0	0	0
Calverley	2	4	8
Shea	1	2	4
Allen	3	4	10
Sciafani	0	0	0
Totals	**16**	**13**	**45**

for so outstanding an individual.

The clock showed forty seconds to play when Calverley fouled Beard. As Calverley walked to the bench, Beard calmly caged the free throw that snapped the twelfth tie of the game. Going back a bit farther, it was a foul by Calverley that sent Kenton Campbell to the 15-foot line for a successful penalty toss that enabled Kentucky to tie it at 45-all.

Even after Beard's 1-pointer, the Rams had a chance in the form of a free throw by Dick Hole. Twenty-three seconds remained when Hole flubbed the shot. Between then and the finish, Rhode Island players got their hands on the ball a half a dozen different times, but never got off a shot clearly.

If sloppy at times, this was a feverishly waged contest, in which the lead changed hands eleven times. The Rams, never stopping their running tactics, fell seven points behind, 23-16, but a tremendous surge gave them a 27-26 edge at the intermission.

Thereafter neither side boasted a lead of more than 3 points. There was enough good, spectacular basketball to offset the faulty plays. Kentucky tried to play its own game, but too often was lured into wildness.

For Kentucky, Beard, with his excellent job of defending against Calverley and the 13 points he tallied, was the big man. Besides Calverley, playing in his last college game, Jack Allen, a substitute Ram, turned in a surprisingly good effort.

Jack Parkinson was selected to most all-America squads following the 1946 season.

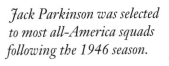

CHAPTER 7

Alex Groza reaches above the crowd for a rebound. He added 12 points to the Wildcats' total against Utah.

Utah Upsets Kentucky in N.I.T. Final

BY LOUIS EFFRAT
Special to The New York Times

NEW YORK, March 24, 1947 — Midnight still was an hour away, but the clock was wrong — as wrong as all the experts who predicted that Utah didn't have a chance against mighty Kentucky in the final of the tenth annual National Invitation College Basketball Tournament at Madison Square Garden last night.

For at 11 o'clock last night, the Utes, who back in 1944 were called the "Cinderella team," completed their upset victory over the Wildcats, 49-45.

With this unexpected conquest of an all-powerful court aggregation that had won thirty-four of thirty-six games, Utah's undermanned and certainly under-estimated squad sealed for all-time its right to exclusive ownership of the "Cinderella" tag.

The Utes came from nowhere to win in 1944, and

some may have felt they were lucky to have reached last night's final. But some sixty minutes before the legendary hour of midnight, they didn't ask the Cinderella team to try a golden slipper for size. It was a crown and it fit perfectly.

Utah, it will be recalled, survived the first round by virtue of a 45-44 triumph over Duquesne. Against West Virginia in the semi-finals, the Utes prevailed, 64-62. Last night, four points divided the finalists, so that an overall margin of 7 points brought to Utah its second National Invitation Tournament championship.

There was little of the sensational connected with the final, but Utah's performance against a heavily favored, high-scoring group that looked like a cinch to annex its second successive N.I.T. diadem, won the admiration of 18,467 fans.

Undoubtedly, Coach Vadal Peterson had instructed his men to slow down the pace and stress possession at all times. The Utah plan of battle never deviated although the Wildcats tried to force the Utes into faster action. The Utes knew what they wanted to do and did it — handsomely.

Vern Gardner, the blond bombshell who was named the most valuable player in the tournament, did an excellent job for the winning team. He captured most of the rebounds, fed the ball to his teammates and still found time to share, with Arnold Ferrin, individual scoring honors. Each made 15 points.

Little Wat Misaka, American-born of Japanese descent, was a "cute" fellow intercepting passes and making the night miserable for Kentucky. Leon Watson and Fred Weidner, the other two starters, and Lyman Clark, the lone substitute, who did everything asked of him, also came in for applause.

And what of Kentucky? The Wildcats did not play poorly, but they did not match Utah's all-around superiority. Trailing at the half, 27-21, Adolph Rupp's lads three

THE LINE-UPS

KENTUCKY (45)

	FG	FT	Pts.
Holland	1	0	2
Jones	2	4	8
Groza	5	2	12
Tingle	0	0	0
Barker	0	0	0
Rollins	3	0	6
Line	6	0	12
Beard	0	1	1
Jordan	1	2	4
Totals	**18**	**9**	**45**

UTAH (49)

	FG	FT	Pts.
Watson	3	7	13
Misaka	0	2	2
Gardner	5	5	15
Ferrin	6	3	15
Weidner	1	2	4
Clark	0	0	0
Totals	**15**	**19**	**49**

times were confronted with 7-point deficits. They rallied to within one point of the leaders, 45-44, with little more than three minutes remaining. If Utah was destined to crack, this was the spot.

But Ferrin caged a twisting, underhand lay-up. Wah-Wah Jones caged a Kentucky foul that brought the Wildcats a point closer, but not close enough. The Utes held the ball as the precious seconds ticked away.

Obviously, the 2-point lead was sufficient, but five seconds before the end, Ferrin spied Gardner underneath and alone, so he fired the pass that produced the cushion.

Alex Groza and Jim Line, the freshmen with the southpaw one-handed shot, counted 12 points each for Kentucky, but Ralph Beard was limited to a mere point by Misaka. They say Kentucky goes as Beard goes. Last night he just didn't go.

Jim Line was known for his southpaw one-handed shots.

From Old Kaintuck

By Arthur J. Daley
The New York Times

New York, March 24, 1947 — Fast horses, strong whiskey and fine tobacco are not the only products of superlative quality found in Old Kaintuck. There also is the University of Kentucky basketball team, which probably is the best in the land. Anyone seeking corroboration need turn no further than Col. Adolph Rupp, a transplanted hillbilly from Kansas, who can extol the virtues of the Bluegrass Country with even more vehemence than Col. Matt Winn, one of the survivors of Daniel Boone's first expedition into the territory.

But where Col. Winn will stress the fast horses and his beloved Kentucky Derby, Col. Rupp will expound at length — and just try to stop him! — on his Wildcat dribble artists. He's got a good talking point, too. His "pore lil' country boys" are the very best — unless some team can prove differently.

It will be up to Utah tonight to attempt to prove it as the Utes square off against the lads from Lexington in the final of the National Invitation Tournament in Madison Square Garden. However, the Rocky Mountain contingent has made a habit of proving such unprovable propositions.

Eliminated in the first round of this same tournament three years ago, Utah was named as a last-minute substitute for Arkansas in the national collegiate title show. Thereupon the Utes scored a couple of upsets to win the Western final, scored another upset in the East-West final and then scored another upset to win the unofficial national championship. So far in this tournament, they've surprised by upending both Duquesne and West Virginia, heavy favorites. If the clock hasn't yet stuck midnight, the Fairy Godmother again might wave her magic wand for this Cinderella team.

Surplus Talent

However, it will take a feat of magic to beat Old Kaintuck. The droll and delightful Col. Rupp, suh, is more heavily loaded than a moonshiner's shotgun. He has all-America players picking up splinters on his bench and one such operative quit the squad in disgust because he couldn't even make the second team. The Colonel can always use one foolproof system. He can keep substituting until he finds which performers are "hot." Then he yanks the luke-warm boys and leaves the super-heated ones in there.

In that respect, he almost reminds you of the Joe McCarthy of old. And, like Marse Joe, he has the admirable trait of

Adolph Rupp and his long-time assistant, Harry Lancaster.

being extremely adroit in his shuffling of his talent. Fred Russell, the Nashville sportswriter, tells the tale of the excitable Rupp being detected coaching from the bench. A technical foul therefore was called against Kentucky.

"By crimminey," exploded the never-shy Col. Rupp, "my coaching is worth a technical foul any time." Doggone, but he's really got something there.

The truth of the matter is that the Colonel never would win a popularity contest among his fellow coaches, especially in Dixie, where he's been such a dominating figure for so long. He's well liked personally but professionally he has the same approximate appeal as a man with the bubonic plague. Most coaches can — and do — avoid scheduling him, but the chaps in his own Southeastern Conference are stuck. They have to play against him.

So they cheer violently for every team in the league except Kentucky, hoping against hope that the Wildcats will be beaten in some miraculous fashion so that the rest of them will have some sort of chance.

Embarrassing Moment

A story filtered down to Florida a week or so ago — maybe true, maybe apocryphal but surely illustrative.

Gen. Bob Neyland, the Tennessee football coach and ordinarily not a demonstrative man, was rooting hard for the Volunteers during the Southeastern Conference tournament. His fervor so amused the lady in back of him that she couldn't resist the remark: "My, but you certainly are for Tennessee, aren't you?"

"Madam," said the gallant General, "I'm for everyone but Kentucky."

For a while the General couldn't understand the frosty silence that enveloped his section of the stands. It was almost as though an icy blast from the Arctic had struck him in the back of the neck. Then a neighbor whispered in his ear that the query had come from none other than Mrs. Adolph Rupp.

Yet you can better understand the feeling that the Wildcats engendered in the hearts of all non-Kentuckians during that tournament when you look at the scores. Col. Rupp's "pore lil' country boys" edged out Vanderbilt in the first round, 98-29; barely beat Auburn in the semi-final, 84-14; and virtually had the blind staggers in nosing out Georgia Tech in the final, 75-53.

It's a team so good that you wonder how any quintet managed to beat it at all this season. Two of them did, though, the Oklahoma Aggies and DePaul — in thirty-six games. That would indicate that Kentucky is human and that the job can be done. In neither of its preliminary games here did the Wildcats look overpowering except in the final quarter of its semi-final. Then Col. Rupp's boys hit their stride and won going away.

Somehow or other, however, you can't escape comparing Old Kaintuck to the old-time Yankees. Although the emphasis always was placed on the scoring abilities of each, it was the overlooked but truly extraordinary defensive play that weighted the scales so heavily in their favor. Col. Rupp has in the person of Col. Ralph Beard one of the finest all-around stars of this generation. He also has super-players in Col. Wah-Wah Jones, Col. Alex Groza and a dozen other Kentucky colonels of incomparable skill.

Utah still can win, of course, but only if the Fairy Godmother still has a powerful lot of magic hidden away in her wand.

CHAPTER 8

Ralph Beard (12) soars for a lay-up against Holy Cross.

Kentucky Topples Holy Cross, 60-52

BY LOUIS EFFRAT
Special to The New York Times

NEW YORK, March 3, 1948 — A Kentucky quintet that never stopped driving until the final two minutes, when victory was clinched, rode over scrappy Holy Cross, 60-52, and into the N.C.A.A. championship round last night at Madison Square Garden.

Wholly merited and earned, the triumph gave Adolph Rupp's Wildcats first place in the Eastern regional competition and qualified the Kentuckians for Tuesday night's final at the Garden against Bay-

lor, the Western regional survivor. The Bears upset Kansas State, 60-52, at Kansas City last night.

Top-notch basketball was displayed by both sides at the Garden last night, but the Wildcats had the speed, the size and the shots. More important, they knew how to utilize these assets and, at one stage in the second half, enjoyed a 14-point margin. That the Crusaders from Worcester, Mass., fought back into contention later, cutting the deficit to four points, was indicative of their ability and determination.

In the end, however, Kentucky had what it needed to protect its advantage — stamina. Two minutes before time ran out, the Wildcats were ahead, 57-50. The Crusaders, pressing all over the court, attempted to knock the leaders off stride, but they succeeded only in committing a half dozen fouls, all of which were waived. Poise, so vital in basketball, never deserted the Wildcats.

The 18,472 fans on hand saw more than an ordinary court struggle. Students of the game were thrilled by the individual duels that were going on, as the rival coaches, Rupp and Alvin (Doggy) Julian, master-minded every minute. Rupp's strategy prevailed because Ken Rollins and Dale Barnstable turned in magnificent jobs of defending against the brilliant Bob Cousy.

Then there was the individual battle between Kentucky's Alex Groza and Holy Cross' George Kaftan. There, again, the Wildcats finished on top, Groza outplaying Kaftan by a wide margin and tallying 23 points to annex the game's scoring laurels. And while all this was going on, Ralph Beard and Wallace (Wah Wah) Jones were running the Crusaders dizzy.

Because the Holy Cross players, vainly trying to add to a 19-game winning streak and protect an unbeaten record on the Eighth Avenue hardwood, were unable to stop Groza, Jones and Beard, it was inevitable that victory go to Kentucky. On the other hand, once it became apparent that the Wildcats had the formula to minimize the effectiveness of Cousy and Kaftan, the decision belonged, more or less, to Kentucky.

Cousy, limited to one field goal, wound up with five points, practically a shut-out for the prolific scorer whose outstanding work throughout the year sparked the Crusaders to one of their greatest records — 25 wins and 3 losses — up to last night. Cousy, who scored 472 points prior to this engagement, seldom was allowed room to get off his shots and much credit for a fine guarding chore must go to Rollins.

Kentucky, a 5-point favorite, lived up to its billing.

THE LINE-UPS

KENTUCKY (60)

	FG	FT	Pts.
Jones	4	4	12
Barker	2	0	4
Line	0	0	0
Groza	10	3	23
Holland	0	0	0
Beard	6	1	13
Rollins	3	2	8
Barnstable	0	0	0
Totals	**25**	**10**	**60**

HOLY CROSS (52)

	FG	FT	Pts.
Oftring	4	4	12
McMullan	0	0	0
Cousy	1	3	5
O'Connell	3	3	9
Kaftan	6	3	15
Bollinger	1	0	2
Curran	3	1	7
Forman	0	0	0
Mullaney	0	0	0
Laska	1	0	2
Totals	**19**	**14**	**52**

From the outset, Rupp had his charges running at top speed and making the most of a fast break. But Holy Cross, with Kaftan doing a nice job, capitalized on slick ball-handling and, after three and a half minutes of the most spirited play witnessed all season, it was a 7-7 standstill.

Then the Wildcats, with Beard contributing handsomely, clicked for 5 straight points for a 12-7 lead and a headstart toward conquest. Never again did the Crusaders pull into a tie. At the half the count favored Kentucky, 36-38, and there was every indication that it might go higher.

However, following the rest period, the Crusaders came out full of fight, drove in for two quick baskets and suddenly it was a real contest again. Four points to the good, Kentucky called for a time-out. The Wildcats must have realized that Holy Cross, counting the closing minutes of the opening period, had amassed nine consecutive points.

That cessation did it. When play was resumed, the Wildcats hit for seven in a row. Jones succeeded with a one-hander, followed with a 2-pointer from the keyhole and, after a one-hander by Groza, Jones tossed in a foul shot. The Crusaders could not retrieve those points, and though they continued to battle, it was in a losing cause.

Groza's tap-ins were spectacular and the maneuvers of Beard won the fancy of the crowd, but if one were asked to point to the strongest feature of Kentucky's play, it would have to be its relentless driving. The Wildcats did a lot of digging and never tired. It was the inability of Holy Cross to cope with this power that led to defeat.

One thing is certain — the East will have the strongest representation possible in Tuesday night's final. That's a fair-to-middlin' outfit that Rupp has assembled, an outfit which now has gained a berth in the Olympic playoffs.

Kenny Rollins' superb defensive effort against Bob Cousy was the key to stopping Holy Cross. In this contest, Rollins allowed the Holy Cross star to score only 5 points.

CHAPTER 9

The 1947-48 Wildcats, with a record of 36 wins and 3 losses, defeated Baylor, 58-42, in the final game of the N.C.A.A. Tournament. This victory gave Kentucky its first N.C.A.A. championship in basketball.

Kentucky Defeats Baylor in N.C.A.A. Final at Garden

BY LOUIS EFFRAT
Special to The New York Times

NEW YORK, March 23, 1948 — Kentucky's Wildcats, at no time in jeopardy, easily conquered Baylor, 58-42, last night at Madison Square Garden and romped to their first N.C.A.A. basketball championship. Off to an early 17-point lead, Adolph Rupp's powerhouse completely outclassed the Bears from Waco, Texas.

The second smallest turnout of the season, 16,174, witnessed this one-sided East-West final, in which Baylor's strategy — slowdown and stress possessions

— succeeded only in holding down the score. Baylor, lightly regarded at the outset of the Western Regionals, qualified for the title clash with a pair of upset victories over Washington and Kansas State, but last night ran out of surprises.

Perhaps the best way to describe Kentucky's thirty-fourth and certainly most important triumph of the campaign is to report that form held up. Nearly every pre-game prediction pointed to the size, speed and depth of the Wildcats from Lexington and figured that these would determine the outcome. They did, too, even if Coach Rupp, who wanted to win this one above all others, saw little need to turn to his bench. He did not substitute until 6:30 of the second half, by which time the decision was just about clinched.

Alex Groza, the tallest man on the floor, was the high scorer for Kentucky and the game. His 14 points were two more than Ralph Beard tallied and four more than Bill Johnson made for Baylor. The latter was unable to handle Groza's height and most of the rebounds were dominated by the 6-foot 7-inch center who was voted the outstanding player of the tournament.

But Groza was far from being the only Wildcat in a starring role. Beard, an irrepressible digger; Ken Rollins, an all-around ace; Wallace (Wah Wah) Jones, a dependable workhorse, along with the steady Cliff Barker — all contributed handsomely toward a victorious cause.

That Baylor, because of Kentucky's height advantage, would resort to a deliberate style of attack, was anticipated. The Bears, reluctant to risk forfeiting possession, attempted to make certain that every shot be a clear one and from close range. As a result they had taken only one chance in the first four minutes and six in the first seven and a half, not one finding the target.

Thus Kentucky enjoyed a 13-1 spread — Jim Owen caged a foul shot at 5:25 — and Baylor followers foresaw a rout.

Finally, when the clock showed 7 minutes and 35 seconds gone, Don Heathington dribbled in with a lay-up and the Texans, on their seventh attempt from the floor,

THE LINE-UPS

KENTUCKY (58)

	FG	FT	Pts.
Jones	4	1	9
Line	3	1	7
Barker	2	1	5
Groza	6	2	14
Holland	1	0	2
Beard	4	4	12
Rollins	3	3	9
Barnstable	0	0	0
Totals	**23**	**12**	**58**

BAYLOR (42)

	FG	FT	Pts.
Owen	2	1	5
Pulley	0	1	1
Dewitt	3	2	8
Hickman	1	0	2
Heathington	3	2	8
Preston	0	0	0
Johnson	3	4	10
Srack	0	0	0
Robinson	3	2	8
Totals	**15**	**12**	**42**

achieved their initial basket.

However, this was not repeated often enough to lighten Baylor's burden and at 12:35 Kentucky's lead was 17 points at 24-7. This shrunk slightly to 29-15 at the intermission and later the Bears rallied to cut the deficit to 9 points, but the Wildcats packed too many weapons and triumphed going away.

Kentucky, obviously superior in all departments, was most impressive during the early stages. One 2-minute spurt netted 7 points as Jones, Rollins and Groza excelled.

The Wildcats were driving hard and harassing the Bears at every turn. Thereafter they performed commendably enough, but their rallies were intermittent and the Kentuckians did not again look that superb.

Probably the reason for this letup was lack of incentive. They were en route to victory and knew it, and no end of grimaces from Rupp on the bench sufficed to reawaken them. Baylor, on the other hand, did not have the power to take full advantage and suffered its sixth setback of the year.

In victory, Kentucky attempted a total of 83 shots, clicking with 23, as compared to 15 out of 64 for the losers. Both teams automatically qualified for the Olympic Trials which get underway Saturday afternoon at the Garden.

Third place in the competition went to Holy Cross, despite an early 16-point lead, staggering to a 60-54 victory over Kansas State in the preliminary encounter

----

Ralph Beard (left) and Alex Groza were a one-two punch against Baylor.

Top: After the 1948 N.C.A.A. Tournament in New York City, a large crowd awaited the Wildcats' return to Lexington.

Right: Alex Groza, with the national championship trophy under his arm, was the most valuable player in the 1948 N.C.A.A. Tournament.

CHAPTER 10

Powerful Cats Crush Louisville's Hopes, 91-57

BY LARRY BOECK
Special to The Courier-Journal

NEW YORK, March 27, 1948 — Louisville's courageous Cardinals gave it the ol' college try here tonight. But spirit and scrap weren't enough to match the power and punch of Kentucky's pulverizing Wildcats.

So the Wildcats, unleashing their fury early in the game, mastered the Cardinals, 91-57, in the opening round of the Olympic Trials.

By virtue of their victory, their 35th in 37 games, the Wildcats again clash with Baylor Monday night. The Bears upset N.Y.U., 59-57, in a thrilling afternoon game.

Baylor, the N.C.A.A. runner-up, lost the title to Kentucky last week, 58-42.

As irony would have it tonight, it was a Louisville youngster who wrought the most devastation in the carnage before 15,297 fans in Madison Square Garden.

Gum-chewing all-American Ralph Beard, the former Louisville Male High pepper-pot, was the chief-executioner in Louisville's demise. Beard, whose play in New York has sent him right along on the road to becoming one of the game's all-time greats, poured in 22 back-breaking points. And his floor game, his defensive work, also sparkled.

The combination of Beard, Wah Wah Jones (19 points), Cliff Barker (13) and Alex Groza (12), was just too much for the Cardinals, the N.A.I.B. champions. That, plus the loss of their towering star, Jack Coleman, who fouled out after eight and one-half minutes of the second half.

But, just as they had played in winning that title, the Cardinals tonight refused to give up. After they had lost an early 5-0 lead, and the Wildcats went on to roll up a 21-point margin after 15 minutes of play, the Cards adamantly wouldn't admit they were a beaten team.

The combination of Cliff Barker (above), Ralph Beard, Wallace (Wah Wah) Jones (below) and Alex Groza was too much for Louisville to handle.

They fought back. They continued to run with the Wildcats, to give and to take. As a result, they whittled UK's lead down to 11 points — 51-40 — early in the second half.

After eight and one-half minutes of play, however, the rampaging Wildcats had gone on to a 16-point lead, 63-47. And Coleman, the six-foot-five spark-plug of the team, fouled out elbowing Groza under the Kentucky basket.

Without their rebounder and scoring threat — Jack Coleman had tallied 10 points — the Cardinals were in hopeless straits.

Right there time ran out on Louisville's "Cinderella kids," who had come out of nowhere to win the Cardinals' first national cage championship.

The Kentucky Wildcats, meanwhile, continued to toll the hour of midnight for the Cardinals. True, they were without their playmaker, Kenny Rollins, who had accumulated five personals after three minutes of the second half. But that didn't make any difference.

They still had explosive scoring punch.

They still had their tight defensive screen intact.

They still were a basketball blitz as they took off on the fast-break.

And they still drove with relentless aggressiveness.

Minus Coleman, and with their one do-or-die challenge early in the second half decisively repulsed, the Cardinals floundered and the Wildcats romped along to amass the highest scoring mark of the season at Madison Square Garden.

It was, in the final analysis, a case of a boy sent on a man's errand.

Kentucky, the scourge of the nation's hardwood, rated by basketball experts here as one of the great college quints of all-time, had too many things the Cardinals didn't have.

THE LINE-UPS

KENTUCKY (91)

	FG	FT	Pts.
Barker	4	5	13
Jones	7	5	19
Line	4	0	8
Stough	0	0	0
Groza	5	2	12
Holland	2	1	5
Rollins	2	0	4
Beard	10	2	22
Barnstable	3	0	6
Jordan	0	2	2
Totals	**37**	**17**	**91**

LOUISVILLE (57)

	FG	FT	Pts.
Coleman	4	2	10
G.Combs	3	4	10
Borah	0	3	3
Edwards	0	0	0
Compton	3	3	9
Johnson	1	1	3
Reeves	1	3	5
Knopf	3	1	7
R.Combs	3	4	10
Walker	0	0	0
Totals	**18**	**21**	**57**

They had height, although that wasn't as important as the reserve strength they could pour into the fray. Dale Barnstable, for instance, who went in for Rollins, tabbed six while Oz Johnson, who replaced Jackson Coleman for the Cardinals, could amass but three points.

The Wildcats, too, were capable of matching power with scrap and punch over spirit. And, additionally, they had plenty of fire themselves tonight.

They knew their reign as king of the national and state hardwood was at stake, and they were ready to accept the challenge.

They knew they would have to fight to beat the Cards, for whom they voiced a healthy respect before the game, and that's just what they did.

Louisville fought, too. But, as it was tonight, there are times when fight alone, heroic as it may be, is not sufficient.

When the Cardinals went on the offensive, for instance, there was aggressive Wah Wah Jones, a fighter himself, after Jack Coleman, Alex Groza took Dee Compton, Ralph Beard took Kenny Reeves, Cliff Barker was on Johnny Knopf and Kenny Rollins on Glen Combs.

With that wall, the Wildcats were able to throw up a tight defensive screen, of which they are masters besides the art of scoring.

True, Louisville hopped to a 5-0 lead on Compton's two field goals and a free throw. Kentucky, however, quickly re-organized itself. Barker and Groza hit, Jones wired a free throw with two field goals, and Beard drove through for two quick ones.

At the end of five minutes of play, it was Kentucky, 12-5. And at the end of 10 minutes, Kentucky was out front, 20-9. They were hitting from all angles, as their healthy 35.9 percentage of shot attempts made good shows.

Louisville, meanwhile, was having a hard time finding the range, although it rarely had time for a set-shot and found it difficult getting in for crips. For the night, they hit 22.5 percent of their field-goal attempts.

When 15 minutes of play elapsed, Kentucky was making a rout of it. The Wildcats led, 41-20.

Undaunted, Louisville scrapped back, as it had in Kansas City in coming from behind in four out of the five games it won. The Cards shaved UK's lead to 14 points — 43-29 — at the half.

They came out for the second half with grim determination, too. And they succeeded in getting back into the ball game, pulling to within 51-40 of the Cats after four minutes of play.

But Jones, who turned in a great performance along with Beard, coupled to reestablish Kentucky's dominance.

When Coleman left after eight and one-half minutes of play, following Rollins, who departed after three and one-half minutes, Kentucky had regained a comfortable 63-47 margin.

Coleman's departure put the iron-bound clinches on the game, however. From there on — even with substitutes playing most of the way — the Wildcats still were complete masters of the situation.

Kentucky's dazzling Ralph Beard graced the cover of the inaugural issue of Stanley Woodward's original Sports Illustrated *in February 1949.*

End of The Trail

By Arthur J. Daley
The New York Times

New York, March 31, 1948 — Don't look now but the college basketball season is almost over. Honest Injun. It had seemed for the longest while as though it never would end but would settle down for a more enduring run than "Tobacco Road" or "Life With Father." Even the writers were beginning to show signs of being dribble drunk, an occupational hazard akin to being punch drunk. The spots they were seeing before their eyes were merely basketballs sailing through the air. Complete rest is the only known cure. By golly, they're gonna get it.

But the sport is at least finishing with a flourish since it will present the finest attraction of the campaign for its farewell showing, the Olympic tryout final between the University of Kentucky, the national collegiate champion, and the Phillips 66ers, the national A.A.U. champions. It's a most intriguing match between two most skillful teams and the suggestion is hereby offered to the British Organizing Committee that it stage a special exhibition after the United States has won the Olympic title. All it need do is split the American squad in two and have it play a game so that the foreigners can see basketball at its very best.

The dribble addicts are quite excited about the clash between the Wildcats and the 66ers, and there are quite a few who are of the opinion that Kentucky's speed will be able to offset the 66ers' height. That height is really awesome, though. The ten Phillips players merely average 6-feet-5 and there's only one undersize operative in uniform, Lew Beck, who must have sneaked in a back door on a dark night. He's only 5-feet-10 and should be ashamed of himself.

Two Opinions

How good are the 66ers anyway? Joe Lapchick, the frank and outspoken coach of the professional Knickerbockers, declared, "They'd do all right in our league, mainly because of Bob Kurland, the 7-footer." More

vehement by far is Lou Varnell, the coach from Southern Methodist. "The 66ers would blow that league apart," he snapped. "I've seen the Chicago Stags often and Andy Phillips is the only fellow on the entire squad who could even make the 66ers' team. That's how good they are."

The 66ers are a rather strange phenomenon anyway in the rather strange phenomenon which is A.A.U. basketball. The industrial play, which has its deepest roots in the Western hinterlands, is amateur in a technical sense. The athletes don't get paid for playing basketball but they do get their jobs because of their court skills. The purists can unravel that situation at their leisure.

What Price Amateurism?

The large Mr. Kurland, for instance, turned down the initial offer of $11,000 that Ned Irish made him to join the New York Knicks. There also have been reports that he turned his back on other offers which purportedly went as high as $15,000 a season. That sort of thing makes amateur idealism sound slightly expensive.

But if anyone is to blame for that odd situation it has to be Kenneth (Boots) Adams. A star court performer at the University of Kansas, he joined the Phillips company in 1921 and, mainly for his own amusement and exercise, started a team there. The first thing he knew, though, he no longer had time to devote to the dribble diversion because he was moving from one responsible post to another. An now he's the president of the concern at $75,000.

That's the attraction that the Phillips 66ers have to offer the college graduates, a lifetime job where the sky is the limit if the athletes have the off-the-court ability to go with their on-the-court savvy. The turnover in talent is fairly steady each season because there's a company rule that executives cannot play and an astonishing number of dribble artists become executives.

An Ex-Goal Tender

So perhaps Kuland is doing the smarter thing in

refusing professional blandishments. The payoff for him might come in the long run. Yet he must come pretty close to being the best basketball player in the world. It's his size, of course, which makes him such a standout. After all, he's seven feet tall and those long arms of his reach far. In fact, he's the chap who is chiefly responsible for the rules committee's ban on goal tending. Large Kurland not only could score in his college days at Oklahoma A&M but he'd also acquired the habit of deflecting from the hoop sure-fire baskets by the opposition.

As one who saw him operate as a freshman some five years ago, this reporter is amazed at the way he's developed. In that season the gangling youth was so tall and ungainly that he rarely could play more than five minutes at a stretch. But now he has his full strength at the tender age of 22 and has become a poised and polished performer. Not only is he a demon at grabbing off the rebounds at either basket but he's an accomplished ambidextrous shot and a deadly performer from the pivot post.

"They have five pivot men," is the rueful comment of Col. Adolph Rupp, the maestro of the Bluegrass contingent, "and we have only one. I still don't know how we're going to counteract their height."

Seeking an Antidote

Perhaps he can hit on the system for stopping Kurland & Co. But if he can, he'll be unique. They've been trying everything at one time or another and nothing has worked yet. Back in Long Bob's goal-tending days, the Oklahoma Aggies played Tulsa and the Hurricanes refused to take any foul shots, except the first of two. Instead, they preferred to take the ball out of bounds because Kurland always seized the missed tries. The final score was 31 to 24 in favor of the Aggies. Each team made twelve field goals but Tulsa didn't score once from the free throw line. That was the difference.

So you can see what a terrific problem, psychological and physical, is confronting the Kentucky Wildcats at the Garden tonight. They've won thirty-six of thirty-eight games this season. But the 66ers have won sixty-one of sixty-five, their four defeats being clean oversights. This should be a rousing finish to the campaign. And none too soon, either.

CHAPTER 11

A.A.U. Squad Defeats
Cats in Olympic Trials Final

BY LOUIS EFFRAT
Special to The New York Times

NEW YORK, March 31, 1948 — As the fourteenth season of college basketball at Madison Square Garden ended last night, and 18,475 fans filed out of the arena, the buzzing was not about the 53-49 victory of the Phillips 66ers over the University of Kentucky. It did not concern individual exploits, nor did it speculate about the personnel that will emerge from the Olympic Trials to wear our colors at London next summer.

"Greatest game of all time!"

These five words that cover a lot of years and a lot of thrills were heard all over the Garden, undisputed by anyone. For this finale, pitting the best of the A.A.U. and collegiate quintets, was, indeed, more than an exciting, tense, spectacular contest, in which fortunes rose, sagged and rose again. It was basketball at its very best — sharp, smart, daringly aggressive.

Only the tremendous height-advantage of the amateur champions from Bartlesville, Okla., prevented this game from winding up in a dead heat. The Wildcats, because they were unable to cope with Bob Kurland's 7-foot frame, forfeited a 47-45 edge six minutes before the finish. Kurland was a menace, contributing three vital field goals in the final six minutes.

Without Kurland, the 66ers, though endowed with remarkable talent — Jesse Renick, Gordon Carpenter, Gerald Tucker, etc. — might have been upset. But Kurland's 20 points

for the night proved the crusher, even if Ralph Beard netted 23 points for Kentucky. Nothing that Beard could accomplish, and that was plenty, sufficed to minimize the importance of Kurland's scoring and rebounding.

A seven-time national A.A.U. ruler, including the

Ralph Beard (12) outduels a Phillips player en route to a lay-up. Beard led the Wildcats in scoring with 23 points.

last six years, the 66ers, surrounded by superb players, who formerly starred on college courts, did not wilt under the terrific pace set by the Kentuckians.

Unruffled at any time, though they were behind, 20-13, at the 12-minute mark in the opening period, the 66ers did not lose their poise. Rather, it was the Wildcats who bogged down, the Oklahomans clicking eleven straight points within the next five minutes for a 24-20 advantage. Kentucky, it appeared, had tightened and paid heavily for its attack of jitters.

A bad break for Kentucky came at 9:20 in the first half. Cliff Barker, a magnificent performer who had just fed Beard for an electrifying field goal, suffered a fractured nose and had to retire. The Wildcats missed Barker immeasurably. In the second stanza Wallace (Wah Wah) Jones fouled out and his absence, too, was felt.

THE LINE-UPS

KENTUCKY (49)

	FG	FT	Pts.
Barker	1	2	4
Holland	2	1	5
Rollins	2	2	6
Gross	1	2	4
W.Jones	1	3	5
Line	0	0	0
Barnstable	1	0	2
Beard	11	1	23
Totals	**19**	**11**	**49**

PHILLIPS 66ERS (53)

	FG	FT	Pts.
Beck	2	0	4
G.Jones	0	0	0
Pitts	0	1	1
Renick	4	3	11
Kurland	9	2	20
Carpenter	1	1	3
Beisner	0	0	0
Nash	0	2	2
Tucker	3	3	9
Reich	1	1	3
Totals	**20**	**13**	**53**

Intermission found the teams deadlocked at 26-all, but Kurland and Renick sparked the 66ers to a 10-point, 37-27 spread within the first five minutes after play was resumed. Then it was up to Kentucky to prove its mettle. Could the Wildcats erase this mountainous deficit? They did.

With Beard, a speedy guard, turning in a sensational exhibition of set- and drive-in shooting, the Kentuckians slowly supplied the answer. At 13:44, Beard, an all-American if ever there was one, drove in with a sensational one-hander. Fouled on the play, he added the points and now Kentucky was on top, 47-45.

The 66ers could have cracked right there, but did not. At the fourteen-minute mark, Kurland hit from under the bucket, tying the issue. Fouls by Tucker and Renick followed and exactly at sixteen minutes, Kurland again succeeded from the keyhole, so that the Oilers enjoyed a 51-47 advantage.

Now the Oklahomans, feeling none too secure, adopted sound tactics. They went into a freeze. This they achieved in masterful fashion and with 43 seconds left, Kurland scooted underneath with a sleeper-pass from Renick. Eight seconds later Dale Barnstable came through with an angle shot, but the Wildcats had no time to draw closer.

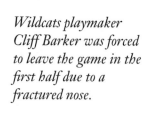

Wildcats playmaker Cliff Barker was forced to leave the game in the first half due to a fractured nose.

The 1948 U.S. Olympic basketball squad was composed of 5 players each from Kentucky and the Phillips 66ers, and 4 players from other A.A.U. and college teams.

U.S. Squad of 14 in Olympics Named

BY LOUIS EFFRAT
Special to The New York Times

NEW YORK, April 1, 1948 — It is with no feeling of relief that the basketball-playing nations of the world learn that the United States will be able to hurl the greatest one-two punch since Davis and Blanchard into the Olympic tournament this summer.

The United States squad, selected yesterday following tryouts in Madison Square Garden, includes the five regulars from each of the two best amateur teams in the country — the Phillips 66ers of Bartlesville, Okla., and the University of Kentucky at Lexington.

That means the United States, which probably could defend its Olympic basketball title successfully with any of its better high school teams, will go into the London games with two separate units, each carrying an added advantage of long experience together.

The 66ers, the national Amateur Athletic Union champions the past six years, won the Olympic tryouts Wednesday night, defeating Kentucky's N.C.A.A. title holders, 53-49, in one of the best games ever. In addition to strengthening their prestige, the Okla-

homans earned for their coach, Omar (Bud) Browning, the honor of coaching the Olympic team.

Here is the fourteen-man United States Olympic squad, chosen by the Olympic Basketball committee, headed by Lou Wilke of Denver:

	Team	Age	Height
Bob Kurland	Phillips 66ers	22	7'
Jesse Renick	Phillips 66ers	29	6'2"
G. Carpenter	Phillips 66ers	29	6'7"
R.C. Pitts	Phillips 66ers	28	6'4"
Lew Beck	Phillips 66ers	25	5'10"
Alex Groza	Kentucky	21	6'7"
Wallace Jones	Kentucky	21	6'4"
Cliff Barker	Kentucky	26	6'1"
Ken Rollins	Kentucky	24	6'
Ralph Beard	Kentucky	20	5'10"
Vince Boryla	Denver Nuggets	20	6'4"
Don Barksdale	Bittners	22	6'5"
Jack Robinson	Baylor	20	6'
Ray Lumpp	N.Y.U.	22	6'1"

Adolph Rupp, the Kentucky coach, will serve as Browning's assistant. Actually, the two coaches probably will operate their respective units in London, with Browning directing the over-all strategy and making substitutions from among the other four members of the squad.

Browning said yesterday he would call the Olympic players of his Phillips squad together for a workout each week between now and the time the full United States team reassembles here for practice prior to its departure for London in July.

Rupp also plans to keep his boys in training through the remainder of the college year. Some time during the summer the full Phillips and Kentucky teams will meet in an exhibition series of two or three games — one in Lexington, one in Bartlesville and possibly a third on a neutral court.

These exhibitions are expected to add at least $20,000 to the Olympic basketball fund, already enriched by approximately $35,000, cleared on the eight-game tryouts. The Olympic fathers are happy to contrast this financial situation with that of 1936, when the tryouts did not pay expenses.

Thirteen alternates also were named in case any of the Olympic cagers cannot go to London. They are Gerald Tucker, Martin Nash and Ed Beisser of the 66ers; Joe Holland, Jim Line and Dale Barnstable of Kentucky; Ray Lipscomb and Jim Darden of the Denver Nuggets; Les O'Gara and Warren Taulbee of the Oakland Bittners; Jim Owens and Bill Johnson of Baylor; and Adolph Schayes of New York University.

CHAPTER 12

U.S. Cage Team Routs France, 65-21, For Olympic Crown

BY EARL RUBY
Special to The Courier Journal

LONDON, Aug. 13, 1948 — The United States won the Olympic basketball championship tonight, apologetically collecting a 65-21 advantage over thoroughly outclassed France.

The lopsided contest climaxed a string of eight successive triumphs by the American representatives. The other victims were Switzerland, Czechoslovakia, Argentina (which scared us with a close game), Egypt and Peru in preliminary tests, and Uruguay and Mexico in the quarter- and semi-finals.

The crowd of about 3,500 in Harringay Arena, which seats 9,000, came to see the fabulous Americans. But they got their biggest thrill out of a preliminary game in which Brazil bested Mexico, 52-47, for third place.

The demonstrative Brazilians, true to the South American way, collapsed on the floor at the end. They rolled and wept and kissed each other, and they didn't get up until reserves came out and gave them assistance befitting the occasion. There weren't enough reserves to go around. This left one prostrate fellow languishing unattended. He finally sat up and left on his own steam but did not leave the court until his coach came over and solicitously helped him to his feet and placed a strong arm around him.

Coach Bud Browning started his Phillips 66ers, as he figured he would after starting the five University of Kentucky boys in the semi-final. These athletes — Bob Kurland, Jesse Renick, Louis Beck, Gordon Carpenter and R.C. Pitts — couldn't get into the swing of things. And, after eight minutes, they were ahead by only 9-4.

Browning sent Kenny Rollins of Kentucky in for Carpenter and Vince Boryla of Notre Dame in for Pitts. Then Donald Barksdale, the Californian, replaced Kurland, and Jackie Robinson from Texas

Alex Groza led the U.S. Olympic team in scoring in the 65-21 gold-medal victory over France.

1948
UNITED STATES
OLYMPIC BASKETBALL TEAM

SOUVENIR PROGRAM   25 Cents

THE LINE-UPS

KENTUCKY (65)	FG	FT	Pts.
Beck	2	2	6
Pitts	3	1	7
Boryla	1	1	3
Robinson	1	0	2
Beard	1	2	4
Lumpp	5	0	10
Kurland	2	0	4
Barksdale	3	2	8
Groza	5	1	11
Carpenter	0	2	2
Renick	1	0	2
Rollins	1	0	2
Jones	1	2	4
Barker	0	0	0
Totals	**26**	**13**	**65**

FRANCE (21)	FG	FT	Pts.
Guillon	0	1	1
Pierrier	2	1	5
Even	0	0	0
Quenin	0	0	0
Girardot	0	0	0
Desaymonnet	0	0	0
Derency	0	1	1
Thiolin	1	1	3
Buffiere	0	0	0
Chochet	3	2	8
Offner	1	0	2
Rebuffic	0	1	1
Barrais	0	0	0
Totals	**7**	**7**	**21**

was sent in for Beck.

With the count 21-8, Coach Browning sent in Wah Wah Jones to give him a complete new outfit on the floor. These boys took the score to 23-8, when Ralph Beard replaced Robinson and Alex Groza went in for Barksdale. Then, with the count 27-8, Cliff Barker subbed for Boryla and the Kentucky Wildcats had the court. Two minutes later, the half ended 28-9.

The five Kentuckians started the second half and were on top, 36-10, when Ray Lumpp, the New Yorker, was sent in for Rollins. This gang ran the count to sizable proportions and then a rotation of substitutions began in earnest. All the 66ers got back in for another period of about three minutes and all five Kentuckians were on the floor at the finish.

As the bell jangled ending the game and bringing the Olympic championship to a close, the band stuck up the American National Anthem in honor of the triumphant boys in red, white and blue.

Everybody stood politely, but with the last strain the crowd broke for the doors, then stopped when the musicians began playing the French National Anthem. The rush started again only to be brought up abruptly once more when the band started to play "God Save The King."

High point men were Groza and Lumpp with 11 each. This gave Groza, the Martins Ferry Wildcat, top honors for the Olympics with a grand total of 76. Kurland, who tabbed four tonight, was second with 65 for the Olympics. Then followed Barksdale with 43, Jones with 42, Renick with 39, and Lumpp with 38. Carpenter finished with 35, Beck with 33, Pitts with 31, Boryla with 28, Beard with 27, Rollins with 20, Barker 19 and Robinson with 13.

Before the game, the two coaches agreed to permit all 14 players on each squad to play. In other games only 10 of the 14 have been allowed in uniform.

The cagers will receive their Olympic medals in traditional Olympic style at Wembley Stadium tomorrow and will fly to France for a vacation on Sunday. They will sail for America on August 20.

Rupp and his "Fabulous Five" Kentucky players — Ralph Beard (12), Wah Wah Jones (27), Alex Groza (15), Cliff Barker (23) and Ken Rollins (26) — who won gold medals in the 1948 Olympics.

After defeating Oklahoma A&M for the Wildcats' second straight N.C.A.A. title, Rupp and his squad admire their national championship trophy.

Groza Leads Kentucky to 2d N.C.A.A. Crown

BY THE ASSOCIATED PRESS
The New York Times

SEATTLE, March 27, 1949 — Back to the Bluegrass state goes the national collegiate basketball championship, which was won by a great University of Kentucky team that broke the heart of the fighting Oklahoma Aggies last night, 46-36.

A big, hulking bear of a man who moves with deceptive grace was the key to the Wildcats' victory.

When 6-foot 7-inch Alex Groza fouled out five minutes before the end of the game, he had poured in 25 points and carried Kentucky to its triumph on his burly shoulders.

There was no doubt in the minds of sportswriters who had watched the all-America senior center in action. They unanimously voted him the most valuable player award for the second straight National Collegiate Athletic Association tournament.

Before the title game, watched by a turn-away crowd of 12,500 at the University of Washington Pavilion, the Big Nine champions from Illinois had taken third

Wah Wah Jones scores despite being closely guarded by Oklahoma A&M's Jack Shelton (45) and Joe Bradley (22) during the 1949 N.C.A.A. final game.

Groza his chance to crack the all-time N.C.A.A. single game scoring record of 31 set in 1941 by George Glamack of North Carolina. With four personals against him, Groza was benched for eight minutes in the second half, then got back in just past the midway mark and finally went out via the foul route five minutes before the gun.

Oklahoma A&M stepped off to a 5-2 lead with its ball-control style of play. Then Groza started to roll. At the half it was 25-20 for Kentucky and the big guy had accounted for 15 points.

The Aggies' battle was lost when lanky Bob Harris, who matches Groza in height but is 28 pounds lighter at 198, was whistled to the sidelines with five personals early in the second half. Then near the end of the game A&M's scrappy J.L. Parks went out on fouls and it was all over. Kentucky stalled to the finish.

Kentucky's triumph, its second in a row, gave the East its fifth N.C.A.A. championship against six for the West. The Wildcats joined the Aggies as the only two-time winners since the tournament started in 1939.

place by defeating Pacific Coast Conference champion Oregon State, 57-53.

The jubilant Kentuckians, heading back by chartered plane today to Lexington, took with them half of basketball's double diadem for which they had been aiming.

Twelve days earlier, they lost their chance at a twin sweep in the National Invitation Tournament at New York, where they were rudely dumped on their press clippings by unawed Loyola of Chicago.

But in the roaring finish that carried them through the Eastern N.C.A.A. finals and the championship here, the Wildcats proved their No. 1 rating in the eyes of the fans.

After it was all over, beaming Coach Adolph Rupp said:

"It was a tough game all the way. We had to play this one the hard way, almost to the finish. We beat a good team and we're mighty happy about it."

The Aggies' coach, Hank Iba, shrugged off defeat with "We just had a bad night; we were way off on our shots."

But hitting or not, Oklahoma A&M would have still had that Groza edge to overcome. Fouls cost

THE LINE-UPS				OKLAHOMA A&M (36)			
KENTUCKY (46)					FG	FT	Pts.
				Yates	1	0	2
	FG	FT	Pts.	Jaquet	0	1	1
Jones	1	1	3	Shelton	3	6	12
Hirsch	1	0	2	McArthur	0	2	2
Line	2	1	5	Harris	3	1	7
Groza	9	7	25	Bradley	0	3	3
Beard	1	1	3	Parks	2	3	7
Barker	1	3	5	Pilgrim	0	2	2
Barnstable	1	1	3	Smith	0	0	0
Totals	**16**	**14**	**46**	**Totals**	**9**	**18**	**36**

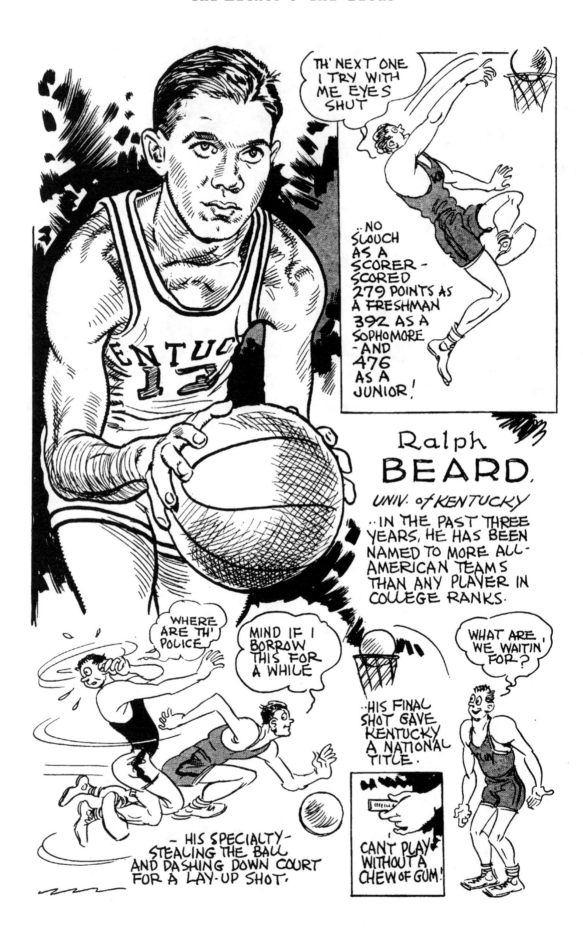

CHAPTER 14

Bill Spivey (77) attempts a hook shot against a stingy C.C.N.Y. defense in the 1950 N.I.T. at Madison Square Garden.

C.C.N.Y. Trounces Kentucky, 89-50

BY LOUIS EFFRAT
Special to The New York Times

NEW YORK, March 14, 1950 — More vividly and eloquently than words, the figures tell the story of the worst defeat ever pinned on any Wildcat basketball team since the court sport was introduced at the Lexington university back in 1903. It happened last night

at Madison Square Garden, where 18,000 fans saw Nat Holman's busy Beavers rout the second-seeded team, 89-50, in a quarter-final encounter in the thirteenth annual National Invitation Tournament.

Following another upset, in which Duquesne conquered La Salle, 49-47, the City College victory qualified the Lavender to oppose the Pittsburgh Dukes in one of tomorrow night's semi-finals. St. John's will engage top-seeded Bradley in the other.

The City College-Kentucky clash pitted two of the nation's recognized master strategists, Nat Holman and Adolph Rupp, against each other in a battle of wits, which failed to materialize, for the C.C.N.Y. players, with a furious first half, gave neither celebrated coach time for thinking.

The Beavers turned the trick with baskets, some of them so spectacularly made that they left everyone, including Holman, breathless. On the other hand, Rupp, who had been named "Coach of the Year" by the Metropolitan Basketball Writers Association, would have had to be a magician to save the night.

Never in all his twenty glorious years as head man at Kentucky had a team tutored by Rupp been so humiliated. Run into the boards by the speedy Beavers, the Wildcats were virtually beaten in the first four and a half minutes. At this stage, C.C.N.Y. enjoyed a 13-1 spread, as Ed Warner, Ed Roman and Floyd Layne — the first with his amazing shooting and feeding accuracy, the second with his flawless defense against the 7-foot Bill Spivey, and the third with his incredibly successful handling of rebounds — completely dominated the struggle.

The Kentucky players were not permitted to catch their breaths. Seldom were they allotted too much room to get off their shots and except for one short span in the second half — when they had cut a 26-point deficit to 16 — as Spivey belatedly found the range, were made to look pitifully weak.

City College was great. None will question the superb play of the Beavers, who

THE LINE-UPS

KENTUCKY (50)

	FG	FT	Pts.
Line	2	1	5
Linville	5	3	13
Hirsch	1	0	2
Morgan	0	0	0
Spivey	4	7	15
Watson	1	0	2
Pearson	3	1	7
Townes	0	0	0
Barnstable	3	0	6
Whitaker	0	0	0
Totals	19	12	50

C.C.N.Y. (89)

	FG	FT	Pts.
Dambrot	9	2	20
Warner	10	6	26
Watkins	1	0	2
Roman	8	1	17
Mager	2	2	6
Roth	3	3	9
Cohen	0	1	1
Wittlin	0	1	1
Smith	0	0	0
Layne	1	1	3
Nadel	2	0	4
Glass	0	0	0
Totals	36	17	89

after they had dropped to a mere 54-38 advantage, clicked for sixteen straight points in slightly more than three minutes. Warner, Irwin, Dambrot, Roman, Layne — every man in a City College uniform, in fact — carried out his part sensationally. All this against a squad that Uncle Adolph had proclaimed "potentially the greatest team I ever have had."

When the Beavers needed to fast-break, they did. When the set-up called a slowdown, they did. And when a pass or a rebound was required, they were there, on time and at the correct spot. Against such magnificence, there was little the Wildcats could do. Spivey, charged with four fouls in the first half, had to proceed with caution, and Jim Line, Walt Hirsch, Bobby Watson and Dale Barnstable were just "names" in so far as the victors were concerned.

Long before halftime, when C.C.N.Y., the Metropolitan ruler, but unseeded in this tourney, had a 45-20 lead, the Beavers had this one solidly sealed. Warner, feinting and curling in lay-ups from all angles, was the big gun, with a 26-point output. Roman netted 20 and still had time to excel on defense. Spivey's 15 was tops for the losers.

The night was full of surprises, including Holman's decision to start Watkins, who never before had done so at the Garden. However, Holman had Roman poised at the scorer's table and the first-string center replaced him a few seconds after the opening tap. Watkins, a comparative unknown, was employed from time to time thereafter and like all the other Beavers, fared handsomely.

Shelby Linville's performance was not enough to overcome C.C.N.Y.'s scoring prowess.

Rupp of Kentucky Coach of The Year

BY LOUIS EFFRAT
Special to The New York Times

NEW YORK, March 9, 1950 — Adolph Rupp, the veteran Kentucky mentor, has been voted the Coach of the Year by the Metropolitan Basketball Writers Association, it was announced yesterday. At the same time, the scribes named Hal Haskins, the Hamline senior, the winner of their Gold Star Award as the outstanding visiting player among the many who performed here.

The trophies will be presented to Rupp and Haskins at the association's annual dinner, Sunday night, March 19, at Jack Marin's Bear Mountain Inn.

Third in last season's polling behind Hank Iba of the Oklahoma Aggies and Pete Newell of San Francisco, Rupp becomes the third recipient of the writers' award. It was inaugurated after the 1948 campaign, when Howard Cann of N.Y.U. finished on top.

Rupp, in his twentieth season as head man of the Kentucky Wildcats, accomplished an excellent rebuilding job this year. Undaunted by the loss through graduation of Alex Groza, Wallace Jones, Ralph Beard and Cliff Barker, Uncle Adolph proceeded to win twenty-five games while losing only four, with only three lettermen, Dale Barnstable, Jim Line and Walter Hirsch. Of course, the Wildcats

have gained a berth in the forthcoming National Invitation Tournament.

Runner-up to Rupp in the balloting was Bradley's Forrest Anderson, who netted 44 points, eleven fewer than Rupp on a 5-3-1 basis. Frank McGuire of St. John's was third with 33 points, while others high in the voting were Clair Bee of Long Island University and Ken Loeffler of La Salle.

The victory of Haskins was decisive. His total of 63 points virtually doubled that of the second man, Chuck Cooper of Duquesne, who got 32. Sam Ranzino of North Carolina State was third with 31, George Stanich of U.C.L.A. fourth with 27 and Bob Cousy of Holy Cross fifth with 13.

Haskins, possessor of an assortment of soft shots, earned the laurels by scoring 32 points against Long Island University in a losing cause. A native of Alexandria, Minn., Haskins is a 6-foot 3-inch athlete. He has tallied more than 500 points in three consecutive campaigns.

Originated in 1945, the Gold Star Award first was won by Howie Dallmar of Pennsylvania, where he now is head basketball coach. Then the trophy went, in order, to George Mikan of DePaul, Ralph Beard of Kentucky, Ed Macauley of St. Louis and Vince Boryla of Denver. The latter currently is with the professional New York Knickerbockers.

At the UK Alumni Association's banquet in Spring 1949, Rupp announced that the Fabulous Five's jerseys would be retired.

CHAPTER 15

Spivey Wins Battle of Skyscrapers

BY LARRY BOECK
Special to The Courier-Journal

LEXINGTON, Dec. 16, 1950 — A record-breaking crowd of 13,000 sang Christmas carols at the halftime intermission here tonight. And when they left Memorial Coliseum after Kentucky had staggered Kansas, 68-39, they caroled the praises of the Wildcats' Bill Spivey.

For Spivey emerged from this "battle of the giants" with Kansas' Clyde Lovellette as a truly big man in basketball in more ways than simply height. And the Wildcats as a whole showed they potentially are one of basketball's great teams in handing the No. 4-ranked nationally Jayhawks their first loss in five starts.

Spivey, a demon on defense and a back-breaker on offense, left no doubt as to who was the big man on the floor tonight. The 7-foot one-inch Georgian outscored the 6-foot 9-inch Lovellette, 22 points to 10; and, perhaps more important, he stuck to the Kansas star like glue. His defensive game was one of the most exciting and effective ever turned in by a Wildcat.

Kansas was destroyed during a flaming five-minute assault by Kentucky that began midway of the first half with the Wildcats ahead, 8-5. After this siege, the Cats possessed a commanding 20-6 lead. And this was increased to 16 points at the half, 28-12. Kentucky extended even this lead, to 64-33, as substitutes carried on in the last seven minutes.

During the first half, to demonstrate the tremendous effort of Spivey, the Wildcat giant scored 14 points while Lovellette was tallying four. What's more, Spivey guarded the Kansan so masterfully that the Jayhawks had a most troublesome time attempting to feed Lovellette the ball. On 11 occasions, Spivey thrust his hand out and deflected the ball away from Lovellette.

Lovellette fouled out in the second half with more

Bill Spivey envelopes Kansas' Clyde Lovellette in their big showdown in December 1950. Playing perhaps the finest game of his career, Spivey outscored the Kansas star, 22 to 10.

than 13 minutes left. When he left the game, Coach Adolph Rupp also benched Spivey for the remainder of the game. At this point, Spivey owned 22 points and Lovellette 10. The tall Kansan tried hard and had tough luck with his shots in the first half. He dunked three quick buckets early in the second half and seemed to have found the range, but he soon fouled out.

Spivey, of course, wasn't the whole show tonight as the Wildcats notched their fifth triumph against no defeats this season and their 88th straight on the home floor.

There was sophomore Frank Ramsey, who accumulated 19 points, a number of them in the clutches, and turned in a top performance on the floor and boards. There was Shelby Linville, whose forceful rebounding allowed Kentucky to get the ball away from the Jayhawks, who like to play a slow, deliberate game; what's more, Linville tabbed eight points. There was Walter Hirsch, the Kentucky captain, who directed his teammates with confidence and was the Wildcat who fed the ball into Spivey.

Kentucky connected on 30 of 94 shots for a percentage of 31.9 before the biggest crowd ever to see a regularly scheduled season's game in the state. Kansas fired 62 times and could hit on just 14 shots for 22.5 percent as Kentucky demonstrated one of its finest defensive games. Kansas rarely had time to get set for a shot; it didn't have the speed, either, to match UK and so hard pressed, it found itself having difficult in attempting to set up its plays.

Spivey attempted 16 shots and cashed in on nine, a percentage of 56.3. Lovellette tried 17 shots, completed four for 24.5 percent.

Someone asked Rupp after the game why he pulled Spivey when Lovellette left on fouls.

THE LINE-UPS

KENTUCKY (68)

	FG	FT	Pts.
Hirsch	5	0	10
Linville	4	0	8
Price	0	0	0
Newton	0	0	0
Spivey	9	4	22
Tsioropoulos	1	0	2
Ramsey	8	3	19
Watson	3	0	6
Whitaker	0	1	1
Castle	0	0	0
Totals	**30**	**8**	**68**

KANSAS (39)

	FG	FT	Pts.
Linehard	3	0	6
Kenney	1	2	4
Beck	0	1	1
Bull	1	2	4
Hoag	1	0	2
Enns	0	0	0
Lovellette	4	2	10
Houghland	2	3	7
Waugh	0	0	0
Schaake	1	1	3
Engel	1	0	2
Wells	0	0	0
Totals	**14**	**11**	**39**

"We wanted the playing time to be exactly even — we wanted it just that way," he responded. "We had a commanding lead, too."

Kentucky and Kansas fought on even terms for the first 10 minutes of the opening half, and the battle of the giants — Spivey and Lovellette — was a defensive one. They were on each other like glue, with neither able to get many good shots at the basket.

So, midway of this half, Kentucky led, 8-5. Both teams fired erratically, but both were pressed by the tight defense of the opposition.

Kentucky got its fast break working during a flaming five minutes that ensued. Ramsey cut loose with two buckets. Then Spivey found the range, too, with his hooks and spins, and he connected on three straight buckets. On the first, he stole the ball from Lovellette under the Kansas basket. Breaking loose from the surprised pack, Spivey dribbled the length of the floor and scored in the clear.

Ramsey came back with another basket on a crip. By now, Kentucky had constructed a 14-point lead these torrid five minutes and was ahead, 20-6.

This margin was boosted to 16 at the half — 28-12. Spivey had accounted for 14 points and Ramsey eight. Lovellette had four points on two fielders and two free throws.

Spivey and Hirsch hit to open the second half, and Kentucky increased its advantage to 20 points — 32-12. However, Lovellette began to operate, and with him chipping in three field goals, Kansas narrowed the UK lead to 36-21.

But Kentucky retaliated with Ramsey and Linville scoring buckets and Spivey accumulating two more, too. This boosted Kentucky to 44-21, and then Kansas got a tough break. Lovellette fouled out with 13 minutes 33 seconds of playing time left.

At a height of 7 feet, Bill Spivey's domination of opposing teams made him a Kentucky legend of epic proportions.

Memorial Coliseum, with a seating capacity of 11,000 plus, opened in 1950. For the next 25 seasons it was the place where many Kentucky basketball legends were born and opposing teams' fortunes buried.

The issue now no longer was in doubt. And to clinch things, the Wildcats spurted to a 26-point lead, at 49-23, with 10 minutes remaining. With Spivey out, Ramsey now was sparking the Wildcat offense.

Shortly after this midway point of the second half, Rupp started substituting. With six minutes left, only Ramsey and Watson of the regulars still were in action. Even so, the hot Wildcats continued to hit, and they rolled on to a 64-33 lead behind some long range

shooting by Watson.

Watson soon left the game, too, and Kentucky finished up with subs on the floor.

Thus, this first meeting between two of the games most colorful personalities resulted in a victory for the pupil — Adolph Rupp. Rupp had played basketball under Phog Allen, the Kansas mentor, in the early 1920's.

CHAPTER 16

After scoring 22 points in the Wildcats' 68-58 win over Kansas State in the N.C.A.A. Tournament final, Bill Spivey is congratulated by his coach, Adolph Rupp.

Kentucky Rolls Over K-State to Win 3d N.C.A.A. Title

BY LARRY BOECK
Special to The Courier-Journal

MINNEAPOLIS, March 27, 1951 — They earned the right tonight, did these current Wildcats, to stand erectly alongside other immortal Kentucky basketball teams.

These courageous Wildcats did it by creating basketball history as they came from behind to subdue big, fast Kansas State, 68-58, before 15,438 in the Min-neapolis Fieldhouse.

They won for Kentucky its third National Collegiate Athletic Association championship — the first time it ever has been achieved by one school.

And the Kentuckians did it the hard way once again, coming from behind for the fourth time in four hectic tournament games.

Kentucky previously had won the N.C.A.A. crown with the "Fabulous Five" in 1947-48 and 1948-49.

Kentucky came into this game as the underdog, the

first time it had been cast in that role in 10 years. For fans here, impressed by the way Kansas State had stormed through three tough foes in gaining the final, gave the nod to the Kansans.

This seemed to be the correct call in the first half, when poor-shooting and perhaps over-anxious UK trailed by five and six points, then lost a two-point lead and went in at the half behind, 29-27.

Kentucky stormed back in the second half, looking like the sharp team it had been in mid-season. In a matter of seconds, these battling, racing, shooting Kentuckians grabbed a 35-30 margin after two minutes.

They never trailed again. They were outrebounding and outfiring the Kansans, outracing and outscrapping them. Led by Bill Spivey and Cliff Hagan, the Wildcats romped along to a 15-point lead, 54-39, after 10 minutes of play in this second half.

Here, Kansas State employed a full-court press for a few hazardous moments. This rattled Kentucky. And Kansas State, which had been cold, started to find the range, whittling the Kentucky lead to 58-48 with 4:40 left and seemingly were on the way.

But not against a bunch like the Wildcats, who struggled hard to gain the finals and were fighting now. Hagan scored on a spin shot, then on a crip after receiving a long, nifty pass from Spivey. Spivey followed with a free throw and Skippy Whitaker with a crip.

That was it. It broke the back of a fine Kansas State team, one which Coach Hank Iba of Oklahoma A&M called "one of the finest in basketball history."

But tonight the Kansans encountered a Kentucky squad that was keyed to a feverish pitch. The Wildcats wanted desperately to win this one, and so, perhaps, they were tight in the first half when they hit

THE LINE-UPS

KENTUCKY (68)

	FG	FT	Pts.
Whitaker	4	1	9
Linville	2	4	8
Spivey	9	4	22
Ramsey	4	1	9
Watson	3	2	8
Hagan	5	0	10
Tsioropoulos	1	0	2
Newton	0	0	0
Totals	**28**	**12**	**68**

KANSAS STATE (58)

	FG	FT	Pts.
Head	3	2	8
Stone	3	6	12
Hitch	6	1	13
Barrett	2	0	4
Iverson	3	1	7
Rousey	2	0	4
Gibson	0	1	1
Upson	0	0	0
Knostman	1	1	3
Peck	2	0	4
Schuyler	1	0	2
Totals	**23**	**12**	**58**

just 28 percent of their shots.

The Wildcats shook off this tenseness in the second chapter, while Kansas State, closely guarded, could never get going and failed to set off its vaunted offense.

Spivey, as Coach Adolph Rupp said after the game, was the big gun. The seven-foot "Georgia Pine" accumulated 22 points — many in the clutches. More than this point-production, however, was his terrific work under the boards. He got 21 vital rebounds — almost half of Kentucky's 45 — while Kansas State got just 30.

Tonight's victory tied the 1948-49 record of the Fabulous Five at 32-2, but in 1947-48 the Fabulous Five won 36 and lost 3.

Behind Spivey and Hagan, who did not start because he had a touch of the flue yesterday and today, came Skippy Whitaker and Frank Ramsey with nine points each, and Bobby Watson and Shelby Linville with eight each. Linville, terrific throughout the entire tournament, snared eight rebounds as well.

Six-foot-nine Lew Hitch, who opposed Spivey at center, nabbed 13 points. Jack Stone had 12. All-America Ernie Barrett was limited to four by the close-guarding of Watson, Linville, Ramsey and Whitaker, who alternated on the job.

Kentucky, in hitting a fine 40.5 percentage of their shots from the field (about 46 the second half), conquered Kansas State for the third time in the history of this series. K-State, which had been hot throughout the meet and in blasting Illinois in a warmup, hit just 28 percent.

It was the fourth loss in 26 games for K-State, which wound up third in the combined A.P. and U.P. ratings.

An elated Coach Rupp said after the game he was proud of his boys.

"They sure can make your hair stand on end," he said, "but they come through in the clutch. They

Bill Spivey (77) and Frank Ramsey (30) battle against Kansas State's John Gibson (21) for a rebound in Kentucky's 68-58 victory in the 1951 N.C.A.A. final.

nipping at their heels at from two to four points but never catching up. Finally, near the half's end, they forged ahead, 24-22, on Spivey's lay-up. Then back came Kansas State to build another four-point lead at 29-25 while the few agonized Kentucky fans in the Fieldhouse, which was wildly pro-Kansas State, sat back and chewed their nails.

The Wildcats came back as killers the second half. Linville got a free throw and then once more Spivey gave the Cats a lead — 30-29.

Kansas State tied it up on a free throw. And Linville countered with a free throw to return the lead to Kentucky.

Running briskly, and bewildering the Kansans while their fans sat surprised, Kentucky was off and running.

Quickly, they surged to a 10-point lead, 48-38, with 13:16 left. Now the Cats, sluggish in the first half, were rolling. They were rebounding well, shooting terrifically and running at a speed that amazed the Kansas State team and stunned onlookers.

The Wildcats piled it on, while Kansas State could do nothing right, and went out front, 54-39, with 10 minutes left.

showed they have a lot of courage, a lot of determination, in this tournament.

"Was it one of our best games? Well, in the second half, it came close to being. But we still didn't play as well as we are capable. But that's not to be construed as a criticism from me, please. How ya' gonna criticize a great bunch of boys like this after the great season they've had?"

Five points separated these Cats from an undefeated season, losing only by one point in overtime to St. Louis in the Sugar Bowl and by four to Vanderbilt in the Southeastern Conference tourney.

At the outset they fell behind, 9-4. And once again, as in the Illinois semi-final, they hounded the Kansans,

Here, things appeared to take a desperate turn for UK. Shelby Linville, Frank Ramsey and Cliff Hagan had four personal fouls each. What's more, Kansas State went to a full-court press.

Kentucky appeared to be rattled. Kansas State narrowed the gap to 10 points, 58-48, with 4:40 to go. They appeared now to be rolling, to be finding the range, and they were taking advantage of Kentucky mistakes.

What's more, Linville had fouled out with 5:57 left.

Kentucky, however, once more was equal to the task. It quelled the rebellion. Hagan's two field goals, a free throw by Spivey and Whitaker's field goal, while Kansas State was not scoring, sealed the issue.

Rupp receives Kentucky's third N.C.A.A. championship trophy in 4 seasons.

CHAPTER 17

The Wildcats won 29 games, lost only 3 and were ranked No. 1 in the country at the end of the 1951-52 season by both The Associated Press and The United Press. However, in the 1952 N.C.A.A. Tournament St. John's dethroned the Wildcats.

Wildcats Topple Redmen for 100th Straight Home Win

BY THE ASSOCIATED PRESS
The New York Times

LEXINGTON, Dec. 17, 1951 — Kentucky smashed St. John's, 81-40, in a battle of the nation's Nos. 1 and 2 basketball powers before a crowd of 12,000 here tonight.

Cliff Hagan, a leaping, twisting whirlwind, and little Bobby Watson scored 25 points apiece in Kentucky's triumph.

Hagan and Frank Ramsey controlled the rebounds on both boards and Watson fired from the outside to humiliate St. John's, previously unbeaten in five starts.

The crowd that expected a tight duel saw Kentucky go to the front at the outset and gradually build its command to 10, 20, 30 and finally 41 points. Kentucky was hot. It hit 44.4 percent of its tries to a 16.6 shooting mark for St. John's.

Though it conceded the visitors some height, Kentucky worked under both boards like it owned them

With Bill Spivey unable to play due to injury, Cliff Hagan stepped forward and led the Wildcats to victory.

and there was little doubt that St. John's was a beaten club after the first period.

Bob Zawoluk, the St. John's center who has a chance to become collegiate scoring leader, got only one field goal and wound up with seven points.

Hagan was hitting tip-ins, rebounds and wide-open lay-ups, and little Watson was firing them in from far and near as Kentucky took its 100th consecutive home-floor victory.

St. John's acted at the start as if it would make a game of it. Solly Walker, a sophomore guard, hit six of the first seven points for the Redmen with leaping shots. But Hagan had fired in nine and Kentucky was ahead, 14-7.

By the quarter, the count moved to 17-8 and Watson began to warm up. In the middle of the second period the score was 26-16 and Kentucky went on a spree that ran it to 39-19 at the half.

It took Kentucky only four and a half minutes in this frame to get a 30-point edge. St. John's began to slow the game near the end of that frame and the crowd yelled for the Redmen to "freeze the ball."

Starting the last frame, the game lost much of its luster and the ragged play was reflected in the scoring, with Kentucky gaining a 14-9 advantage for the period.

Shelby Linville, Ramsey and Watson fouled out in the last half for Kentucky, but the game was under control before their exit.

The crowd treated Walker, the first Negro to play in the Coliseum, like any other player and he got a big hand when he went out for a rest in the second period.

Bill Spivey, Kentucky's 7-foot center, who is suffering from a knee injury, sat this one out. Hagan was more than adequate as his replacement.

THE LINE-UPS

KENTUCKY (81)

	FG	FT	Pts.
Linville	2	1	5
Tsioropoulos	3	1	7
Evans	1	0	2
Hagan	10	5	25
Ramsey	4	4	12
Whitaker	1	0	2
Watson	11	3	25
Rose	1	1	3
Neff	0	0	0
Totals	**33**	**15**	**81**

ST. JOHN'S (40)

	FG	FT	Pts.
McMahon	0	3	3
Davis	3	0	6
Duckett	0	0	0
Coyle	0	0	0
Sagons	1	1	3
Zawoluk	1	5	7
Dunn	1	2	4
McGilvray	0	4	4
Walker	3	0	6
Giancontieri	1	2	4
McMurrow	0	3	3
Walsh	0	0	0
Totals	**10**	**20**	**40**

Frank Ramsey (30) fights with St. John's Bob Zawoluk for the ball late in the first quarter.

CHAPTER 18

Rupp's Wildcats won 25 games and lost none in the 1953-54 season. Kentucky also won its 16th S.E.C. title in 21 seasons. Five heroes of this memorable campaign were (left to right) Phil Grawemeyer, Bill Evans, Lou Tsioropoulos, Cliff Hagan and Frank Ramsey.

Kentucky Wins, But Pulls Out of N.C.A.A. Tourney

BY LARRY BOECK
Special to The Courier-Journal

NASHVILLE, March 9, 1954 — Kentucky froze a hot Louisiana State out of the Southeastern Conference championship here tonight by 63-56. The school then announced it will not compete in the National Collegiate Athletic Association tournament.

Louisiana State was chosen to go instead and accepted.

The Wildcats, who did not lose in 24 previous games this season, tottered near an upset before 7,300 excited fans. But, led by Frank Ramsey's sensational play and a big contribution by Cliff Hagan, Kentucky overcame a 40-36 deficit midway in the third quarter of this frantically contested game.

Then, leading 55-51 with only 4:52 left, the Wildcats started to freeze the ball. Aided by some dazzling dribbling by Gayle Rose, they stalled it out and still stretched their edge a little.

As cheerleaders and Kentucky partisans carried the Wildcats from the floor on their shoulders in a gleeful celebration, newsmen were handed the school's prepared statement on the N.C.A.A. tournament.

Pointing out that three boys were ineligible for the tournament (the N.C.A.A. Tuesday afternoon officially ruled Ramsey, Hagan and Lou Tsioropoulos cannot compete in the collegiate playoffs) the school added:

"The Athletics Board and athletic officials at the University of Kentucky doubt that in the absence of the three boys, its team would be the strongest in the Southeastern Conference. Accordingly, the Athletics Board has unanimously voted that the University of Kentucky withdraw from the N.C.A.A. Tournament and requests the conference to designate some other team to represent this district."

The three boys are ineligible under N.C.A.A. rules because they are postgraduates, but under S.E.C. rules they have been eligible for conference play.

Kentucky coach Adolph Rupp, who has been ailing with a heart condition, suffered what was a possible mild heart attack in the locker room after the game. He was forced to rest.

Dr. V. H. Jackson, of Clinton, Ky., attended him at the hotel later and said the coach's blood pressure and heart "checked out O.K."

Rupp's illness might signal the end of a fabulous, excitement-packed basketball career. Friends have been urging Rupp to quit for some time.

It was generally believed he would do so if he won the N.C.A.A. title this year.

However, he now might settle for the Wildcats' brilliant record of 25-0, the longest undefeated, one-

THE LINE-UPS

KENTUCKY (63)

	FG	FT	Pts.
Tsioropoulos	1	1	3
Evans	1	1	3
Grawemeyer	0	0	0
Hagan	7	3	17
Ramsey	13	4	30
Puckett	1	1	3
Rose	1	5	7
Rouse	0	0	0
Totals	**24**	**15**	**63**

LOUISIANA STATE (56)

	FG	FT	Pts.
Clark	6	2	14
McNeilly	1	0	2
Belcher	3	3	9
Pettit	6	5	17
Magee	0	1	1
Sebastian	4	0	8
McArdle	1	3	5
Jones	0	0	0
Zinser	0	0	0
Totals	**21**	**14**	**56**

season winning streak in basketball history.

The Wildcats had to sweat to pull this one out of danger in a game in which both teams stressed what was supposed to be a lost art in basketball — defense.

L.S.U.'s defense, however, could not stop one man — Ramsey, who has been nicknamed "The Blond Bombshell." He was a bombshell, indeed, as he scored 30 points.

Hagan collected 17 points, although he was guarded by the 6-foot-9 Bob Pettit and another Bengal as L.S.U. employed a sagging defense. L.S.U. also jammed the middle lanes to the basket, attempting to cut off Kentucky's drives.

Pettit almost matched Ramsey in luster. He scored 17 points, much below his season's average of 32, but he was a tyrant on the boards, getting rebound after rebound. He grabbed 21 for the night.

Like Hagan, Pettit was closely guarded, and Kentucky, for the first time this season, almost used a sagging defense. Tsioropoulos was on Pettit and was helped by Hagan.

Despite Pettit's heroic rebounding, Kentucky collected more. It also got 14 more shots than L.S.U., 67-53. The Wildcats hit on 24 of these shots for a 36.8 percent average. L.S.U. hit on 21 for 39.6 percent.

Thus, the game story is wrapped up in that vital figure — those 14 more shots. For had this hot L.S.U. had the opportunity to fire more often, the Bengals obviously could have staged the upset.

They came uncomfortably close, for Kentucky fans, to doing just that after Kentucky appeared to be coasting toward victory when it had piled up an 11-point lead, 25 to 14, with 6:17 left in the first half.

Nonetheless, Ben Clark, who had 12 points for the night, and New Albany's Don Belcher, who scored nine, sliced the Kentucky margin to 30-28 and went into the halftime intermission behind by that score.

Frank Ramsey, an all-American in 1952 and 1954, led the Wildcats with 30 points in their win over L.S.U. in 1954.

bit flustered.

Kentucky finally regained the lead, as both teams fought fiercely, when Hagan stole the ball, dribbled almost the full length of the floor and then drove in for the vital lay-up.

This appeared to restore their poise to the champions. And, although the teams traded buckets until Kentucky made it 53-51 with 5 minutes left, they appeared to control the situation.

Hagan then hooked in a shot. And at 55-51, Kentucky began then to freeze the ball. However, with 4:14 to go, Ramsey saw an opening, darted through it, and scored on this driving crip shot.

Now ahead, 57-51, Kentucky really put on the freeze. And Rose put on that clever dribbling act. Frantically, Bengals went after the ball. Whenever they closed in on him, Rose faked and dribbled around and away.

He was helped by Willie Rouse, who went into the game after Billy Evans fouled out with 7:25 of game time left.

Thus Kentucky, in a dramatic playoff, won its 16th Southeastern Conference championship in the 21 years of the league's life. The teams staged tonight's playoff because they had tied by finishing unbeaten during the regular conference season.

Finally, with 6:45 to go in the third quarter, Clark hit from the side and Kentucky was tied, 36-36. Don Sebastian then looped in a 30-footer and Pettit followed with a tip as a disorganized UK scrambled all over the floor in confusion as L.S.U. led, 40 to 36.

It was here that Kentucky put on its all-court press — that is, going after the ball even when L.S.U. had it in the back court.

And the strategy paid off. L.S.U. started getting a

Bernie Moore, the S.E.C. commissioner, immediately after UK's statement, offered Louisiana State the N.C.A.A. tournament berth vacated by Kentucky.

Later, L.S.U. coach Harry Rabenhorst polled the team back at its hotel and the boys voted to accept the offer.

Lou Tsioropoulos (above), along with Cliff Hagan and Frank Ramsey, were ruled ineligible to play in the 1954 N.C.A.A. Tournament. Because of this problem, the school withdraw from the tournament.

CHAPTER 19

Tech 'Iron Men' Lead 59-58 Win

By Larry Boeck
Special to The Courier-Journal

Lexington, Jan. 8, 1955 — Georgia Tech employed no witchcraft in strategy, in surprising Kentucky, 59-58, here tonight.

"Strategy? Naw, naw. Those kids just went out and played their hearts out," said joyous Tech coach Whack Hyder of the amazing victors.

"Those five kids who went all the way — they deserve all the credit. All I did was pray in those last five minutes."

Pulling the "Iron man" stunt for Georgia Tech were Bobby Kimmel, the sophomore captain and former Valley High star, Joe Helms, Dick Lenholt, Lenny Cohen and Bill Cohen.

"We didn't prepare anything special for Kentucky on offense," added Hyder, who recorded only his 17th victory in 76 games at Tech over four seasons.

"The only thing we did do that we hadn't done before was to switch off on the guards on defense, that's all."

When the final buzzer sounded, the supremely happy, flushed-faced Engineers whacked each other heartily — so lustily, in fact, that Kimmel suffered a cut lip that bled freely. It wasn't serious though.

"Lenny! Lenny! We beat em! We beat em!" shouted one Engineer, who appeared as disbelieving of the result as the crowd of 8,500.

Down a dimly lit corridor off the playing floor, there was disbelief, too — silent and agonizing instead of hysterically happy — around UK quarters.

Puffy-eyed Coach Adolph Rupp, who leaped from the bench to congratulate Hyder before even the Engineers could get to their coach, gave Tech all the credit.

"They deserve everything they got," he said. "We have no one to blame but ourselves. We had the game won three times and lost it."

Kentucky led by seven points early in the going. They lost that lead by six with some eight minutes left and had a 58-55 margin with 1:30 remaining. Outside the room where the Cats glumly dressed, Wildcat football coach Blanton Collier appeared as grief-stricken as the basketball coaching staff of Adolph Rupp.

"I'm sorry, Adolph," he said. "It's too bad — too bad."

Players filed out of the dressing room one at a time, not talking to one another and preferring not to talk to other people.

"We didn't work as a team tonight," said disconsolate Jerry Bird. "We were individuals, not a team."

Most of the arena was deserted when Louisville's Phil (Cookie) Grawemeyer came out to see his

Kentucky vs **Ga. Tech**

MEMORIAL COLISEUM

Saturday, January 8, 1955 — 8:00 p.m.

OFFICIAL PROGRAM—10 CENTS

parents, Mr. and Mrs. Ernest Grawemeyer.

"We didn't click on anything, on our plays, shooting, rebounding, passing — nothing," said Grawemeyer.

This first defeat on the home floor since January 2, 1943 — to Ohio State by 45-40 — surprised many but it didn't catch some members of the football squad without their wits.

Outside the Coliseum, in the coldish night, the gridmen assembled a study body of several hundred and, while Wildcat basketball players filed out, the assemblage sang "On, On, U. of K." and other pep songs.

One of the leaders was football co-captain Joe Koch of Louisville.

There was good reason for the shock and disbelief among UK followers. For here was a team that had knocked off La Salle, Utah and Xavier this season — and then lost to an outfit that had won just two of its

THE LINE-UPS

KENTUCKY (58)

	FG	FT	Pts.
Bird	3	1	7
Grawemeyer	8	3	19
Burrow	7	2	16
Mills	0	0	0
Puckett	5	0	10
Evans	1	3	5
Rose	0	1	1
Totals	**24**	**10**	**58**

GEORGIA TECH (59)

	FG	FT	Pts.
L. Cohen	5	0	10
Lenholt	0	4	4
B. Cohen	2	0	4
Helms	7	9	23
Kimmel	4	10	18
Totals	**18**	**23**	**59**

last six games.

So lightly regarded were the Engineers that Kentucky didn't even scout them. The Wildcats had chalked up 28 straight victories over Tech since 1940.

But most observers agreed that Kentucky was a very flat team tonight — and very smug.

It had taken this victory for granted and was looking ahead, quite possibly to a tough session with strong DePaul here Monday night.

"It just goes to prove that Rupp was right when he said last week he'd stricken the word 'impossible' from his vocabulary," said one writer. "I'm striking if from mine, too."

Among the few elated observers in the assemblage was George Kimmel of Columbia, Ky., a brother of the sensational Bobby Kimmel.

"I'm happy for my brother's sake," said George Kimmel. "If Kentucky had to be beat, this is the best way."

Kimmel's parents moved from the Louisville area last year to Panama City, Fla.

When did the Engineers get the feeling they could whip the Cats, we asked Bobby Kimmel.

"In the last five minutes, we knew we really were after a big upset and could get it," he said.

Kentucky was on the ropes then, added Kimmel, and the Engineers figured one good punch could do it. The Engineers got it and landed.

Among the last to leave the arena was Hyder.

"They probably won't believe that score down in Atlanta," he said. "Especially since we got beat by Sewanee our last time out. But, you know, I've said that this bunch could beat any given club on any given night.

"Yep, they probably won't believe that score down in Atlanta."

"Or anywhere else," added a hurried sportswriter on the press bench.

Phil Grawemeyer was a pivotal anchor in the Wildcats' defense in the 1954-55 season.

CHAPTER 20

Wildcats Smash Dogs, 143-66

BY LARRY BOECK
Special to The Courier-Journal

LEXINGTON, Feb. 27, 1956 — Kentucky broke more records last night than a 3-year-old bundle of mischief left alone in a music shop.

The Wildcats' basket barrage crumbled Georgia, 143-66, at the Armory before a crowd of approximately 5,000. What made the score all the more impressive was that UK regulars played for approximately just 15 minutes.

That was enough to send the Wildcats to a 53-49 lead. Here, Kentucky coach Adolph Rupp started to pour in substitutes. They were hot, too, against inept Georgia. And so at halftime the Cats led, 75-33.

Second stringers opened the second half and by the time this carnage had ceased every Wildcat had seen combat. The starters never returned.

Georgia made just one run at the Wildcats. UK led, 17-8, at the end of five minutes. Then the Bulldogs chopped this to 17-15. Kentucky quickly applied the pressure and that was that.

Here are some of the records the Wildcats set, although more will come to light as historians check through the record book:

1. Cracked the S.E.C. record of 120 points, scored by Louisiana State last season.

2. Broke the Armory's high of 115 points, scored by Louisville against Mississippi State in 1954.

3. Shattered their own team high of 116, set against Ole Miss at Owensboro in 1952.

4. Poured in the most field goals ever in an S.E.C. game, connecting on 60.

5. Set a conference record of total points for both teams, the 209 surpassing the 188 UK and Auburn constructed in 1954.

Jerry Bird, with 22 points, led the Wildcats' scoring attack against the Bulldogs.

THE LINE-UPS

KENTUCKY (143)

	FG	FT	Pts.
Bird	10	2	22
Grawemeyer	5	3	13
Brewer	2	0	4
Johnson	3	3	9
Smith	4	2	10
Mills	5	0	10
Burrow	8	5	21
Beck	3	2	8
Hatton	2	2	6
Calvert	3	2	8
Cassady	8	0	16
Ross	3	2	8
Collingsworth	0	0	0
Crigler	4	0	8
Totals	**60**	**23**	**143**

GEORGIA (66)

	FG	FT	Pts.
Bell	3	0	6
Allen	5	1	11
Hearn	1	0	2
Gleaton	3	0	6
Cabaniss	8	7	23
Hartsfield	3	4	10
Dinwiddie	3	2	8
Hester	0	0	0
Totals	**26**	**14**	**66**

Bob Burrow and the Baron. Burrow scored 21 points in the Wildcats' rout of Georgia in 1956.

The Wildcats' 143 points compiled by 14 players also is believed to be the second highest ever scored by a major college team. Furman last season trounced The Citadel, 154-67. The N.C.A.A. last night was checking UK's status as No. 2 in scoring.

The victory was Kentucky's 18th victory opposed to five losses. Georgia, which never came close to UK in any department, has achieved just three victories.

The Wildcats connected on 60 of 105 shots for a percentage of 57.1. This also is believed to be a UK record in firing. Georgia sank 26 of 55 field goal attempts for 29.5 percent. Kentucky gathered 80 rebounds, Georgia 36.

The scoring leader for the night, although he was on the losing team, was Georgia's Henry Cabannis with 23 points. Jerry Bird led the Wildcats with 22 and Bob Burrow tallied 21.

This didn't stack up as much of a contest and, brother, it sho' wasn't! After the second stringers matched the starting bunch in firing, Coach Rupp combined elements of the third team with that of the second. Even this couldn't withhold the avalanche of buckets.

Cookie Grawemeyer, who didn't start last night, went in as the first sub with five minutes to go in the half and wound up with 13 points, although he was withdrawn from the game with 10 minutes to go. Billy Cassady tossed in 16 points.

CHAPTER 21

The Wildcats posted a record of 23 wins and 6 losses and won their fourth N.C.A.A. Tournament championship in 1957-58.

Hatton's Heroics Let UK Win in 3 Overtimes

BY LARRY BOECK
Special to The Courier-Journal

LEXINGTON, Dec. 7, 1957 — Vernon Hatton's incredible, 47-foot field goal with one second left in the first overtime and his six points in the third overtime gave courageous Kentucky a heart-pounding 85-83 victory over valiant Temple here Saturday night.

This thriller — which will be recorded among basketball's all-time classics — was an uphill struggle for the Wildcats virtually all the tense 55 minutes.

It was Hatton, the crew-cut, 6-foot-4 senior guard from Lexington, who will be remembered as the star (although he also could have been a bit of a goat). But this truly should be chronicled as a team victory.

Hatton, though, will be remembered for years for his fantastic shot in the only overtime game in the Memorial Coliseum since the imposing building was first put into use in 1950.

He'll be remembered, too, for sinking a free throw that put the game into overtime and for his six points in the third overtime.

The regulation-time game ended at 65-65 when Hatton sank a one-shot free throw with 49 seconds remaining. It was a portent of Hatton's subsequent role as the hero, although twice during the upcoming three overtimes he lost the ball on errors at critical moments.

But nothing can ever dim the memories of the 12,300 nerve-shaken fans of that 47-foot shot. Nor the six points Hatton threw in — two on field goals — to push Kentucky out front 85-81 with 1:28 to go in the third overtime.

Here was the scene of that memorable shot — one that Hatton figured to have less chance of making than buying a winning ticket in the Irish Sweepstakes.

Kentucky trailed, 71-69, with three seconds left after Temple's Guy Rodgers, a magnificent all-around guard who tallied 24 points, sent through a 15-foot push shot.

Kentucky signaled time-out with one precious — although seemingly futile — second glimmering red on the scoreboard.

The Wildcats took the ball out at mid-floor. The Wildcats lined up evenly, about a yard apart, on the white stripe at mid-floor, except John Crigler. He threw the ball in from out-of-bounds to Hatton.

Hatton, with a 45-degree angle or so at the basket, fired immediately. The ball arched high, power behind it. It thumped into dead center of the hoop, bounced violently between the iron circle but was trapped and fell through.

Bedlam then broke loose.

The teams ended at 71-all this first overtime, and 75-75 after the suspenseful second overtime, in which Temple came from behind on Mel Brodsky's two free throws with 53 seconds left.

Temple now was operating without that indescribable Rogers — a scoring threat, leader, playmaker and ball-hawk. He had fouled out with 55 seconds remaining to go in the second extra five-minute period. His running mate, sophomore Bill Kennedy, fouled out

THE LINE-UPS

KENTUCKY (85)

	FG	FT	Pts.
Cox	10	2	22
Crigler	6	5	17
Beck	2	3	7
Smith	6	5	17
Hatton	5	7	17
Adkins	2	1	5
Totals	31	23	85

TEMPLE (83)

	FG	FT	Pts.
Brodsky	9	6	24
Norman	5	2	12
Fleming	0	0	0
Franklin	1	0	2
Van Patton	1	0	2
Kennedy	8	3	19
Rodgers	11	2	24
Peppe	0	0	0
Totals	35	13	83

with 1:30 left in the third overtime.

Crigler gave UK the lead at 77-75 to open the third overtime with two free shots, but Temple evened it on Jay Norman's 15-foot jump shot.

Adrian Smith made it 79-77 with 3:05 left on two free throws but Brodsky hit on a spin shot from the circle to tie the game the 13th time.

Here Hatton went to work — first on a 20-foot overhead pot shot. Kennedy tied it 81-81 on a fading jump shot from the corner. But Hatton retaliated with a 20-foot shot and two free throws to make it 85-81 with 1:28 remaining.

Temple scored again — but now the ball game was over.

Kentucky rescued it on that miraculous 47-foot shot, for Temple should — and would have in 10,000 other such situations — won the game with that second to go in the overtime.

It was a planned play that Kentucky used, said Coach Adolph Rupp afterwards.

"We used it a couple of years ago to beat Utah," he said, his coat now off in the locker room and his white shirt soaked with sweat.

"When people make shots like that, it just isn't' your night," said Coach Harry Litwack of Temple, sadly.

Kentucky beat Utah, 70-65, in the UK Invitational Tournament in 1954. It lined up the same way near the game's end but the pass went to a Wildcat who had broken free off the pass.

With one second left, time was out and the clock doesn't start again until a man on the floor touches the ball.

After a 2-0 lead, Kentucky trailed most of the frantically fought game. It was behind by eight at 21-13 with 9:23 left in the half but went into the intermission trailing only 35-34.

Temple opened a five-point, 47-42 margin after five minutes in the second half. Then the battle became a see-saw thriller.

Vernon Hatton, an all-America selection in 1958, had many memorable shots against Temple.

Kentucky appeared ready to sew it up against a poised, clever, race-horse and hot-shooting (during regulation time) Temple when it opened a 63-60 lead with four minutes left in the regular game. But it was behind, 65-64, with 49 seconds remaining. Here, Hatton set the stage for the chillers to come.

Temple sank 35 of 91 shot attempts for a 38.5 percent average. Kentucky, who for the second time this season won at the free throw line, made just 31 of 90 field goal attempts for 34.4 percent. But the Cats sank 23 of 33 free throws to 13 of 19 for Temple.

Kentucky, in winning its third game in as many outings, outrebounded Temple, which now is 1-1, by 63-58.

It was a UK team victory, as noted. For Johnny Cox finally cut loose after 12 rebounds and three-point efforts by turning in 22 points and 16 rebounds. Smith, Hatton and Crigler each had 17, with Crigler gaining 17 rebounds, and Beck accounted for 20 rebounds.

Rodgers — an all-American if ever there was one — tabbed 24 points and Brodsky 24 as well. Norman was the game's top rebounder with 23.

CHAPTER 22

Hatton Fires Goal in Final 16 Seconds For 61-60 Win

BY LARRY BOECK
Special to The Courier-Journal

LOUISVILLE, March 21, 1958 — Vernon Hatton did it to Temple again last night — this time from right under the basket and with 16 seconds left.

The imperturbable, dead-pan guy who sank an incredible 47-footer with a second left in overtime in December to help beat Temple, did it again last night on a huddle-planned, driving lay-up that gave Kentucky a 61-60 triumph over the Owls.

That victory sends the Wildcats against Seattle tonight at 9 o'clock for the N.C.A.A. championship. The underdog, but sharp-shooting Chieftains upset giant Kansas State in last night's second game of the National Collegiate Athletic Association semifinals, 73-51.

Temple will meet Kansas State in the consolation game at 7 tonight.

A record N.C.A.A. Tournament crowd of 18,586 thundered in exultation or despair when the senior guard from Lexington took a pass at the circle, swerved to his right behind a screen by Ed Beck, cut down the baseline, leaped and laid in the game-winning basket.

So once more, as in Lexington in December, the crew-cut Hatton spelled heartbreak for the speedy, ball-hawking Owls. Last December, the Owls seemed a cinch winner until Hatton's 47-footer that led to an 85-83 triple overtime victory.

Johnny Cox (24), the only All-S.E.C. player on the Wildcat squad in 1957-58, was the top scorer for UK against Temple.

Last night Kentucky again appeared a doomed club as Temple led by 4 points with 2:56 remaining. But again, the Owls collapsed under the pressure of the relentless Cats.

Thus, Kentucky — which had a mediocre 19 and 6 regular season — appears in its fourth N.C.A.A. final with a team that has no all-American and which could place just one man (Johnny Cox) on one of three All-Southeastern Conference teams released. And for the fourth time, Kentucky seeks the national championship.

Another packed-house at Freedom Hall — which took the 1946 N.C.A.A. record of 18,479 away from Madison Square Garden — is expected for the duel with Seattle.

The smaller but faster and deadlier shooting Chieftains — 8-point underdogs — outfought the rangy Kansas State Wildcats on the boards. And their chances of winning this title were set at 4 to 1 before the meet opened.

Those odds tumbled as Seattle grabbed 56 rebounds to Kansas State's 34.

Led by the remarkable shooting Elgin Baylor and by Charley Brown, an Indiana U. transfer, the Chieftains overcame an early Kansas State lead, went into the half ahead, 37-32, and then poured it on at the second half's onset.

UK — a team that fought and bled and scraped its way all this pressureful season to get this far — appeared a doomed ball club in the final minutes.

Once more, and once again in a classically dueled, tenseful battle, Temple needed but to control the situation to triumph.

In a frantically fought contest that was close all the way, Temple led by 4 points at 59-55 after erasing a seven-point UK first half lead and a five-point Wildcat early second-half margin.

The magnificent Guy Rodgers, an all-American guard, got hot with 10:53 to go in the second half and the teams tied for the third time at 42-42 in a defensive battle.

THE LINE-UPS

KENTUCKY (61)

	FG	FT	Pts.
Crigler	3	0	6
Cox	6	10	22
Collingsworth	0	0	0
Beck	3	2	8
Hatton	5	3	13
Smith	2	8	12
Totals	**19**	**23**	**61**

TEMPLE (60)

	FG	FT	Pts.
Norman	7	2	16
Brodsky	2	0	4
Van Patton	1	1	3
Fleming	3	3	9
Rodgers	9	4	22
Kennedy	3	0	6
Totals	**25**	**10**	**60**

Rodgers sank four buckets from outside in the next five minutes to give Temple temporary mastery of the situation.

Then, with the count 59-55, Temple coach Harry Litwack of the Owls jumped from the bench, stretched out both hands, palms upward, in a slowdown signal, and Temple went into a stall.

This was its undoing.

Adrian Smith sank two free throws after sophomore Bill Kennedy — the eventual goat of the game — charged into him. This made it 59-57.

Now 1:30 remained on the scoreboard clock.

With 55 seconds on the clock, Dan Fleming hit a free throw on the bonus to make it 60-57.

Rodgers fouled Smith — and again Smith hit two free throws to make it 60-59 with 29 seconds left.

Lincoln Collingsworth then fouled Rodgers — but this time Rodgers missed on the first free throw of the bonus.

Ed Beck jumped high, tipped the ball to Smith, and UK called time-out with only 23 ticks left. In the time-out huddle, Coach Adolph Rupp told the Cats how he wanted it played. Hatton's clutch field goal followed.

Temple got possession and quickly called time-out, then put the ball into play with 12 seconds left for a final important shot. But Kennedy bobbled a pass, the ball bounced out of bounds, Kentucky took over and that was it.

The defeat was all the more bitter for Temple because the Owls outscored UK from the field, 25 to 19. They outshot Kentucky, too, sinking 25 of 61 field goal attempts for a solid 41 percent while the Cats sank just 19 of 63 field goal attempts for a meek 30.2 percent.

But the Cats did out-rebound Temple, 44 to 36, and shot well from the free throw line in sinking 23

John Crigler (32) glides for a lay-up against Temple in the N.C.A.A. Tournament semi-final.

of 28 shots.

Johnny Cox, showing no ill effects from an injured shooting hand, led UK with 22 points, Hatton followed with 13 and Smith with 12.

Guy Rodgers didn't seem to be impaired by an ailing back as he fired home 22 points.

Each team committed nine turnovers.

The teams were nip-and-tuck until the end, although Temple did open up a 7-2 early lead and Kentucky went to the fore, 23-16, before the teams went into halftime tied, 33-33.

The score was tied eight times and changed hands 10 times.

CHAPTER 23

UK Stops Seattle, 84-72, For Its 4th N.C.A.A. Title

BY LARRY BOECK
Special to The Courier-Journal

LOUISVILLE, March 22, 1958 — Kentucky's "Fiddling Five" came right out of the barnyard to join the "Fabulous Five" and other great UK teams as champions of college basketball.

Described by Coach Adolph Rupp early in the season as "fiddlers, not violinists," battling Kentucky poured forth symphonic strains last night to conquer Seattle, 84-72.

In another come-from-behind victory, these kings of basketball erased an 11-point Seattle lead to triumph in the N.C.A.A. final.

Trailing almost all the way until only 6 minutes remained in the second half, sophomore Don Mills sank a short hook shot to put UK ahead, 61-60.

The N.C.A.A. title is Kentucky's fourth.

UK captured this title in a heroic uphill struggle — one typical of its season as a whole — before a record N.C.A.A. crowd of 18,803 who roared approval at Freedom Hall. Vernon Hatton, the UK guard, led all scorers with 30 points.

Stamped as a mediocre team, one not in the great tradition of past Kentucky teams, after compiling a 19 and 6 regular-season record, the Wildcats caught fire in the N.C.A.A. tourney.

After annexing their 19th Southeastern Conference title in one of the toughest fights for a Wildcat team in

Johnny Cox (24) leaps high for a tip-in against Seattle in the 1958 N.C.A.A. Tournament final.

Fresh from cutting the victory net, Vernon Hatton (52) is greeted by Gov. A.B. (Happy) Chandler.

many years, UK swept on to win two regional games at Lexington and then two more here.

Thus the bunch regarded as fiddlers — Rupp had said he needed violinists for a "Carnegie Hall schedule" — ended the season blissfully and sounding like Hiefetz playing Brahms on a Stradavarius.

Running their overall season mark to 23-6, this senior club had a tough time getting started.

A team that never has quit, UK battled back when, during a cold streak, Seattle streaked to a 29-18 lead with 7:44 to go in the first half.

Seattle then went into a zone and Kentucky managed to cut the margin to 39-36 at the halftime.

Seattle had slowed down play, Chieftain coach John Castellani said, because star Elgin Baylor — who collected 25 points — had injured ribs.

Nonetheless, Seattle pushed its lead to 44-38 with 16:44 left in the game.

Then Baylor picked up a fourth personal foul, and Johnny Cox — who had a bruised shooting hand — began to hit from outside as Seattle, after switching from the zone to a man-to-man defense, went back into a zone to protect Baylor.

The Wildcats began to hit the free throws and outfight the tiring Chieftains on the boards.

And, despite the fact that Mills had to play the last 17 minutes 44 seconds after Ed Beck collected his fourth foul, Kentucky started to crack away.

Mills helped tremendously on the boards and hit the shot that gave UK the 61-60 lead.

Cox immediately followed this with a push shot from the circle.

Adrian Smith added a free throw to make it 64-60.

Hatton then sank a free throw to make it 65-60, missed the second free throw, but grabbed the rebound and fired in a field goal.

That made it 67-60 with 4:18 remaining.

Suddenly, the Chieftains began to collapse.

Seattle would make one last threat with 3:14 left when it came within 68-65, but Cox hit two free throws to put the victory out of Seattle's reach.

Led by all-American Baylor, Charlie Brown, a transfer from Indiana U., and Jerry Frizzel, Seattle played poised basketball until those final frantic 6 minutes.

The tournament grind — the Chieftains had to play one more game than the other teams and travel farther in getting here — told near the end.

The game was the last for UK starters Hatton, Beck, Smith and John Crigler.

Crigler wound up with 14 points. Most of these came in the first half and allowed Kentucky to stay reasonably close to Seattle.

UK outrebounded Seattle, 55 to 46. It was one of the rare times that Seattle, one of the nation's rebounding leaders, had been beaten on the boards.

Moreover, Kentucky won with Seattle having something of a "home-floor" edge. True, most fans at vast Freedom Hall were for the Cats, but the 2-point underdog Chieftains had a rather large and vocal gathering for the game, which was tied six times and in

THE LINE-UPS

KENTUCKY (84)

	FG	FT	Pts.
Cox	10	4	24
Crigler	5	4	14
Beck	0	0	0
Mills	4	1	9
Hatton	9	12	30
Smith	2	3	7
Totals	30	24	84

SEATTLE (72)

	FG	FT	Pts.
Frizzel	4	8	16
Ogorek	4	2	10
Baylor	9	7	25
Harney	2	0	4
Brown	6	5	17
Saunders	0	0	0
Piasecki	0	0	0
Totals	25	22	72

which the lead changed hands five times.

But Seattle was playing its fourth game on the Freedom Hall floor, having played twice here during the Bluegrass Tournament.

With that record crowd of 18,803 — Friday night's 18,586 had broken the N.C.A.A. Madison Square Garden attendance of 18,479 set in 1946 — the tourney as a whole set a mark of 176,878.

Kentucky outshot the Chieftains 41.2 percent to 36 percent.

Cox had 24 points, 16 in the last 15 minutes of play.

Seattle, in its fifth N.C.A.A. final, was led by Baylor with 25.

A cold-shooting Kentucky, with no one scoring field goals except Crigler — on driving crips — fell behind, 18-10 after 10 minutes and then by a perilous 11 points at 29-18.

Then Seattle slowed down the pace and went into a semi-stall, but it didn't work.

For Kentucky, which caught fire after trailing, 29-18, with 7:44 to go in the first half, began getting help from Hatton. Chopping away at the Chieftains, the Cats finally pulled to 33-32 with 2:37 remaining in the half.

Once more, though — running a bit again — Seattle pulled to a 7-point margin at 39-32 with 1:12 left.

Kentucky battled back and went into the intermission trailing by 3 points at 39-36.

The Cats weren't able to stop Baylor, who had 12 points, and Frizzel and Brown were causing trouble with 12 and 9 points, respectively.

Hatton had 13 for UK, Crigler 11, and Cox with 6 as Kentucky — which went almost 5 minutes without a field goal when Seattle compiled its first lead — hit 39.4 percent of its shots.

Seattle, outscored by one field goal, hit 40.7 percent and had a free throw edge on Kentucky. The Cats missed three straight charity shots near the half's end.

Both teams were in trouble on fouls.

An excited crew of UK cheerleaders and Gov. Happy Chandler celebrate the Wildcats' 4th N.C.A.A. championship.

Beck and Smith had three each for U.K and Baylor three for Seattle.

UK and Seattle were rather lightly regarded in final season polls by the experts. UK was 14 in The United Press poll of coaches, ninth in The Associated Press survey; Seattle was 19th in the U.P., 18th in the A.P. poll.

CHAPTER 24

UK Rally Surprises Ohio State

By Larry Boeck
Special to The Courier-Journal

Lexington, Dec. 28, 1959 — This time it was Kentucky's Bennie Coffman playing with a broken nose, yet he teamed with Bill Lickert to break the back of big Ohio State, 96-93, here Monday night.

These guards scored 55 points between them to lead the Wildcats to victory in one of the most courageous comebacks ever seen on the Memorial Coliseum floor.

And there were a thundering 13,000 here to watch these gallant Cats overcome a 15-point Buckeye lead near the end of the second half and then win out in the final frantic five minutes, 13 seconds of play.

Paced by the remarkable Jerry Lucas and his 34 points, the rangy and powerful Buckeyes — firing incredibly — sped to a 57-42 margin with 1:50 left in the first half. Refusing to buckle here, the gritty Kentuckians sliced the margin to 59-49 at intermission behind Lickert and Coffman who, like Jerry West of West Virginia in the recent UK Invitational, had a great night playing with a busted nose.

The Cats were hitting well enough to be ahead at this point as they sank 51.3 percent of their field-goal attempts, but the flaming Buckeyes at this juncture sizzled with an amazing 64.1 percent.

Kentucky came out in the double pivot to start the second half. This slowed the tempo of the blitzing battle. The Cats began to dominate the boards and guards Lickert and Coffman — with 29 and 26 points, respectively, for the night — began to get slashing shots and other good ones.

Kentucky also began to hit with a fury. And the Buckeyes cooled off — UK hitting 61.5 percent in the second half and Ohio State 34.2.

Playing with a broken nose, Bennie Coffman's 26 points boosted the Wildcats over the powerful Buckeyes.

Battling the Buckeyes to start the second half, Kentucky pulled within 67-66 with 13:58 left. However, Ohio State jumped back to an 80-72 margin with 9:07 remaining and seemingly had Kentucky on the ropes again.

But back stormed the Cats, doggin the Buckeyes relentlessly.

With 5:13 remaining, Coffman hit a 14-foot jump shot to give UK an 85-84 margin. Ohio State nudged ahead, 86-85. Then Don Mills tied it at 86-86 with one free throw on the bonus. Moments later, again coming through in the clutch, Mills sank a spinner from the circle.

Kentucky now led, 88-86, with 3:06 remain-

THE LINE-UPS

KENTUCKY (96)	FG	FT	Pts.
Mills	5	3	13
Burchett	5	3	13
Jennings	3	2	8
Coffman	10	6	26
Lickert	12	5	29
Feldhaus	1	1	3
Pursiful	0	0	0
Cohen	0	4	4
Totals	**36**	**24**	**96**

OHIO STATE (93)	FG	FT	Pts.
Havlicek	7	4	18
Roberts	7	0	14
Lucas	13	8	34
Nowell	5	2	12
Seigfried	5	3	13
Hoyt	1	0	2
Gearhart	0	0	0
Furry	0	0	0
Totals	**38**	**17**	**93**

ing as the lead changed hands for the 10th and last time. The Cats never lost the lead thereafter. They built a 90-86 margin with 2:16 to go in this hectic thriller in which UK desperately stalled to protect the four-point bulge and Ohio State just as desperately fouled to try to get the ball. The scrambling in the final minutes was blood drumming and furious and felt like an eternity to UK followers.

Twice the Cats missed on the one-and-one in the clutch and Ohio State pulled within 90-89 in the final 45 seconds as the smooth, potentially great Lucas hit

Bill Lickert was the Wildcats' high scorer with 29 points.

his 34th and last point on a free throw. However, Sid Cohen then sank a pair of free throws, Carrol Burchett hit two at the charity line and Cohen came back with two more as the Cats hit six of six free throws in the final 35 seconds to triumph.

Thus, in what Coach Adolph Rupp later described as one of the greatest games ever played here, Kentucky made its record 6-3 in knocking off the Buckeyes. Ohio State, rated No. 3 in the last Associated Press poll, is 7-2.

And helping to save Kentucky from an embarrassing December was senior Coffman. He had broken his nose — it's a hairline fracture — against West Virginia when the Cats lost to the Mountaineers in the UK tournament final here before Christmas.

West also suffered a broken nose in that game, but scored 37 points.

CHAPTER 25

Bravo For The Baron

By Frank Deford
Sports Illustrated

New York, March 7, 1966 — A governor cannot succeed himself in the Commonwealth of Kentucky, and a horse can run only once in the Derby, but as long as Adolph Rupp is around the Bluegrass will never suffer from a lack of continuity. For 36 years, in a land of colonels, he has been the only Baron, a man of consummate pride and well-earned privilege. One might think that Adolph Rupp would be satisfied now to retire to his estate in the pleasant, rolling country outside Lexington, there to tend his prize Herefords and Burley tobacco, to rest amid his affluence and such souvenirs of glory as no other basketball coach ever has gathered. Instead, at the age of 64, he continues to pursue the only challenge left — trying to top himself. And that is some tough act to follow.

Rupp has won 743 games, 22 Southeastern Conference titles and four N.C.A.A. national championships, as well as enough acclaim (and censure, too) to serve most men, barons

Rupp and Cotton Nash, an all-American in 1962, 1963 and 1964, pose with Kentucky's four national championship trophies.

and otherwise, for all their years. Yet his persistence in staying at his job has won him this year something more than just another trophy or a few fresh statistics. He is threatening to become the grand old man of basketball.

Nearly everywhere his undefeated, No. 1 team has played, in the old hellholes and new fieldhouses throughout the South, where he has been hooted and despised for decades, Rupp has been accorded ovations of respect merely upon his appearance on the court.

Adolph Rupp offers his opinion to an uncompromising referee.

Though he does not admit it, he must sense his new status. Typical was the scene in Nashville four weeks ago after his Wildcats beat Vanderbilt, virtually assuring themselves a berth in the N.C.A.A. tournament and crushing the hopes of the home fans for a championship of their own. After shaking hands with the losing coach Rupp turned and, as the Vanderbilt partisans responded with applause for their conqueror, he threw an arm about Kentucky forward Larry Conley, received Conley's arm around his shoulder in return, and together — beaming — they marched down the length of the court.

Everyone's explanation for Rupp's new phase is that he has mellowed. "That's what they're saying," he concedes, indicating nothing except that it is interesting, at least, to be called mellow after all those years of antonymous description. But then he moves on, into

voluntary, eager praise for his team. "These boys are coachable," he says. "They listen and they do what they're supposed to. They're a pleasure and they're all regular. They are regular to the last man. It would be mean if they lost a game."

There has been a great deal of fuss in the Commonwealth about the matter of finding a nickname for this team, in keeping with those that have distinguished former Wildcat clubs. Mrs. Mary Simmerman of Lexington even wrote to the paper insisting that all the players be commissioned, so that they could simply and rightfully be proclaimed "The Kentucky Colonels." Most suggestions have featured alliteration, and so far "Rupp's Runts" seems to be leading in popularity. Regardless of the final public choice, however, it is clear from his behavior that this is Rupp's favorite five.

Adolph's mellowing has had little effect on the famous Kentucky practices, those taut lessons in efficiency which the Baron and his assistants preside over, all dressed in outfits of starched khaki. But this year Rupp's sarcasm, which used to endanger sensitive eardrums, is being held to a minimum. And, off the court, the players, a remarkably intelligent and personable bunch, are accorded attention and solicitude that no other Rupp team has ever been granted. "The other day," says senior guard Tommy Kron, "I heard him ask Conley what he was going to do after graduation. I never heard of that before. Coach Rupp always sort of found those things out. He was interested, but there was never anything like that." The attitude is unanimously reciprocal, too. "I really want to win this thing for him," says junior forward Pat Riley. "We all do. We're very close. It seems like we've all grown this year, and he's just grown into us."

Rupp gives Kron the hardest time on the practice floor ("Someday I'm going to write a book on how not to play basketball, and I'm going to devote the first 200 pages to you"), but the mellow Baron quickly takes over. The night before the Tennessee game last week the team met outside Rupp's office to receive encouragement from the cheerleaders. On behalf of the players Kron accepted a prize for "a special team, a special Kentucky team, something special." It was decorated giant-size box of the cereal Special K.

Shortly afterward Rupp came by on his way home. "Now, Tommy," he said. "No courting tonight." Kron had been fighting a virus and had hardly been out of his room for the last three days. "Now, you get your rest," Rupp added.

"Well, I don't know if I can get to sleep, but I'll just lie there," Kron said.

Rupp's UK Invitational Tournaments, which were held in mid-December, always attracted the country's best teams.

"Well, then," Rupp replied, almost paternally by now, "you get a good supper." Then he saw the cereal box.

"The cheerleaders gave it to us," Kron explained, handing it to Rupp for inspection. "See — K, Special K — for Kentucky. Why don't you keep it, Coach?"

"No, it was meant for the team," Rupp said.

"No, sir, really, you take it. None of us could eat it anyway. I mean, you know, none of us have refrigerators." Rupp was examining the contents label. "It's full of proteins," Kron urged.

"Well, all right, Tommy. Thank you," Rupp said. And then, bidding everyone good night, he moved

Michigan coach Dave Strack (second from left) visits with Rupp, Harry Lancaster and Joe B. Hall (far right).

on, the cereal box with the big bow and the bright-blue ribbon around it clutched to his bosom. If the scene after the Vanderbilt game was surprising, this one was stunning, and also touching, to anyone familiar with Rupp's previous relations with his players.

The point has been made, often cynically, that it would be impossible for any coach not to warm up to a team that was 23-0 and had no academic or disciplinary problems. But the change in Rupp is not so easily explainable. "With us," says Alex Groza, the all-America center on the "Fabulous Five" champs of the late 1940's, "there was no joking, no laughing, no whistling, no singing, no nothing. Just basketball. When we traveled, for instance, he often communicated with us through the team manager."

But there was one time this year, in Alabama, when Rupp positively enthralled some of the starters with an enchanting discourse about how his mother used to prepare fried chicken. On another occasion Louis Dampier, the little guard, came up to Rupp before practice and said blithely, "Hey, Coach, a professor told me a funny story about you today." Rupp was delighted. He asked to hear the tale, laughed throughout it and then told Dampier it was absolutely true.

At times this season Rupp has solicited and then used advice on strategy from his players. He did it at halftime in the St. Louis game, when Kentucky led by only a basket. He has gone so far on some occasions as to ask the players if they approved of his strategy. There is virtually no precedent for this. "I can't ever remember us offering suggestions in a game," says Frank Ramsey, the star of the undefeated 1953-54 team. "We did discuss things with him, but you have to remember that was a special situation. Since the N.C.A.A. suspension kept us out for that year, we could do nothing but practice, and three of us were

Rupp accepts a bid from Elliott Lauderman to play in the 1963 Sugar Bowl Tournament.

five-year men. We'd known Coach Rupp for a long time."

One reason for the change in Rupp is his health. He has had trouble with his blood pressure for a decade. Last year he endured his worst record (15-10) and was physically debilitated as well. "Why, I'd just be sitting there dictating a letter, and in a third of a second I'd be all dizzy," he says. "Just to get on the court was hard. I was breathing like a panther all the time." Often he was dopey from a variety of medications, and some observers thought he was falling into senility. This year Rupp is 20 pounds lighter, the blood pressure is down, the dizziness is gone and he has never felt better.

He knocks on wood when he says that. He knocks on wood with almost every optimistic statement he makes, a strange habit for a man who is so majestically self-assured. He is as vigorous and as cantanker-

ous as he wants to be and positively delighted with all the new attention he is receiving. "I'm just so busy," he says. "Why, we have so much mail we had to hire another secretary." There always seems to be someone waiting in his outer office to see him, and he greets all visitors — the men with energy, the women with a genuine courtliness. It is obvious he is overjoyed that the world has come back to see Adolph Rupp once more. There are silver threads across the bald head and a punch of diminished but still impressive girth, but his outlook is so cheerful that he blanches at the thought of having to leave coaching.

"He's so loose now," says Harry Lancaster, Rupp's assistant and comrade for the last two decades. "I don't believe he's ever been so relaxed. I think this is important for this team, too. He's made it their ball club. He's given them the credit."

The credit has been earned, since this team was

generally picked about third best in the S.E.C. Only one new starter, 6-foot-5 sophomore center Thad Jaracz, has joined last year's unsuccessful quartet: Kron, the 6-foot-5 passing guard; Dampier, the 6-foot shooting guard; and the 6-foot-3 forwards, Conley, who passes, and Riley, who shoots and rebounds. That they have become the slickest basketball unit in the country is a metamorphosis at least as pronounced as that of their coach. "There was dissension on this team last year," Dampier says. "We were always bickering, and by the end of the season we knew we were holding onto the ball for ourselves instead of passing it."

The key to Kentucky is Conley, a frail and unusu-ally perceptive young man who is that rarity, a play-making forward. More accurately, he plays smart and is what the N.C.A.A. means when it uses the term "student-athlete." Conley leans toward becoming a dentist, but he majors in political science and has taken a curriculum that includes Russian, art, music and most anything else he thought might be interesting.

"I came to college," he said, "thinking that I should make it as broadening, as enlightening an experience as I could." This year, applying that kind of reasoning to basketball, he has chosen — along with his roommate, Kron — to sacrifice his scoring in order to set up the underclassmen. In a typical game Saturday

Prior to the 1968-69 season, Rupp poses with Mike Casey (34), Dan Issel (44) and Mike Pratt (22).

against Tennessee, he added six assists to his team-leading total, passing up at least a dozen respectable shots of his own. The performance prompted Tennessee coach Ray Mears to say that Conley was as unselfish a player and as fine a college passer as he has seen.

In this game, against the Tennessee 1-3-1 zone, Rupp stationed Riley in one corner and brought Dampier down to the other, moving Conley out to a backcourt position. With Conley and Kron hitting first Riley and then Dampier (as the defensive emphasis changed), Riley and Dampier got 28 and 29 points bombing over the zone and brought Kentucky an easy 78-64 victory. The Wildcats not only outshot Tennessee, which they do to everybody (Conley's shooting percentage of 47.5 is the poorest among the starters), but they also showed again how position, fight and timing can enable a little team to outrebound a bigger one. The Wildcats won the boards, 46-27, with the guards, little Dampier and big Kron, leading the way with 20 rebounds between them.

Riley, the team's best all-round player, also handles center-jump duties, and though he is only 6 feet 3, he has won all but seven of 46 jumping duels. He leads Dampier, whom Rupp calls "the best outside shooter I ever saw," by a hair (21.7 points to 21.4) in scoring. Dampier is the best percentage shooter; Kron, who also specializes in defense, is the top free throw man.

The team is marked, obviously, by versatility and balance, making it difficult to defense. For example, as soon as Tennessee ignored Kron as a shooter to concentrate on Dampier and Riley, he promptly popped in two 20-footers. When the Vols fell back on him, Kron immediately returned to feeding. Putting pressure on playmaker Conley, as one team (St. Louis) did with fair success, may be the best way to play the Wildcats.

Such teamwork plays a large part in providing Rupp with his first reliable center in years, the hometown kid Jaracz. He gets many easy baskets off passes from Conley. "They all treat Thad like a baby brother," Lancaster says. "They call him the Bear, which makes him think he is a lot tougher than he really is." Jaracz has fallen into a slump lately. "I told him," Rupp says, "that he had been making so many of those crazy shots that he thinks he is Hank Luisetti, and he's just not that kind of boy yet." A year ago the Baron would not have added the "yet."

Rupp has good back-up help for Jaracz in another sophomore, 6-foot-8 Cliff Berger. Jaracz beat out Berger because he has better hands and a better shot, even if he does shoot it off the wrong foot. And though he is heftier than Berger — at 230 lbs. — he can keep up with his running teammates better. Berger played the last three quarters of the Tennessee game, after Jaracz got into foul trouble, and did a good job against big Red Robbins.

The shooting roommates, Dampier and Riley, are virtually unstoppable — they have been held to less than 33 points only once this season. Dampier, in fact, is such an excellent shooter that in a scrimmage earlier this year the whole team reflexively headed back on defense as soon as he threw up his jumper. When it missed and Rupp suddenly discovered his rebounders milling about in midcourt, the Baron abandoned his new mellow image for a spell.

The other scorer, Riley, "the Irishman," may be Rupp's favorite. Riley has been enamored of Kentucky since his childhood, though he comes from Schenectady, N. Y., where he was a high school all-America quarterback. He wears contact lenses on the court, horned rims off the court, and might be accused of being Clark Kent, except that he could never fit into a phone booth to change clothes.

Trying to explain the team's success, Conley says, "It's simply that we know each other. Instinct, I guess. It's instinct. It's really lucky that we ended up together. A lot of it has been the old man, too. Let's put it this way — there have been times I hated him, but we all know what he has meant to us. Consider the abuse that he gives us in practice. Well, if you can't take it, you can't take it in a game. I think it's certain that we never would have won at a place like Mississippi State unless we had what we learned from him and what we had taken from him"

Oh, yes, about that story Louis Dampier heard and related to the Baron. It seems that Rupp, who has never been encumbered by modesty, used to teach a basketball course at UK, and he would always give all of his students "A's." Rupp's reasoning was simply that no one could learn basketball from Adolph Rupp and not get an A. The reasoning is as sound today, although this bunch of Wildcats would deserve their A's. The teacher should get an A, too.

Wearing his customary brown suit, Rupp visits the Kentucky spotlight in 1972 at Memorial Coliseum one last time.

CHAPTER 26

Texas Western Upsets Kentucky For N.C.A.A. Title

By Gordon S. White Jr.
Special to The New York Times

College Park, Md., March 19, 1966 — Texas Western, overlooked in preseason ratings last December, became the collegiate basketball champion for the first time by whipping long-time powerful Kentucky, 72-65, tonight in the final of the National Collegiate Athletic Association tournament.

The Miners never lost their poise in the face of a strong comeback attempt by the team rated No. 1 in the nation. Their shooting kept them ahead after 9 minutes 40 seconds of the first half until the end of the game.

It was a glorious moment for the flashy players of Coach Don Haskins. The El Paso college got its first taste of the glory that Kentucky had fed upon four times. The Wildcats have won more national collegiate basketball championships than any other team.

Kentucky never before went as far as the final of this tournament without winning. But, before 14,253 fans at the University of Maryland's Cole Field House, Coach Adolph Rupp's little men, who had done so well against taller teams all season, failed in their biggest game.

Duke defeated Utah, 79-77, in the game for third place.

Nevil Shed, a New York boy, sank the free throw that put Texas Western into the lead it never relinquished. Few in the capacity crowd believed this was the beginning of the end for the Wildcats.

Pat Riley (42) and Cliff Berger (45) reach for a rebound in the 1966 N.C.A.A. Tournament championship game against Texas Western.

But the Texans, rated No. 3, believed in themselves and kept a tight grip on the situation. Kentucky, usually a fine shooting team, was off its usual marksmanship.

Dave Lattin, a strong 240-pounder from Houston, had too much power under the boards for Kentucky to cope with. Though in foul trouble in the late stages of the game, Lattin managed to keep off the Wildcats' big man, Thad Jaracz.

Yet it was a little man who filled the hero's assignment for Texas Western. He was Bobby Joe Hill, who used his cut-and-go skills to run around and through Kentucky. The 5-foot 10-inch junior from Detroit dropped in some of the fanciest shots of the tourney and scored 20 points. He also was a demon on defense, often taking the ball away from Kentucky players.

THE LINE-UPS

KENTUCKY (65)

	FG	FT	Pts.
Dampier	7	5	19
Kron	3	0	6
Conley	4	2	10
Riley	8	3	19
Jaracz	3	1	7
Berger	2	0	4
Totals	**27**	**11**	**65**

TEXAS WESTERN (72)

	FG	FT	Pts.
Hill	7	6	20
Artis	5	5	15
Shed	1	1	3
Lattin	5	6	16
Worsley	2	4	8
Flourney	1	0	2
Cager	1	6	8
Totals	**22**	**28**	**72**

The championship quality of the Texans appeared in full in the second half. When Lattin sank a pair of fouls with four minutes to go in the first half, the Miners had an 8-point lead. Then the Kentuckians came charging back.

Point by point, the Wildcats moved closer to the Texans. All season long Kentucky has managed to overtake team after team that dared to gain a lead against the squad backed by the aura of a great basketball tradition.

But the Texans didn't panic. After their lead was cut to a single point with 3 minutes gone in the second half, the Miners rallied themselves. Orsten Artis and Hill combined for 6 straight points.

The lead was increased to 9 points and remained safe enough for the fancy ball handler to slow the game

An intense Adolph Rupp observes at courtside.

The disappointment is obvious for Kentucky players following the loss to Texas Western.

during the last three minutes.

Louie Dampier and Pat Riley, two of Kentucky's short but excellent players, scored 19 points each. Dampier, only 6 feet tall, led the Wildcats in rebounds, with nine.

But all of Kentucky's efforts, so good for a small squad all season, were to no avail against a squad that measured 6-7 and 6-8 in a couple of spots. However, Hill and 5-6 Willie Worsley, another of the three New Yorkers on the Texas team, were the shortest men to reach the semi-finals of this tournament.

Both Kentucky and Texas Western reached the final after much of the same type of season. Each squad ran up undefeated strings of 23 games before suffering their first losses. Each lost two weeks ago tonight, just before the start of the N.C.A.A. tournament.

Texas Western then got into action in the first round of the tournament and progressed to the semi-finals, where the Miners beat Utah. Kentucky, with a bye in the first round, went through the second and third rounds to the semi-finals, where the Wildcats defeated Duke in a game between the No. 1 and No. 2 teams in the nation.

As the Texans seemed sure of victory in the last minute, their fans began chanting, "We're No. 1." And as they left the arena, many were yelling, "We won this one for L.B.J."

Rupp gave Hill credit for the inevitable "turning point of the game." The Baron referred to Hill's stealing the ball twice within 10 seconds for lay-ups just after Shed sank the foul shot to give the Miners the lead they never lost.

Rupp's Runts at centerstage prior to the 1966 N.C.A.A. championship game against Texas Western.

The Runts Rupp Won With

BY C. RAY HALL
Special to The Courier-Journal

LOUISVILLE, March 30, 1986 — A child of the 1970's recently came upon a photograph of the 1966 University of Kentucky basketball team. She studied the players' snug-fitting blazers with the tiny lapels, their white shirts and dry-look hairstyles. A flicker of amusement crossed her face as she announced, "They look like the Beatles."

In Kentucky, they were bigger than the Beatles.

Taller, too — though not by much. So they were called Rupp's Runts, a name that suggests that they

were adored. They were. When they lost the national championship game 20 years ago, grief covered Kentucky from Pineville to Paducah. Somehow that team had worked its way so deeply into the state's psyche that losing a basketball game seemed like losing a life. "If I could change anything about my life," says one of the players, "even if I could change everything, that game is the only thing I would change."

To look at the five starters from that team today, you would guess they have been blessed many times over — surely enough to make amends for one basketball game. Maybe not enough to heal the hurt from two infant deaths, one divorce and three forced retire-

The Runts enjoy a movie prior to a 1966 game against Alabama in Tuscaloosa.

ments from pro basketball. But surely enough to cover one basketball game.

They have loving wives, bright children and swell jobs. By practically any measure, they are successful. And yet they are famous for failure. "We're probably better known for losing that game," says Larry Conley, "than we would be if we'd won."

The best-known work of art in sports, "Casey at the Bat," is about failure, too. Perhaps it's because failure gives a human dimension to athletes, who so often are set apart from the rest of humanity. Not above, necessarily, but apart.

One reason for the enduring fame of Rupp's Runts is that they suffered one of the biggest upsets in the history of the championship game. Another is that they were the only all-white team ever to play a black

team for the title. Five of Texas Western's players were white, but they watched from the bench as the seven blacks — David Lattin, Bobby Joe Hill, Orsten Artis, Willie Worsley, Willie Cager, Harry Flournoy and Nevil Shed — won the championship for the school that is now known as the University of Texas - El Paso.

Pat Riley, who coaches the professional Los Angeles Lakers now, was a UK forward. That night in College Park, Md., he quickly realized that the team in the orange uniforms was playing for more than the national championship. Texas Western's first dunk was an emphatic eye-opener. "I was right below the dunk, and the Texas Western player said, 'Take that, you white honky —!' "

Riley was a tough guy, though: Joe B. Hall, a UK assistant coach then, describes him in four words: "He could withstand intimidation."

When Riley was growing up in Schenectady, N.Y., his brothers would take him to the roughest part of town and leave him to fend for himself. His father wanted him to be tough. He managed to grow tough and tender. For a while, he wanted to be an Olympic skater, which probably contributed to his grace on the dance floor.

When he was cut after nine years in pro basketball, he was still tough and tender. He took a year off to write down his rage in a book. The rest of his rage he took out on his house, which he practically rebuilt.

When he arrived at UK, Riley must have looked like a rebuilding job to Coach Adolph Rupp. He would spend hours in the student center hunkered over a pool table shooting with his custom-made cue. "I never saw him lose," says Louie Dampier, the guard, who was Riley's roommate for four years.

"I could make 20 to 25 dollars in an afternoon," Riley says. "Then Adolph found out about it and took my pool cue away."

When he left UK for the pros, Riley bought a yellow Corvette convertible. One of his first passengers was Rupp. "Pat, this is not exactly my style," said Rupp, whose taste ran to deep-blue Cadillacs.

Riley, who was 6 feet, 3 inches tall, jumped center at UK During one stretch, he won 46 of 51 jumps against players who were usually 5 to 6 inches taller. He accomplished this through a simple expedient some people would call cheating. "Harry Lancaster (then a Rupp assistant) taught me a little trick," Riley says. "As I went up, I would plant my elbow in the other guy's shoulder, and he'd lift me up."

Nothing in Lancaster's bag of tricks — or in Riley's formidable constitution — worked the night of UK's 72-65 loss to Texas Western. "It was a violent game," Riley says. "I don't mean there were any fights — but they were desperate, and they were committed, and they were more motivated than we were. They were playing for identity, for respect. They were angry, and we weren't. They had more passion and commitment."

Until that night, Kentucky's own passion and commitment had usually been enough. UK entered the game ranked No. 1, with 27 victories and one loss (a 69-62 defeat at Tennessee after 23 straight wins). Ranked third, Texas Western had also lost once — to Seattle.

Entering that season, Kentucky had been in the most barren stretch of Rupp's 42 years. Only once in the previous seven seasons had UK won a Southeastern Conference championship outright. The year before, it had lost 10 games. The next season it would lose 13. So for UK fans, Rupp's Runts were astonishingly good in an astonishingly bad time. Hence, part of its charm.

None of the players was more beguiling than Tommy Kron, a senior guard from Tell City, Ind. Like Conley, he now lives in Atlanta. "Tommy was a perfectionist in the tradition of the absent-minded professor, apparently. Perfection on the basketball court and in the classroom did not spill over into the rest of his life.

"There are a lot of advantages in being disorganized," Kron says. "That way every day is a surprise. Besides, if you're organized, you have to organize everybody else. I'd rather be the guy everyone else is looking out for."

One of Conley's treasures from the 1966 season is a picture that appeared in *Time* magazine. The five starters — Conley, Kron, Riley, Dampier and Thad Jaracz — are walking across the campus. In accordance with the photographer's plan, everyone is wearing his blue UK jacket. Everyone except Kron, grappling with the demons of disorganization again.

Once when Kron (rhymes with John) was driving home on the Western Kentucky Parkway, his car ran out of gasoline. On five or six other occasions, he says, he had managed to coast into a gas station on an empty tank. "That time I didn't make it. But I always had faith in my gas tank."

Faith, if not gas.

When he was 20, Kron said, "You know, almost everybody suffers some sort of major setback before he gets to be 40."

Now on the other side of 40, he says, "I really haven't had setbacks, but I guess you could say I've had a varied career — things that have gone up and down. I've made money, and I've lost money."

After four years of pro ball in St. Louis, Seattle and Louisville, he was a stockbroker in Lexington and Dallas. Then he went into real estate in Louisville and opened a restaurant and bar. Then he worked for Gov.

Louie Dampier leads the Runts down the court on a fast break against Duke in 1966.

John Y. Brown Jr. — a year in the Labor Cabinet and a year as state tourism commissioner. Now he is a marketing vice president for an investment company.

"I'm a real survivor," he says. "That pleases me, that I'm able to fight and provide things for my family. I'm fairly well off, but I like the fact that I'm still striving. I never give up."

Lately Kron has been dabbling in television. He was recommended for the job by Conley, who has been a basketball commentator on television games for 10 years. As a color man, Kron says, "You're right on the periphery of the game. It's a way to smell the sweat without getting any on you."

Was Kron ready for the job? "In my mind I've done color commentary on every UK game the last 12 years," he says.

Kron worked two games this season but turned down the chance to do a third. That night he kept a promise to take his son's basketball team to see the Atlanta Hawks play Riley's team, the Lakers.

Like just about everyone else, Riley gives Kron and Conley credit for the success of Rupp's Runts. Both were deft passers who left their imprint on the team not so much by what they did as by what they enabled others to do.

"I don't think I realized how much Tom Kron and Larry Conley sacrificed to allow Louie and me to be the shooters on the team, to become all-Americans," Riley says. "They were the real leaders — the spirit and the glue. Louie and I were just the finish."

Kron, meanwhile, spreads the credit around even more. "There were more than just five players on that team," he says. "Bob Tallent scored more on me in practice than anybody I played against scored in a game. There were some guys that sacrificed more than any of us did — Tallent, Jim LeMaster, Tommy Porter, Cliff Berger, Steve Clevenger, Brad Bounds, Larry Lentz, Gary Gamble, Gene Stewart, Bob Windsor. They sweated as much as we did. They just happened to sweat a little less on game days."

When he played pro ball, Kron was known as "Crash." He fell down a lot on the court. Off court, too. Kron and Dampier were in the same Army reserve unit at Fort Knox. One morning the company mustered for roll call and someone asked, "Where's Crash?" Then they heard a "ka-thunk, ka-thunk, ka-thunk" on the barracks steps, followed by a thud. Practically at their feet, Kron rolled over, righted himself, spread his arms, grinned widely and announced, "Ta-da!"

"Even the captain cracked up," says Dampier. "And he never smiled."

There was a time when Riley thought Dampier might never smile. "He seemed like a sad person," Riley recalls.

If Dampier was a melancholy sort, perhaps he had reason. When he was 16 and a high school junior in Southport, Ind., his mother, Elizabeth, entered the hospital for surgery. She died of shock. The next year, his father, Bill, died of cancer. "Whatever I've had in the way of success," he says, "I'd give it up to have my parents back."

Dampier had begun working at his father's dairy barn when he was 11. He was still working there when Rupp came around to recruit him. By then his father was dying, and Dampier was impressed by Rupp's compassion.

In those days, Dampier rarely spoke. He fit in rather nicely at the UK practices, where an hour could go by without 10 words breaking the silence. "We have a rule," Rupp said. "You don't speak unless you can improve on the silence."

Sometimes Rupp himself couldn't improve on the silence. He would look at Dampier and say, "Steve, go in for Louie!" He often confused Dampier with Clevenger, another guard from Indiana. "Sometimes he would tell us to guard ourselves," Dampier says.

In 1966, Dampier bought a green Dodge Charg-er. He still has the car, complete with the *Kentucky* decal in the back windshield. This comes as no surprise to his friends, because he is known for his thrift. ("I'm not sure if I ever bought Louis a Christmas gift," says Dan Issel, his former roommate with the Kentucky Colonels. "I'm sure he never bought me one," he adds, laughing. Like many of Dampier's friends, Issel was surprised when Louis bought a Mercedes in 1977.)

But then, Dampier has a way of surprising people. Though he was the quietest of the UK players, he was the only one to go into the Texas Western locker room and congratulate the winners. "It wasn't exactly an oration," Dampier says. "I didn't stand in the middle of the locker room and make a speech."

Fans in Texas were so touched by the gesture that they sent him about 100 letters of appreciation. He keeps them in a shoe box. "The things that pleased me about those letters," he says, "is that they were just praising me as a person, not just a player."

He continued to surprise people. Practically nobody thought he would last a dozen years in the pros, but he did. When Dampier was 29, Colonels owner John Y. Brown Jr. told him he was too old. Dampier responded with his best season, and the Colonels won the league championship.

Five years later, he was with the New Jersey Nets on the eve of a new season. At 5:45 p.m., 15 minutes before the deadline for roster changes, he got a phone call saying the Nets had acquired guard Mike Newlin. He was out of a job. Dampier rented a car and drove all night. It took him 12 hours to reach his Oldham County home.

After that, it was a case of "let's go to the videotape." Dampier began distributing tape to radio and TV stations and recording studios. "Then the company I was working for decided to discontinue the line — or discontinue me," he says. "A couple of friends, Bobby Ernspiker and Kenny Dewees, suggested we go into partnership. It was a real good break because I was kind of lost as to what I was going to do."

His company, Dampier Distributing, has an imposing name, but he notes that it is hardly an empire. "I might not have been called Mr. Everything on the basketball court," he says, "but I'm Mr. Everything in the tape-sales business."

After finishing second in the 1966 N.C.A.A. Tournament, Rupp and his Runts pose with their trophy.

Still athletic, Dampier just sort of bounces along when he walks, looking about 25 years old and dewy-eyed. He plays basketball in summer leagues and church leagues, drawing heavy attention from the other teams. "Sometimes," he says, "I pull a Riley and ask myself, 'Why are they keying on a 41-year-old man?'"

To Dampier, "pulling a Riley" means to think about things — especially basketball or life — at great length. Because Dampier went to work at age 11 and lost his parents when he was a teen-ager, it's possible he's trying to grab back a little of the adolescence he missed. He says five people live in his house — "my wife, Judy, and her four boys." By that count, he is one of the boys.

The real boys are Dampier's son Nick, and step-sons Rob and Jay. He married their mother, Judy Stinebruner, after the divorce from his first wife, Marty. A daughter by that marriage, Danielle, is a UK freshman. Dampier himself may become a UK student

again: He is seven hours short of a degree, which he wants so he can become a coach.

The Runt Most Likely to Become a Coach, everyone thought, was Conley, the gregarious blond forward from Ashland. As a 10-year-old, Conley would hang around Rupp's office when his father, George, came to Lexington to referee UK games.

Conley did coach one season. After an uninspired year at the UK law school, he became an assistant coach at George Washington University. When he was recruiting in New York, a high school coach arranged a blind date with a TWA flight attendant name Lorie Vieregge. A year later, they were married and moved to Atlanta, where Conley became a salesman for Converse basketball shoes. In that job, he was a sort of coach, too, conducting clinics for about 30,000 youngsters.

Though Conley works between 35 and 40 television games a year, his real job is being vice president of the General Electric Mortgage Insurance Co. Because of all that basketball in the winter, he spends a lot of Sunday nights at the office. He spends a lot of summer Sundays there, too, because he coaches his two sons' baseball teams.

Another son, Brad, died in infancy 12 years ago. He was born without an esophagus. "He had three operations," Conley says. "He just didn't make it."

Jaracz's first son, Thad, didn't make it, either. Born at the Army hospital at Fort Ord, Calif., he lived three days. Since then, the Jaraczes have had three other children.

Jaracz scarcely imagined he would be a career soldier. After learning he wasn't cut out for Boston Celtic green, he found he was being sized for Army green: He got a draft notice. So he enlisted. He rode a Greyhound bus to Louisville, where he was put up in a barracks-like motel with the other inductees. Someone was listening to a Kentucky game on the radio. Stretched out on a bottom bunk, in the company of all those strangers, Jaracz thought of the coziness of Memorial Coliseum and wondered, "What have I gotten myself into?"

A career, as it turned out. A major now, Jaracz has spent 17 years in the Army, serving in Germany and Korea, among other places. During a tour of duty at Fort Knox, he went to night school on the post and got his degree from UK in 1976.

"I kept getting good jobs with a lot of responsibility for my age," he says of the Army. "I liked the work and I liked the people, so I stayed in."

At 6-foot-5, Jaracz was one of the shortest centers in college basketball. But in the Army, he became one of the tallest tank commanders. "Being tall can be an advantage," he says. "It makes it easier to see when you stand up in the turret."

He's stationed in San Antonio, Texas, now, awaiting word on whether he will be coming to the University of Louisville this summer to begin a three-year assignment teaching military science.

He expects to retire to Kentucky. Perhaps he'll come back to the Fayette County farm where he grew up. When he was a child, his younger brother Chesley would bribe him to come out and shoot baskets. Later Thad and his UK teammates rode sleds over the farm's snow-covered hills and took their dates to the drive-in theater across the road.

When Jaracz arrived at UK in 1964, there was great curiosity about his name, which is spoken as if it rhymes with Harris. A Polish name, it is properly pronounced "Yuh-rotz," though the family hasn't said it that way for a couple of generations.

Jaracz has an interesting family tree: A great-grandmother, Eloise Hance McCaw, was a 9-year-old in the audience at Ford's Theatre the night Abraham Lincoln was assassinated.

Occasionally Jaracz will show his children keepsakes from his own little piece of history — his time at UK. "They look at all those yellowed pictures," he says, "and wonder who I am and what am I doing in that funny suit."

Maybe that's all it amounts to, really, after all these years — just a bunch of guys playing around in funny suits. But Riley suggests it meant much more than that. He recalls a remark by Bob McAdoo, the former Laker who played at North Carolina. "Bob told me that when Kentucky got beat by Texas Western — by those black players — it was more than just a basketball game. He and other black players said that game meant the difference to their being able to feel comfortable about starting to go to predominantly white schools in the South.

"Maybe that's the way we'll go down in history. Maybe we had a hand in the Emancipation Proclamation of 1966," Riley said.

Back in Lexington that spring, the proclamations were not so charitable. At the basketball banquet, sportswriter Billy Thompson rose and declared UK "the best white team in the country, anyway." That remark would not die a quite death: For several years, the student newspaper lampooned it by naming a Best White Team in the Country.

Everything softens with time, though. A few years back, Riley learned that Harry Flournoy, one of the Texas Western players, was working nearby, selling Lakers season tickets. "Come around and talk sometime," Riley said, extending a hand across the years. "The wound is not that deep anymore."

CHAPTER 27

Riley Gets 28 in Rout of 'Bama, 110-78

BY BILLY REED
Special to The Courier-Journal

LEXINGTON, March 6, 1967 — There weren't many dry eyes in the place. The Kentucky band was playing the school's fight song and 11,400 people were on their feet — some laughing, some crying, all applauding.

And out there on the floor, Pat Riley gave a little wave as he jogged slowly toward the bench — leaving his last game as a Kentucky basketball player. "I'll never forget it," Riley said later. "I don't know how to explain the feeling. It was one of the most emotional moments I've ever had."

It was a night for emotion. For one thing, Riley and Louie Dampier — two of the most popular players in UK's history — were ending their careers, along with reserves Brad Bounds and Gene Stewart.

And, besides that, this UK team was just tired of losing, fed up with being reminded that its 13 losses in 26 games make it the worst team in Adolph Rupp's coaching career here. So Alabama never really had a chance.

And, although the fans cheered and applauded, while they laughed and cried, this team closed the season with an awesome, delirious, overwhelming 110-84 victory over Alabama.

Riley, who has played on little more than courage all season because of a bad back, closed his brilliant career with a performance fans will remember for a long, long time.

Thad Jaracz (55) and Pat Riley battle for a rebound against Alabama in 1967.

The 6-foot-3 senior from Schenectady, N.Y., drove and tipped and hit long jump shots for a game-high 28 points . . . crashed the backboards for nine rebounds . . . passed for nine assists . . . and generally played the game like a man possessed. "It's hard to believe that it's over," Riley said after the game. "These have been four good years."

The emotion began building early. Signs bidding the seniors goodbye hung from the Memorial Coliseum balcony. The lights were turned off and a spotlight turned on each senior as he was introduced. The fans cheered everything UK did. Then, in the second half, the emotion spilled over as Kentucky erupted in one brilliant stretch of play that won the game.

Leading only 54-52, Kentucky outscored Alabama, 25-23, to assure itself a break-even .500 percentage. Riley started the streak with a jumper. In the middle, Cliff Berger added two field goals and Riley three more.

Phil Argento finished the stretch with eight straight points — two baskets on wide-open crips after leaving his "point" position in UK's 1-2-2 zone defense to intercept Alabama's passes. It was absolutely dazzling. Soon, Rupp began pulling his starters. Each got a standing ovation and a rare treat — a big smile and handshake from Rupp.

Besides Riley's performance, Argento wound up with 20 points, Thad Jaracz 18, and Dampier and Berger 16 each. UK shot 58.6 percent for the game. Mike Nordholz, the main "culprit" when 'Bama whipped UK, 81-71, in their recent clash at Tuscaloosa, again led Coach Hayden Riley's team. He got 20

THE LINE-UPS

KENTUCKY (110)

	FG	FT	Pts.
Riley	14	0	28
Jaracz	9	0	18
Berger	8	0	16
Dampier	6	4	16
Argento	10	0	20
Porter	0	0	0
Bounds	1	3	5
Stewart	1	1	3
Clevenger	1	0	2
Gamble	0	0	0
LeMaster	1	0	2
Totals	**51**	**8**	**110**

ALABAMA (78)

	FG	FT	Pts.
Jones	5	2	12
Turner	7	4	18
Deppe	3	5	11
Nordholz	9	2	20
Elliott	8	1	17
Ludwig	0	0	0
Caldwell	0	0	0
Wilson	0	0	0
McDaniel	0	0	0
Orton	0	0	0
Totals	**32**	**14**	**78**

points, Guy Turner notched 18 and Gary Elliott added 17.

Even Gene Steward and Brad Bounds got in on UK's scoring act. Stewart, from Brookville, Ind., hit a free throw with 3:37 left for his first point of the season. He later added a jumper. Bounds, the "People's Choice" from Bluffton, Ind., scored five points — including a free throw with 2:38 left that gave UK 100 points.

They got the standing-ovation treatment, too, when Rupp took them out. And, on the sideline, a cheerleader shed a tear. It was that sort of night as the "Long Long Season" drew to an end.

Phil Argento's 8-point stretch in the second half finished off the Crimson Tide.

When Adolph Rupp retired following the 1971-72 season, he had compiled a record of 876 wins and 190 losses to become the winningest basketball coach in history.

CHAPTER 28

Kent Benson (54) of Indiana wrestles away a rebound from Kentucky's Rick Robey (53) during the Mideast Regional finals at Dayton.

Kentucky Ends Indiana String of 34 Wins

BY GORDON S. WHITE JR.
Special to The New York Times

DAYTON, Ohio, March 22, 1975 — Kentucky's powerful team ended Indiana University's 34-game basketball victory streak, 92-90, today and moved to the semi-finals of the 37th National Collegiate Athletic Association tournament.

Without a moment's letup in a game that carried a strong motive for revenge, the Southeastern Conference co-champions and Big Ten Conference champions waged basketball war. The biggest, strongest warriors beat out the normally quicker, more composed men of Bloomington, Ind., in this final of the Mideast Regional competition at the University of Dayton Arena. The Wildcats earned a place against Syracuse in the N.C.A.A. semi-final round next Saturday at San Diego.

Not since the Hoosiers lost a playoff with Michigan for the Big Ten title in March 1974, had the team coached by Bobby Knight known defeat. Now the team that was ranked No. 1 in the nation before today and the only previously unbeaten team, must step aside while Kentucky goes on as a probable favorite to win the national crown.

In a consolation game for third spot in the N.C.A.A.'s Mideast Region, Central Michigan defeated Oregon State, 88-87.

Kentucky is playing in its 22d N.C.A.A. championship, a record. The nearest to the Wildcats is U.C.L.A, which is taking part in its 16th N.C.A.A. championship.

Never before did a team from Lexington, Ky., come into one of these tourneys with such a mass of muscle and height. However, the big men from the Bluegrass Country were supposed to be too slow for Indiana. They were quite sluggish in their Mideast semi-final triumph over Central Michigan last Thursday night.

But they surprised the 13,458 fans in Dayton Arena and shocked Indiana's once mighty defense with agility that disrupted the composure of the Hoosiers. Kentucky forced them into 20 turnovers while committing only 14. Indiana had counted on such an edge in errors to win all if its previous 31 games this season.

The most impressive of the Kentucky giants down the stretch were the two 6-foot 10-inch freshmen, Rick Robey and Mike Phillips. The Wildcats and Hoosiers were racing along neck and neck until there were about 8 minutes to go. The fans kept wondering, "When will something break. They can't keep this up forever."

Then Robey and Kevin Grevey, a mere 6-foot-5, put together 8 straight points for the Wildcats and the pressure was suddenly heavy on the No. 1 team to come back with 5:32 remaining. Indiana just couldn't manage it, although the Hoosiers did spurt from an 89-81 deficit to the final 2-point difference in the last minute and 45 seconds.

Phillip contributed 6 straight points for

THE LINE-UPS

KENTUCKY (92)

	FG	FT	Pts.
Grevey	6	5	17
Guyette	0	2	2
Robey	3	4	10
Conner	8	1	17
Flynn	9	4	22
Givens	4	0	8
Phillips	4	2	10
Johnson	3	0	6
Totals	**37**	**18**	**92**

INDIANA (90)

	FG	FT	Pts.
Green	10	1	21
May	1	0	2
Benson	13	7	33
Buckner	3	2	8
Wilkerson	6	2	14
Laskowski	4	4	12
Totals	**37**	**16**	**90**

Kentucky just after Robey's and Grevey's scoring had put the Wildcats in command. The big youngster from Manchester, Ohio, fouled out a few seconds after his streak. But he and the other tall, husky Wildcats had done their job.

Robey also fouled out shortly before the end and Bob Guyette, Kentucky's 6-9 man of muscle, drew four personal fouls in his 22 minutes of play. Coach Joe B. Hall obviously sent his big men into the game in relays to play hard and rough under the boards.

Kentucky had enough of them to afford more fouls than Indiana could draw inside.

Kent Benson, a 6-foot-1 Hoosier who is more agile than any of the

Jimmy Dan Conner added 17 points in the Wildcats' win over the Hoosiers.

Wildcat assistants Joe B. Hall and T.L. Plain signed Kevin Grevey to a UK letter of intent in Spring 1971.

Wildcats' forwards, played all 40 minutes. He was the game's high scorer with 33 points and had only three personal fouls. But there were times when Kentucky charged the boards and successfully boxed Benson out.

Knight decided to start Scott May, the team's regular-season leading scorer, who broke his left wrist four weeks ago. It had been hoped that May's quickness and shooting would overcome any problems he had. He was wearing a cast over his left forearm. But Kentucky managed to neutralize May, particularly because Grevey kept scoring and getting the ball into the big men by going around May.

May was taken out after 7 minutes of play. He start-

ed the second half but played only a few more seconds.

The Hoosiers' chances came midway in the first half when they moved to a 7-point lead. They were cracking the Kentucky zone as the Wildcats appeared to take a slight pause under the boards to get their wind in a speed game.

Then Kentucky got the big men in motion again, sending the tall ones into the boards quickly while the Wildcat guards harried the Indiana defense by shooting successfully or moving the ball inside. The Wildcats tied the Hoosiers at intermission, 44-44, and the stage was set for the last 20 minutes that was nearly a bloody battle.

CHAPTER 29

U.C.L.A. Five Beats Kentucky, 92-85

BY GORDON S. WHITE JR.
Special to The New York Times

SAN DIEGO, March 31, 1975 — The University of California, Los Angeles won the national collegiate basketball championship tonight for the 10th and last time under the direction of Coach John Wooden.

The Bruins, proving speed more valuable than muscle, raced up and down the court from start to finish to beat a powerful University of Kentucky team, 92-85, in Wooden's final game before retirement.

When it was done, the crowd of 15,153 at the San Diego Arena remained to give Wooden, the Wizard of Westwood, a standing ovation for about four minutes.

In increasing their record of national basketball titles to 10 in the last 12 years and 8 in the last 9, the Bruins beat the school closest to them in national titles. The Wildcats have four.

Although he would not admit it, this victory in his final game of 27 seasons as the U.C.L.A. coach, may have been Wooden's most satisfying. This was a team not as strong as many of his former national champions — one not rated certain of the crown when the season began.

Wooden said following the thrilling triumph, "To say I thought we would win (the title) back then would be stretching a point."

But Dave Meyers, the senior star of the team, said: "I wanted to do it for Coach all season. He's done a masterful job with the team that lost (Bill)

Walton and (Keith) Wilkins," stars of the three preceding seasons.

Most unexpected of all, however, was the fact that U.C.L.A. beat Kentucky using only six players. This was the first time Wooden used only six players in a national championship game. It paid off as the half-dozen slim, tall men kept up an unusually fast pace

U.C.L.A.'s Dave Meyers (34) crashes to the floor after diving for a ball that Kentucky's Rick Robey had picked off.

UK's early version of the Twin Towers: Rick Robey (53) and Mike Phillips (55).

and achieved what U.C.L.A. teams in 1964 and 1965, and from 1967 through 1973, had achieved. And those teams had such star players as Walt Hazzard, Lew Alcindor, Sidney Wicks and Bill Walton.

The mighty six who won this year's crown were Meyers, Marques Johnson, Rich Washington, Pete Trgovich, Andre McCarter and Ralph Drollinger, the man who came off the bench and had the finest game of his career.

The running Bruins took off against the strong but slower Wildcats and managed to go through 40 minutes of hard physical action without losing one man through personal fouls. However, Meyers, Washington, Trgovich and Drollinger finished with four fouls each — one short of banishment.

What they did was beat such big men as Bob Guyette, 6 feet, 9 inches and 240 pounds; Rick Robey, 6-10 and 240; Mike Phillips, 6-10 and 235; and Dan Hall, 6-10 and 235.

They beat them because Washington and Drollinger gained position under the boards. In perhaps the most important statistic, U.C.L.A. out-rebounded Kentucky, 55 to 49. Most of this season, the Southeastern Conference co-champions had been beating teams off the boards.

Other winning factors involved the way Trgovich, a 6-foot-4 guard, defended against Jimmy Dan Conner, the pride of Kentucky's corps of strong, tall guards. Conner was limited to 9 points. Trgovich, meanwhile, had an excellent night on defense and scored 16.

Trgovich, a senior, scored 10 of U.C.L.A.'s 12 points in a five-minute period late in the first half when the Bruins

THE LINE-UPS

KENTUCKY (85)

	FG	FT	Pts.
Grevey	13	8	34
Guyette	7	2	16
Robey	1	0	2
Conner	4	1	9
Flynn	3	4	10
Givens	3	2	8
Johnson	0	0	0
Phillips	1	2	4
Hall	1	0	2
Totals	**33**	**19**	**85**

U.C.L.A. (92)

	FG	FT	Pts.
Meyers	9	6	24
Johnson	3	0	6
Washington	12	4	28
Trgovich	7	2	16
McCarter	3	2	8
Drollinger	4	2	10
Totals	**38**	**16**	**92**

took the lead for keeps. The Wildcats, however, moved within a point with 6 minutes left in the game.

Washington, voted the outstanding player of the tournament, paced U.C.L.A.'s scoring with 28 points. Many of these came on rebounds and the 6-foot-9 sophomore's short field goal from the baseline with 1 minute 23 seconds to go gave U.C.L.A. an 88-83 lead to virtually assure the victory.

Meyers had 24 points, Drollinger 10, McCarter 8, and Johnson 6. It just didn't matter that Kevin Grevey, Kentucky's leading scorer, had 34. He was scoring well off screens set up for him. But the only big man on Kentucky who managed to score well was Guyette, the senior, who had 16 points.

Robey had only 2 points before fouling out. Phillips had only 4 and Hall only 2. Kentucky needed more from its big men.

Drollinger, the 7-foot-1 junior who has been criticized because he was not an Alcindor or Walton, was unusually strong under the boards. The frail Drollinger stood in there for 16 minutes and beat off the Kentucky rebounders Coach Joe B. Hall kept fresh by sending them into the game in relays.

The victory allowed the Bruins to forget some things, such as a 22-point loss to the University of Washington during the regular season that was the third worst defeat the 64-year-old Wooden suffered in his 40 years as a head coach in high school and col-

----

Despite Kevin Grevey's 34-point performance against U.C.L.A. for UK, it wasn't enough to overcome John Wooden's emotional farewell.

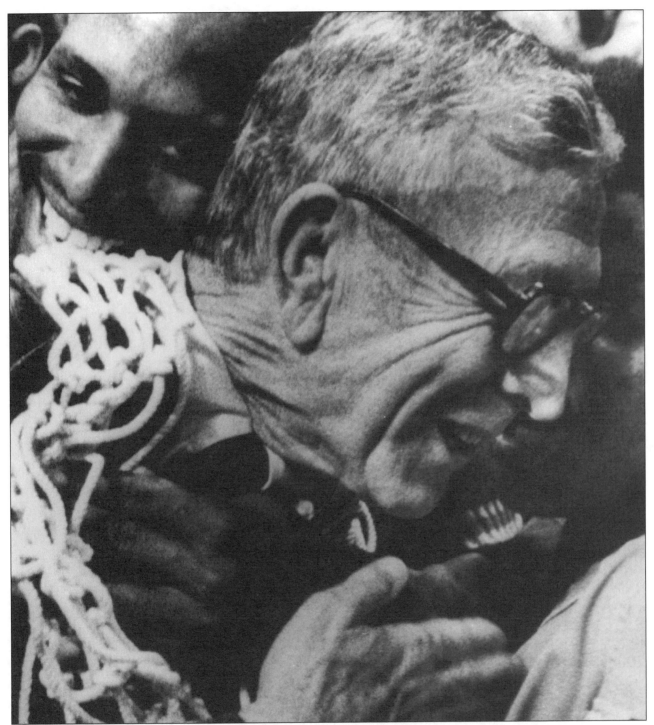

John Wooden savors the Bruins' 92-85 win over Kentucky — his final game as U.C.L.A.'s coach.

lege. For his last season, the Bruins won 28 and lost 3.

Indiana was the favorite to win the title game with Michigan. It was the first time since 1966, when U.C.L.A. was not in the tourney, that the Bruins were not picked to take the title.

U.C.L.A had difficulty getting to the title game, winning a first-round game with Michigan in over-time, another game over Montana by just 3 points and the semi-final thriller with Louisville, 75-74, in over-time when Washington sank the winning basket with four seconds remaining.

CHAPTER 30

UK Closes Coliseum with 94-93 Overtime Win

By Mike Sullivan
Special to The Courier-Journal

LEXINGTON, March 8, 1976 — This will no doubt clash with the sentiments of many red-cheeked, sore-throated basketball fans, but the final monument to Memorial Coliseum may be the courage of Mississippi State's Fighting Bulldogs.

Coach Kermit Davis' Southeastern Conference nobodies walked into a maelstrom of emotions last night, helping the University of Kentucky close out the 26-year history of its arena before 12,200 screaming meemies (capacity is 11,500 screaming meemies).

The visitors were expected to quit. Instead, they played Kentucky off its feet and threatened to embarrass the selection committee of the National Invitation Tournament, in which UK will play Niagara in Saturday's opening round.

Only several minor miracles — and a matching display of grit by Coach Joe B. Hall's UK Wildcats — saved the occasion.

The home team wiped out a seven-point deficit in the final one minute 23 seconds of regulation play — finally forcing an overtime on Jack Givens' 12-foot turnaround jump shot with 8 seconds remaining — then battled to a 94-93 victory in the first five-minute extra period.

"Of course, we planned it that way," Hall joked in the jam-packed UK

Jack (Goose) Givens scored 26 points in this memorable thriller, including a 12-foot turnaround jumper, which forced the game into overtime.

Mike Phillips (55) leaps high for an easy 2-pointer against Mississippi State.

locker room. "With so much nostalgia, we wanted to give the people a game they'd always remember."

It wasn't planned, but what happened will never be forgotten by any eyewitness as UK ended its regular schedule 16-10 overall and 11-7 in the S.E.C. Mississippi State closed out 13-13 in all games, 6-12 in the league.

"Our game plan was excellent and we did the job in every respect," Davis said. "It's a tribute to our three freshmen and two sophomores that they could execute like that with the atmosphere so charged."

What State did was leave Kentucky's defense in shreds, driving to the basket at will and bossing its offensive backboard.

The end result was 24 points from guard Ray White, 23 from forward Gary Hooker (both are 6-foot-5 freshmen), and such firm control of the game that it seemed like an anti-climax when Mike Phillips was thrown out.

Oh yes, UK's 6-foot-10 sophomore center got the thumb all right, taking his 22 points and nine rebounds to the bench and leaving the winners with no player taller than 6-5.

It happened with 6:55 left in regulation and Mississippi State on top, 74-71. Referee Jack Manton ejected Phillips after the big guy's legs had become entangled with the arms of State guard Al Perry, who was on the floor at Phillip's feet.

"Perry was hugging my legs, squeezing them and pulling on them," Phillips said later. "I was trying to free myself to get rebounding position. I never kicked him — I just tried to free my legs. I can't believe a player would do that."

Regardless, the faith of those 12,200 you-know-whats was being tested. State forged ahead by seven on three occasions, the last at 84-77 with only 1:23 to go.

UK's blazing 8-1 finish started with a 23-foot set

THE LINE-UPS

KENTUCKY (94)

	FG	FT	Pts.
Givens	12	2	26
Lee	2	1	5
Phillips	11	0	22
Johnson	6	4	16
Warford	4	4	12
Fowler	3	2	8
Haskins	0	1	1
Casey	0	0	0
Claytor	2	0	4
Totals	**40**	**14**	**94**

MISSISSIPPI STATE (93)

	FG	FT	Pts.
Hooker	8	7	23
Wright	5	0	10
Peck	5	1	11
White	11	2	24
Perry	6	1	13
Dean	0	2	2
Knarr	2	0	4
Moss	0	0	0
Williams	3	0	6
Totals	**40**	**13**	**93**

shot from behind the key by guard Larry Johnson. After a steal by Givens, Reggie Warford sank an eight-foot baseline jumper. Then Perry sank one free throw — putting State ahead, 85-81 — and Johnson answered with a driving flip shot with 43 seconds remaining.

Ten seconds later, Johnson fouled White and the freshman toed the free-throw stripe with a chance to put Kentucky down, 87-83, with just 33 seconds left.

But he missed, and UK's Bob Fowler — another first year man who was brilliant in relief with eight points and four rebounds — grabbed the rebound. UK then took its last time-out, with only 26 ticks remaining.

"We set up a play for Jack to pop outside, take a pass, then hit Fowler cutting underneath."

As Givens explained it, "Fowler cut underneath too soon and we couldn't get the ball to him."

So Givens, instead, passed to Johnson, who went on the dribble and threaded his way among three defenders along the baseline.

Seemingly trapped, Johnson shoveled a short pass to Givens, who whirled and swished the ball in front and to the right of the basket.

State failed to get a shot off and the overtime was on.

"We should have won the game, as far as having the chance to end it at the free-throw line, but I credit Kentucky for never giving up and hitting the big baskets," Davis said.

State took its only overtime lead at 87-85 on Wiley Peck's follow shot, but Givens — who led all scorers with 26 points and added nine rebounds and five assists — answered with a baseline jumper after Merion Haskins' diving hustle had saved a loose ball.

After Johnson and Peck traded jumpers, Fowler put UK ahead, 94-91, making White's last-second lay-up only the signal for a wild celebration and one more rendition of "My Old Kentucky Home."

"I was amazed at what our 'short team' accomplished," Hall said. "Those guys look too small to beat anybody, but their hustle and aggressiveness won for us."

Indeed, Kentucky might have proven itself N.I.T.-worthy by coping with unusual adversities.

Although most of its losses had come in games where it surrendered late leads, UK went nearly 27 minutes of this one without so much as a tie. State moved on top, 31-30, with 6:37 left in the first half and stayed in command until Givens' tying jump shot, often by margins of eight-to-10 points.

Further, UK shot only 46 percent — after hitting between 51 and 65 in its previous five-game winning streak — and overcame an off night by James Lee, a recent tower of strength who was bothered by a sprained wrist and missed 13 of 15 shots.

In one late sequence which started with UK trailing, 80-75, and only 3:05 left, the home team held State scoreless on two straight trips but blew chances to score each time.

It ended with Hooker being fouled under UK's basket and hitting two free throws with 1:59 remaining — a six-point play, really, because UK could have trailed by one (80-79) but went down by seven (82-75) instead.

But somehow nothing State could do was enough to crush the enemy, which maybe is what Memorial Coliseum and Joe B. Hall's fourth UK team are all about.

Larry Johnson keyed UK's blazing finish with a 23-foot set-shot.

The Crowd Roars and UK Rallies

By Dave Kindred
The Courier-Journal

It was your basic Kentucky thriller. Kentucky was seven points behind with a minute 23 seconds to play. On the bench, Adolph Rupp rested his chin on his palm. Nothing to worry about. Sit tight, folks, because Kentucky ain't dead until the basketball goes flat.

It's always been that way, ever since Rupp migrated from Illinois 612 years ago to win 8,795 games at UK, and if last night's goings-on mean anything, it will be that way until Joe B. Hall is old, gray and sitting at the right hand of his predecessor.

Imagine this. With only 33 seconds left, Mississippi State led, 85-83, and had a man, Ray White at the free-throw line shooting one-and-the-bonus. For the assembled 12,200 customers calamity was at hand. The train was bearing down; the buzzsaw moved forward. Was there any way to save the blue-clad nice guys?

For 26 years, Memorial Coliseum crowds have, by the strength of their voices, lifted Kentucky teams to heights beyond their mortal capabilities. So with Ray White at the free-throw line, about to do in the good guys, the crowd set up a clamor designed to unnerve the young man, a freshman to whom this treatment was brand new.

He knew it was coming. Only 18 seconds earlier, the fans had done it to another State player, who missed one of two free throws. As White stepped to the line, he took an imaginary shot without the ball — just to see if he could, under the pressure, move his arm.

The noise grew as the referee handed White the ball. Rising, rising, the thunder filled the arena. White shot. Whether he did it poorly or whether the sound waves threw the ball off course, no one knows. But it barely struck the rim on the right side, and Kentucky took the rebound.

The rest was inevitable. Hall called time-out with 26 seconds left. He drew up a play. If everything went right, high-jumping Bob Fowler would get a lob pass under the basket. If not, Jack Givens was to work one-on-one for a jumper. And with eight seconds left, Givens popped in a 12-footer to tie the game.

Rupp, invited by Hall to sit on the UK bench for this final game in the Coliseum, raised a fist triumphantly in celebration of Givens' work. In the overtime, Mississippi State was no match for the magic that is singularly Kentucky's.

State might have beaten a bunch of guys no bigger than 6-feet-5 (UK played the last 11 minutes with those tykes). But the visitors had no hope of beating Hagan, Ramsey, Spivey, Tsioropoulos, Watson, Strong, Linville, Lancaster, Hall — all those ghosts of 1951 when UK first played in the Coliseum, when UK won the third of its four national championships.

They were all here last night. Time has been kind to them all. They walked tall and erect. Call the names again: all-Americans Cliff Hagan, Frank Ramsey and Bill Spivey; "The Golden Greek" Lou Tsioropoulos; Guy Strong and Bobby Watson and Shelby Linville; Harry Lancaster and Adolph Rupp, "the greatest coach in basketball," to quote the public-address man.

They were introduced before the game. Then the UK band played "My Old Kentucky Home." Rupp sat down on the bench. Hall called Lancaster, once Rupp's assistant, out of the stands to sit on the bench, too. With all that tradition nicely in place, UK was ready to dispatch Mississippi State.

Of late, UK has played well. Its five straight victories before last night, including a 90-85 conquest of Alabama on national television, earned UK a trip to the National Invitation Tournament in New York's Madison Square Garden.

Kentucky in the Garden? In the fall of 1951, some Kentucky players from years before were implicated in a point-shaving scandal. Some of the games involved occurred in the Garden, and UK officials voted never to play there again.

That rule was changed in the summer of 1972. "They figured enough water had gone over the dam," said Hagan, now the UK athletic director.

So Kentucky will be back in New York City. It will return proudly, for in a season of unfortunate circumstances UK has persevered. It lost its best player to an injury six weeks ago, yet by season's end was able to best its league champion, Alabama.

Kentucky plays well now because its center, Mike Phillips, is remarkable offensively; forward Jack Givens can score against anyone; forward James Lee is a 6-foot-5 giant; and guards Larry Johnson and Reggie Warford are efficient and poised at both ends of the floor.

When it was over last night, Hall, in a marvelous gesture, gave the game ball to Rupp. The old coach, 74 now, smiled wonderfully, as if it were Christmas morning and he'd got exactly what he wanted.

"Way to go, Coach," somebody shouted to Rupp as he waled toward the locker room. "Hang onto that ball, Coach," someone else said.

Rupp bounced the ball once, and when somebody asked him if he was worried in the last minute of the game, Rupp said, "Hell, yes." He hefted the ball, then added, "That's a helluva way to treat an old man."

He laughed out loud at that one.

CHAPTER 31

The 1975-76 Wildcats won 20 games, lost 10 and captured the N.I.T. championship.

Kentucky Five Takes N.I.T. Title, 71-67

BY SAM GOLDPAPER
Special to The New York Times

NEW YORK, March 21, 1976 — You can find a Reggie Warford on most any college basketball team in the country. He is the high school hotshot who gets lost in a wealth of other high school hotshots, all recruited for the same position.

But if he is lucky, there comes a day when a Reggie Warford can have his day. Like yesterday, when Reggie Warford, Kentucky's lone senior, led the Wildcats to a 71-67 victory over North Carolina at Charlotte (U.N.C.C.) in the final of the National Invita-

tion Tournament at Madison Square Garden.

The consolation for the upstart U.N.C.C. team, which came to New York seeking national basketball fame, was that Cedric Maxwell, its skinny 6-foot 8-inch forward, was named the most valuable player.

North Carolina State defeated Providence, 74-69, for third-place honors in the preliminary game. Despite the crowd of 12,415, the largest of the tournament, the total attendance of 56,673 for the six sessions was the smallest since 1940, when six teams played over three days.

The stage for Warford, who had scored only 3 points in the previous three games — all on free throws —

was set when Kentucky got into serious second-half foul trouble. Jack Givens, the team's leading scorer all season long, picked up his fourth foul after 9 seconds of the second half. Mike Phillips, the 6-foot-10 center, was charged with his fourth foul 44 seconds later and James Lee, who had sparked the Wildcats to victory in the first two tourney games, was slapped with his fourth violation with 10:37 left.

Warford, a 6-foot-1 backcourt man with a 6.8-point season average, picked up the scoring lag with 10 of his 14 points. His driving left-side lay-up put Kentucky ahead, 60-59, and his 15-foot right side jump shot gave the Wildcats a 64-63 advantage, a lead they never relinquished. On

THE LINE-UPS

KENTUCKY (71)

	FG	FT	Pts.
Givens	3	0	6
Lee	4	0	8
Phillips	5	6	16
Johnson	7	2	16
Warford	7	0	14
Casey	3	0	6
Fowler	2	1	5
Totals	**31**	**9**	**71**

U.N.C.C. (67)

	FG	FT	Pts.
King	3	3	9
Massey	5	6	16
Maxwell	8	8	24
Ball	3	0	6
Watkins	4	0	8
Gruber	1	0	2
Pearce	0	2	2
Totals	**24**	**19**	**67**

Reggie Warford scored 10 points in the game's closing minutes.

that play Maxwell also fouled Phillips and he made both free throws.

Melvin Watkins cut the Kentucky lead to 66-65 with 39 seconds left, but two free throws by Larry Johnson restored the 3-point edge 17 seconds later. When Maxwell's second basket again cut the Wildcat edge to a point with 9 seconds remaining, Phillips' 3-point play 2 seconds later ended all hope for the Forty-Niners.

"It's my win," said Warford after the game, "and no one can take this one away. I'm the only one leaving from this team. It's all over for me. It's back to Drakesboro and the dirt courts where I can do all the shooting I want and there are no 13,000 people watching when you miss."

Drakesboro, Ky., is a town of 1,300 in the western part of the state in where Warford, a sociology major, collected 1,940 career points in leading his high school team to the regional final.

When someone asked Warford if he had any pro aspirations, he said, "I'm too smart for that. At 6-1 you don't think of things like that unless you are a Jo Jo White, a Nate Archibald or a Calvin Murphy and can do the things they can do. I'm realistic. I'd like to coach. I've seen both sides now. I have learned what discipline is all about."

Warford made his first start in three varsity seasons against Alabama in the final Southeastern Conference game. He started in three of the four N.I.T. games, missing against Kansas State when he tore a muscle in the warmup drill.

Warford said he considered leaving Kentucky during his sophomore season, but held out "because all the jokers told me I couldn't make it. I don't have to listen to anybody anymore.

"I took only six shots in the last three games. I don't shoot a lot unless I have to. U.N.C.C. was sagging a lot on Phillips and when that happens the guards must shoot. I made the first shot today. I think if I had missed

Mike Phillips' 3-point play ended U.N.C.C.'s final hopes.

I would have asked the coach to sit me down. I don't think I have taken a bad shot all season."

Even with Kentucky in foul trouble U.N.C.C. was unable to break the game open. When Givens and Phillips returned with 9:48 left, the Forty-Niners failed to drive on them in an effort to get them to foul out of the game, stalling at times, and that hampered their playing style.

In the U.N.C.C. dressing room, Maxwell, the high scorer in the tournament with 109 points in four games, including 24 yesterday, sat with tears streaming down his face.

"We brought the defeat on ourselves," said Maxwell, a junior. "We missed shots and made bad passes at the end. I think in a way we played scared in the final minutes. We didn't do the things we normally do. Everybody was just hoping the clock would run out with us ahead.

"Kentucky went into a 1-3-1 zone in the final minutes and that has been giving us trouble all season. We slowed our game down. It wasn't us out there anymore. We were doing the things Kentucky wanted us to do."

Kentucky finished with a 20-10 record, including the last 10 victories in a row, and U.N.C.C. and Maxwell received the fame they sought.

CHAPTER 32

Macy is Mr. Clutch in UK's Gutsy Rally

BY PAUL BORDEN
Special to The Courier-Journal

DAYTON, March 18, 1978 — Kyle Macy stood up at the podium, blinking at the glare of the bright lights. "How about your foul shooting?" came the first question from the middle of the pack of reporters. The sophomore guard smiled and shrugged his shoulders. Next question, please.

Kyle Macy, Mr. Cool-Calm-and-Collected, Mr. Clutch, if you please, helped Kentucky over a big hurdle in its drive to a fifth national collegiate basketball championship yesterday when his 10 straight second-half free throws helped beat Big Ten champion Michigan State, 52-49, in the title game of the N.C.A.A. Tournament's Mideast Regional.

Down five points at the half, Kentucky changed defenses, forced Michigan State out of its game and won when Macy hit six of his free throws in a tension-packed final three minutes. His last two, with eight seconds left, gave Kentucky an insurmountable three-point lead and sent the Wildcats on to St. Louis, where they will meet Arkansas this Saturday in a semi-final game.

Arkansas beat Cal State-Fullerton, 61-58, for the West title. The other members of the N.C.A.A.'s Final Four will be determined today when Duke plays Villanova in the East Regional and Notre Dame takes on DePaul in the Midwest.

Poise and patience were the keys to Kentucky's 28th victory in 30 games. Michigan State jumped out 29-22 on the first play of the second half, but Kentucky made two changes that stalled the Spartans' drive. One was on defense, where Kentucky abandoned its man-to-man and went to its 1-3-1 zone. That, Coach Joe B. Hall said, took the responsibility of guarding Earvin

Kyle Macy sinks one of his 10 clutch free throws against the Spartans.

After transferring from Indiana, Kyle Macy became a favorite of UK fans.

(Magic) Johnson off Macy and Jack Givens, who had shared the duty in the first half.

"Anyone who is guarding Earvin Johnson is going to have a mismatch," Hall said.

The other change came at Kentucky's end of the court, where Michigan State had shut off UK's inside power with its quick zone.

"We knew we had to get the ball to Macy out front," Hall said. "I told my assistants we wanted to get the ball to Macy for the jumper."

Hall called over Macy and Rick Robey, who would do the actual screening to free Macy, and told them what he wanted done.

"They worked it real well," Hall said. "And Lavon Williams did, too, when Robey was out."

Slowly, but inexorably, Kentucky began getting the game back into its grasp.

"We were in control probably until the last 10 minutes," said Spartan junior Greg Kelser, who had opened the game with two resounding dunks. "Then the tide turned and we couldn't get momentum our way again."

Michigan State held its last seven-point cushion at 31-24 and was sitting on a 35-32 lead when Kentucky made its move. Macy went to the free-throw line at 12:34 and hit one of two chances to make it 35-33. The teams exchanged turnovers on their next trips down the floor, but the next time James Lee and Macy combined to swipe the ball from Johnson at midcourt.

Lee bobbled the ball a bit but spotted an opening to the goal and took it all the way for one of his pattened breakaway dunks. It was tied, 35-35. Michigan State led twice more, at 37-35 and 39-37, but Macy and Givens got Kentucky back even each time — Macy from the line and Givens with a lay-up.

Mike Phillips gave Kentucky its first lead since early in the game with two free throws, making it 41-39 at 7:08. Johnson — limited to six points and only five assists — tied it with one of his two field goals, but Macy's three-point play gave Kentucky the lead for good.

Macy was fouled going up for a jumper, but the shot was good and he hit a free throw for a 44-41 score at 6:16. Michigan State was within a point four times after that, but first Phillips, who hit two at 4:56, and then Macy restored Kentucky's lead to three points with free throws.

"I had all the confidence in the world in Kyle," Robey said. "I know how hard he worked in the off season and how many free throws he shoots in practice. He's the one I want up there. All the close games, after I come down to relieve the pressure from a press, I get the ball back to him. I was glad to see him miss that earlier one. I wasn't at the time, but later I was. I knew he had already missed one, and I'd never seen him miss two in one game."

Each time Macy went to the line, Michigan State called time-out. If the ploy was to make the sophomore guard worry, it failed.

"Personally, I took advantage of it," Macy said. "I could get my breath and rest a little. Coach Hall just talked about our defense. I got my breath and went up there well rested." Thanks to his free throws, Macy accounted for 18 of Kentucky's lowest point production in 11 years. Not since a 52-50 loss to Tennessee on Jan. 23 has a Kentucky team scored fewer points.

Yet, Kentucky also kept Michigan State to the lowest output by a UK opponent since Kansas lost, 54-48, when Robey, Givens, Phillips and Lee were sophomores. The low scoring, of course, resulted from the zone defenses. Kentucky kept working the ball around and around and around in an effort to crack State's zone in the first half.

Kentucky took only 25 shots in that half and hit only 10, a poor 40 percent. And when Kentucky came out in a zone in the second half, Michigan State spread its offense and slowed the tempo even more. But Kentucky wasn't about to come out of the defense that effectively took Johnson out of the game.

THE LINE-UPS

KENTUCKY (52)

	FG	FT	Pts.
Givens	6	2	14
Robey	3	0	6
Phillips	3	4	10
Macy	4	10	18
Claytor	0	0	0
Lee	1	0	2
Schidler	1	0	2
Williams	0	0	0
Totals	**18**	**16**	**52**

MICHIGAN STATE (49)

	FG	FT	Pts.
Johnson	2	2	6
Kelser	9	1	19
Vincent	4	0	8
Donnelly	0	2	2
Chapman	5	0	10
Charles	2	0	4
Brkovich	0	0	0
Totals	**22**	**5**	**49**

"In a 1-3-1 or against any zone that clogs up the middle we like to get inside penetration," said Johnson, who had picked apart Western Kentucky for 14 assists Thursday night. "They didn't let us penetrate and I had to shoot over it. The ball wasn't falling. Against a man-to-man, we can penetrate. That's the difference."

What Michigan State coach Jud Heathcote termed "cheap fouls" made Michigan State's zone less effective than it had been in the first half. State forced Kentucky into 10 turnovers — four in the last three minutes — to turn a 23-22 lead into 27-22 at the break.

"We packed it in and played very aggressive the first half," said Johnson. "In the second, when I got my fourth foul and Bob (Chapman) got

Rick Robey provided the important screens that allowed Kyle Macy to hit his jump shots.

his, we couldn't be as aggressive."

Johnson never did get his fifth foul, but State lost Chapman and guard Terry Donnelly on personals. Both Donnelly and Chapman sent Macy to the line with their fifth fouls.

"Our win probably should be credited to our adjustments in the second half," Hall said. "And Kyle Macy's free throws. Those 10 straight were a clutch performance, but that's not unusual for Kyle. He's a great clutch performer.

"Our shooting in the first half put a lot of pressure on us and that is unusual."

Kentucky picked up in the last 20 minutes, hitting 57.1 percent to finish with 46.2, the first time since a 104-81 win over Auburn on Feb. 6 that Kentucky has been under 56 percent for a game. Michigan State hit 57.9 percent in the first half and 50 in the second, finishing at 53.7 with four more field goals than the Wildcats.

"I thought there were some questionable calls," Heathcote said. "One official made all the calls against us. But the game was well-officiated. I'm not complaining about the officiating, just making an observation." Just as Miami U. coach Darrell Hedric had said after Thursday's semi-final loss to the Wildcats, Heathcote said his club was beaten by a "great basketball team." He also has little doubt where the winner was headed.

"We told our kids whoever won this game would win the national championship," Heathcote said. "Maybe we're stupid, but we included ourselves in that. We could have won it. Now I believe Kentucky will win the national championship."

CHAPTER 33

Joe B. Hall, Successor To A Legend

By Gordon S. White Jr.
Special to The New York Times

St. Louis, March 26, 1978 — For more than a decade, Joe B. Hall has walked in a shadow. It was a bigger-than-life shadow cast by Adolph Rupp, the patriarch of basketball at the University of Kentucky.

That shadow could disappear tomorrow night in the light of a Kentucky victory. It could dissolve in the glow of a St. Louis sun rising on Tuesday over a champion from the bluegrass country.

But will it? Does the memory of the Rupp dynasty overshadow even the ultimate performance in college basketball? Hall will soon find out. Even during this season, his teams have been booed. Was it because he turned off his detractors with a cold and vindictive personality? Or is he, as his cheering section insists, a simple down-to-earth family man?

Simple Needs and Wants

Dennis Crane, who played for Hall at Regis College, has an opinion.

"He's a good man, an honest man," said Crane, who now works for a paper company in St. Louis. "He stays away from his players because he doesn't want to appear to show favoritism. His needs and his wants are simple. He's a good family man. People mistake his desire for privacy as unfriendliness."

Hall's detractors have another term

Joe B. Hall signals for time-out against Indiana in 1975.

Hall shouts instructions to his team.

for his aloofness. They call it paranoia. "He's really difficult to deal with," said one man who has dealt with Hall since Hall arrived in Kentucky in 1965, as an assistant to Rupp.

Hall had been a hotshot scholastic player at Cynthiana, Ky., and great success was predicted for him when he went to Kentucky. But that was the era of the Fabulous Five (Alex Groza, Ralph Beard, Kenny Jones, Wah Wah Jones and Cliff Barker) and who can compete with them?

So Hall transferred to the University of the South at Sewanee, Tenn., where he set a one-game scoring record and was team captain. As a coach, he bounced from college to college before settling down at Kentucky.

He successfully recruited six prep-school all-Americans, including Dan Issel, and turned out a winning freshman team, but being an assistant to Rupp was not the way to attract attention.

The Shadow Remains

Rupp was revered in Kentucky and fought mandatory retirement for as long as he could. But even after time caught up with him and Hall became coach in 1972, the shadow of Rupp stayed on campus.

The pressures on Hall can only be realized with an understanding of what college basketball means in a city like Lexington. Even if Kentucky wins tonight's national championship game, there will be fans who will say that the victory margin — whatever it is — was not high enough.

"Rupp would have done better," they would grumble. This attitude has led Hall to hint guardedly of retirement should he win the title.

Small wonder then that the new 23,000-seat Rupp Arena is part of the shadow cast by the late coach. The arena, built by the city of Lexington, is believed to be the nation's largest basketball facility, and that means that a coach must try to fill the seats or be criticized for his inability to create an interesting and winning team.

Hall is said to favor Memorial Stadium (capacity 11,000), the campus gym facility. He helped raise money for the new university basketball house. When the Wildcat Foundation guesthouse opened, the legend goes, the sign proclaimed "The Joe B. Hall Wildcat Basketball Lodge."

It quickly became "The Wildcat Basketball Lodge."

The explanation: The university does not name its facilities after individuals "until certain requirements have been met."

A Busy Week

Few Kentucky teams worked in the campus gym as hard as this team did this week. The hard practice, complications caused by a death in one player's family, the inevitable request for taped interviews, alumni ticket pressures and ordinary detail work left Hall weary.

On his burley tobacco farm in Harrison County, Hall seems more at home than on the basketball court. With his thick glasses and slow, deliberate manner, Hall offers a counterpoint to such "Eastern establishment" coaches as Digger Phelps of Notre Dame and Bill Foster, who coaches the Duke team Kentucky will face tonight.

A Farm Boy Shows Some Spunk

Hall lives in a fashionable upper middle-class home in Lexington's East End with his wife, Katharine. In addition to a married daughter the Halls have a son and daughter.

Hall will fish with "anyone, anytime, anywhere" on quiet ponds in Harrison County.

The farm boy once showed some spunk in exchange with the impulsive Bobby Knight of Indiana. There was some angry pushing but, though he has a temper, this was not characteristic of Hall.

His admirers prefer to tell of the time when Hall was showing some friends out of his home after a par-

ty. He saw flames gushing from a nearby hose. He rushed over, led his neighbors to safety and tried to extinguish the flames.

And when Crane showed up on Friday for the final Kentucky workout, he stood outside the dressing room with five little boys ("Only two of them are mine"), waiting for Hall to come out.

Would Hall acknowledge his former player and make him a hero in the eyes of his little boys or would Hall ignore him?

Hall whisked out of the dressing room and headed for the court, but saw Crane out of the corner of his eye. He turned and gave him a warm hello.

He talked to all the boys and even put his arms around two of them. The boys were wearing large white buttons that proclaimed, "I'm a Joe B. Fan."

Obviously, Hall didn't like this referee's call.

CHAPTER 34

Joe B. Hall's 1977-78 Wildcats posted a record of 30 wins and 2 losses en route to a 5th N.C.A.A. championship.

Goose Leads Wildcats to 5th N.C.A.A. Title

BY PAUL BORDEN
Special to The Courier-Journal

ST. LOUIS, March 27, 1978 — Kentucky can celebrate now. Jack (Goose) Givens, in the finest performance of his sparkling career and one of the best ever in N.C.A.A. championship game history, led the Wildcats to their fifth national title last night.

Kentucky's 94-88 victory over Duke in the final game of the 40th annual N.C.A.A. tournament climaxed a season of pressure in grand style for the darlings of the Bluegrass. "The pressure's been on six seasons, really," said Wildcat coach Joe B. Hall as he was mobbed by fans, reporters and television crews on the floor of the Checkerdome afterward.

Hall, who took over for Adolph Rupp in 1972 and lived in the shadow of the legendary coach, had spoken of the pressures of coaching at Kentucky a day earlier. He said his team, ranked No. 1 nearly every week of the season, had not taken time to enjoy any of its accomplishments — including a 31st Southeastern Conference crown — this year. It can now.

Givens, the No. 2 all-time Kentucky scorer, put on a tremendous show before a steamy crowd of 18,721 scoring a career-high 41 points. He hit 18 of 27 from the floor in scoring the third highest total for an individual in the N.C.A.A. final. His final-game total is topped only by Bill Walton's 44 in 1973 and Gail Goodrich's 42 in 1965, both for U.C.L.A.

"There's no finer way to go out," said Givens, who

cut the last strand of the netting on the south basket to the cheers of the Kentucky throng. "I'm happy for the team and for the people of the state of Kentucky because they love basketball so much there."

Givens scored 16 of Kentucky's final 18 points in the first half, getting the Wildcats on top, 45-38, at the break. It was a whirlwind finish in the closing minutes of the first half that got Kentucky a fairly comfortable margin.

With 57 seconds left, Duke's Gene Banks, who played despite receiving a death threat before the game, hit two free throws to cut Kentucky's lead to 39-38.

The next trip down, Givens fumbled the ball in the lane but recovered to put in a jumper over 6-foot-11 Mike Gminski, who missed from underneath at Duke's end.

Givens drilled one from the corner to get it up to 43-38 as the final seconds of the period ticked away. Duke rushed the ball down the floor, but Banks was called for charging — Givens, of course.

Givens went to the free throw line and hit both shots with three seconds left to put Kentucky on top by seven points.

"I was really ready," said Givens, "I never felt better before a game than I did tonight."

Duke, probably the youngest team ever to play in the final game with a starting lineup of a junior, two sophomores and two freshmen, hung tough, however, cutting Kentucky's lead to three in the opening minutes of the second period.

Two-time all-American Jack (Goose) Givens scores 2 of his 41 points against Duke.

"Duke played an outstanding game," said Hall, "and we played super."

Kentucky, whose four seniors — Givens, Rick Robey, James Lee and Mike Phillips — had played and lost to U.C.L.A. in the 1975 championship game never faltered.

Lee got Kentucky its first basket of the second half with a hook, and after Duke's Jim Spanarkel got that

Top: An elated Rick Robey, who had 20 points, celebrates following the victory over Duke.

Left: Wildcat coach Joe B. Hall takes the last few snips in the victor's symbolic net-cutting.

basket back, Givens missed a jumper, Lee missed a follow-up shot and Givens tipped it in.

Kentucky got a little more breathing room when Duke coach Bill Foster was called for a technical foul with 17:35 to go. Foster thought Kentucky's Truman Claytor had walked under pressure in the backcourt, but all he got for his protests was the "T" from Big Ten referee Jim Bain.

Kyle Macy, as is his custom, made both free throws, and then bounced a pass into Robey, who dunked one to give Kentucky a 55-46 lead. Kentucky stretched that margin to 12 points quickly at 60-48 and moved the lead up to 16 at 66-50 when Givens hit a follow shot and was fouled. Still, Duke refused to give in.

In fact, in the closing seconds, when Hall pulled his veterans from the game, Duke got the deficit down to 92-88 after Gminski hit a turnaround jumper. Duke called time-out with 10 seconds left to set up a press defense. But by then, Kentucky's regulars were back in the game, and the Kentucky season ended in a most appropriate fashion.

A long pass went to Lee in the Kentucky forecourt, and the big senior from Lexington eluded Duke's Bob Bender and went in for a dunk that made the final margin six points.

Free throws kept Duke in the first period. Duke ran off a string of 12 straight and trailed only 21-20 when the teams went to the bench for a television time-out at 9:41. For the first period, Duke was 20-for-21 from the line and only 9-for-23 from the field — 39.1 percent. Kentucky, meanwhile, was 18-for-34 from the field but went to the line only 12 times and hit nine.

Banks led Duke in scoring with 22 points followed by Spanarkel with 21 and Gminksi with 20. After Givens' 41, Robey followed with 20 for Kentucky. Robey also had 11 rebounds to lead Kentucky. Gminksi led Duke's rebounding with 12 as Duke enjoyed a 35-32 edge on the boards.

THE LINE-UPS

KENTUCKY (94)

	FG	FT	Pts.
Givens	18	5	41
Robey	8	4	20
Phillips	1	2	4
Macy	3	3	9
Claytor	3	2	8
Lee	4	0	8
Shidler	1	0	2
Aleksinas	0	0	0
Williams	1	0	2
Cowan	0	0	0
Stephens	0	0	0
Courts	0	0	0
Gettlefinger	0	0	0
Casey	0	0	0
Totals	**39**	**16**	**94**

DUKE (88)

	FG	FT	Pts.
Banks	6	10	22
Dennard	5	0	10
Gminski	6	8	20
Harrell	2	0	4
Spanarkel	8	5	21
Suddath	1	2	4
Bender	1	5	7
Goetsch	0	0	0
Totals	**29**	**30**	**88**

CHAPTER 35

Macy, Anderson and Cats KO Kansas

By Tev Laudeman
Special to The Courier-Journal

Lexington, Dec. 9, 1978 — There is still much to be learned about the University of Kentucky's young basketball team, but one truth shone through brightly last night: It's a team with heart. Kentucky trailed Kansas by 10 points late in the first half, and it wouldn't have been surprising if Wildcat coach Joe B. Hall had stood up and signalled the band to start playing "I Never Promised You a Rose Garden."

Hall didn't. He had said his players would have to grow up quickly to have a chance to beat some of the strong teams on UK's early schedule, including fifth-ranked Kansas. UK grew enough last night, defeating Kansas, 67-66, in overtime, and the way the 10th-rated Wildcats did it wrote a memorable page in the school's illustrious basketball history.

UK scored seven points in the final 31 seconds of overtime — the last three by junior guard Kyle Macy — to hand Kansas its first defeat in five games. The heroes at the end of the game were a freshman, Dwight Anderson, and Mr. Cool, Macy. UK trailed, 66-60, when the series of events that Hall called "unbelievable" unfolded.

Anderson hit a lay-up to make it 66-62, but he seemed tense with 16 seconds left. He missed on the front end of the bonus free-throw situation.

Mr. Cool — Kyle Macy — scored the Wildcats' final 3 points in overtime in UK's 67-66 win over Kansas.

126

But Anderson drew another foul in a scramble under the basket, and this time he sank both free throws to cut the Kansas lead to 66-64 with only 10 seconds left.

Even then Kansas had a big advantage. All it had to do was get the ball inbounds and upcourt to run out the clock. But somehow, Anderson knocked the ball away from Kansas' Mac Stallcup as the ball came in, and he almost dived to save the ball before it could go out of bounds. He slapped it all the way across court to Macy, who calmly scored from about 15 feet to tie the game with four seconds left.

Kansas' Darnell Valentine, who played a magnificent game and scored a career-high 27 points, called time-out. But he drew a technical foul because Kansas had already used the one time-out the rules allow in overtime. Macy hit the front edge of the rim on the ensuing free throw, but the ball bounced in for the deciding point. Neither Macy nor Anderson saw each other's heroics at the end.

"I really didn't see the play because I was guarding my man," Macy said. "The next thing I knew, it was coming to me. I knew there wasn't much time and I had to shoot. I didn't want to take it in and get it blocked because they'd been blocking a lot of our shots."

Anderson asked reporters: "Did it go straight to Kyle? Oh, it bounced to him. I didn't know that. I'd have to see that one on the film." And he didn't see the shot that followed his remarkable save and pass. "I didn't see anything," he added, laughing. "Somebody told me Kyle had hit the shot and that a technical had been called."

Macy, normally the coolest man on the team, admitted he was jittery on his game-winning free throw. "I kind of had to walk it in," he said. "I've been having a little trouble with free throws. I've been pointing out a little too much instead of pointing toward the

THE LINE-UPS

KENTUCKY (67)

	FG	FT	Pts.
Cowan	4	0	8
Williams	2	6	10
Aleksinas	3	2	8
Macy	6	3	15
Claytor	3	0	6
Anderson	1	2	4
Shidler	4	0	8
Stephens	2	0	4
Verderber	0	0	0
Tillman	2	0	4
Totals	**27**	**13**	**67**

KANSAS (66)

	FG	FT	Pts.
Guy	4	5	13
Crawford	5	1	11
Mokeski	4	0	8
Fowler	0	5	5
Valentine	9	9	27
Stallcup	1	0	2
Neal	0	0	0
Totals	**23**	**20**	**66**

basket. Fortunately, it had enough backspin." That capped a stretch that tested even Hall's imagination.

"The effort to make seven points in 31 seconds is almost unbelievable," Hall said. "I felt all during the game we could win. We'd made a lot of mistakes and we'd had a lot of breaks go against us such as the bounce of the ball and blocking and charging."

Then Hall, who obviously believes in miracles, laughed and said, "I think the technical wasn't important at all, because we would have stolen the inbound pass and scored anyway."

And who's to say he's wrong?

Kansas coach Ted Owens, who seemed reluctant to leave the court after the final horn, was brief in his comments, but his emotions were under control. "First of all, I'm extremely proud of our players," he said. "They played a great game. They took it to Kentucky just as we'd hoped to, and they deserved to win the game. When we had a six-point lead and 31 seconds to go, the officials eased up. They'd called a fine game, in my opinion, up until that point. (UK freshman Clarence) Tillman obviously charged on the basket that cut it to four (before Anderson's basket cut Kansas' lead to 66-62), but no foul was called. On the next possession, there was a scramble and (UK's Lavon) Williams was hanging on the rim. But nothing was called. If they (the officials) had continued the fine work they did the rest of the game, then you'd see a celebration in this locker room."

Hall said Kansas, which had been known for its full-court pressure defense, surprised him with a zone defense it used the entire game. And the strategy was sound, too, because UK's shooting was poor, especially in the first half. "We really struggled. These guys didn't give up," Hall said. "We just weren't hitting against the zone (38.7 percent in the first half and 44.1 in the final half)," he said. "I just can't explain it. They

LaVon Williams (52) scored 10 points in the Wildcats' victory.

were shots we normally hit. They were rimming in and out and that just put tremendous pressure on us, not to be able to hit from the outside." But they hit the ones at the end when they had to have them.

Macy's shooting was off in the first half, although he was UK's high scorer for the game with 15 points. He had hit only two field goals when Hall pulled him out with 3:57 left in the opening half. And Jay Shilder, who was awarded UK's Sixth Man Award for his outside shooting (four for nine), started for Macy in the second half. Macy didn't go back in until 11:32 was left in regulation.

Asked why he held Macy out so long, Hall said, "His leg (a pulled muscle in the right thigh and groin) was bothering him. He could not get his legs under him on his shots. His shooting the first half wasn't good. The last shot he took in the first half, he just armed it up. He had no legs in it at all."

UK, 3-0 and likely to move up in the ratings a notch or two, has a week to get ready for its next game, Saturday at Indiana.

CHAPTER 36

Anderson Leads
Upset of Fighting Irish

BY JOEL BIERIG
Special to The Courier-Journal

LOUISVILLE, Dec. 30, 1978 — "I was scared," Dwight Anderson said. "I was nervous." That was understandable. Until tonight, Kentucky-Notre Dame basketball games were something he watched on television. When they were over, he could turn off his set and dream.

Tonight, however, there was no way out. Dwight Anderson was part of the real, live drama being acted out before a throng of 16,869 at Freedom Hall. With the fans and his coach, Joe Hall, yelling in his ears, Anderson knew it was a case of produce or else. So he responded by scoring 17 points — all in the second half — and something virtually unbelievable happened.

No. 13-ranked Kentucky, down by 12 points midway through the second half, rallied to upset No. 2 Notre Dame, 81-76. The people in Hollywood couldn't have enjoyed the script anymore than Hall.

"Happy is not the way I feel about this ballclub," Hall said as his team savored its fifth victory in seven games. "They've come back from the dead so many times, I don't know who you'd compare them with."

The Wildcats, who found a way to upset Kansas in overtime earlier this season, seemed out of miracles when they lost to Indiana and Texas A&M in their next two outings. But they rebounded to beat Syracuse in the

Dwight Anderson's dreams came true when he led the Wildcats with 17 second-half points as UK defeated Notre Dame, 81-76.

consolation game of the UK Invitational, and tonight they were back to their old scheming ways.

"Coach Hall told me to go straight to the hole," said Anderson, a 6-foot-3 guard-forward from Dayton, Ohio. When the freshman missed his first four shots, however, Hall almost told him to go straight to the bench. "I thought he was going to pull me," Anderson said.

That would have been fine with Notre Dame, which came in with a 5-0 record and hopes of moving into the top spot in The Associated Press poll. After Ohio State upset top-ranked Duke on Friday night, Notre Dame's chances seemed good.

And they seemed even better when the Irish, ahead 40-37 at half-time, took a 61-49 lead with 10:23

THE LINE-UPS

KENTUCKY (81)

	FG	FT	Pts.
Verderber	2	1	5
Williams	4	4	12
Aleksinas	6	0	12
Macy	4	3	11
Claytor	8	2	18
Anderson	5	7	17
Shidler	0	0	0
Tillman	3	0	6
Cowan	0	0	0
Totals	**32**	**17**	**81**

NOTRE DAME (76)

	FG	FT	Pts.
Woolridge	2	0	4
Tripucka	7	7	21
Laimbeer	4	0	8
Branning	2	9	13
Hanzlik	5	2	12
Wilcox	1	0	2
Jackson	4	0	8
Flowers	4	0	8
Totals	**29**	**18**	**76**

remaining. "The place got quiet," Notre Dame center Bruce Flowers noted. "I'd never seen it that quiet."

Anderson eliminated the library atmosphere by hitting two free throws to make it 61-51, then brought the crowd to its feet with a driving lay-up that narrowed the gap to 61-53. "There was a letdown," Flowers said when asked why Notre Dame's 12-point lead suddenly dissipated. "There's always a letdown here."

The Irish, who are 1-7 against UK since Digger Phelps became their coach, watched Anderson fly through the air with the greatest of ease for a dunk with 8:10 remaining. There was little cause for worry, though, because UK still trailed by eight, 65-57.

An Anderson lay-up and a three-point play by guard Truman Claytor brought the Wildcats within 67-64, and UK stayed three behind when another freshman, Clarence Tillman, hit a jumper to make it 69-66.

With 4:33 left, Anderson hit a short jumper and was fouled by Notre Dame's Tracy Jackson. He missed the free throw, but Tillman tipped it in for a 70-70 tie.

At that point, Phelps instructed his team to go into its spread offense. "That means we try it once — spread it — look for penetration and then go back to our regular offense," Phelps said.

"Why didn't I go into it when we were 12 points up? I didn't think it would do any good. The foul totals were against us at that point, and I didn't think the spread would help us."

"Yes, I was a little surprised they went into it," said Hall, "but we like to see that. It gave us an opportunity to rest a little, and we felt the momentum of the game changed at that point."

With 2:43 remaining, Anderson was fouled by Kelly Tripucka — the game's leading scorer with 21 points. His first shot rolled ominously around the rim before

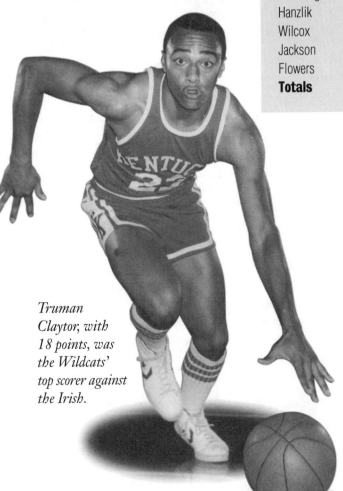

Truman Claytor, with 18 points, was the Wildcats' top scorer against the Irish.

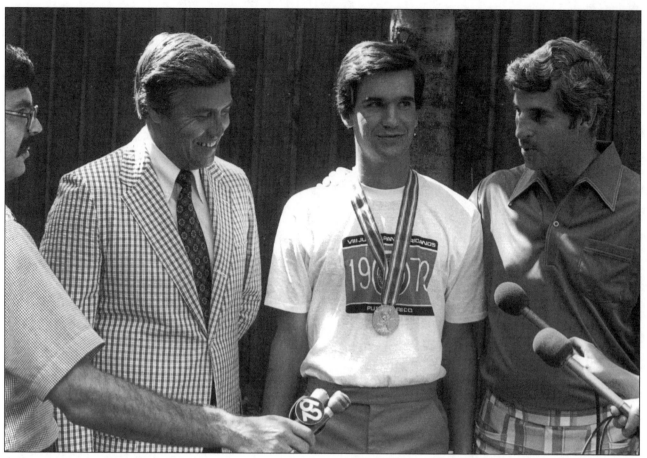

Kyle Macy, wearing his 1978 Pan-Am Games gold medal, fields questions from the press. He is flanked by UK athletic director Cliff Hagan (left) and Indiana coach Bobby Knight.

consenting to go through, putting UK ahead for good at 71-70. He hit his second free throw with far less difficulty, then stole the ball as Notre Dame tried to transport it downcourt. The result was another daredevil dunk that gave UK a 74-70 edge — and Hall a bad case of the goose bumps — with 2:32 left.

"His steal, fullcourt dribble and dunk was a big play," Hall said. "I think it broke them."

"We just broke down in the second half," said Phelps.

"We made some errors and didn't execute well. We didn't get any offensive rebounds of any significance in the second half. Too many shots of ours were 'bump blocked,' " Phelps added.

Asked if that meant Notre Dame was fouled and

the refs didn't blow their whistles, Phelps said, "Yes."

The Notre Dame coach said he wasn't surprised by the performance of Anderson, who was five-for-12 from the field, seven-for-10 from the foul line and was voted the game's most valuable player.

"We knew he could penetrate well," Phelps said. "I don't think his ability surprised any of us."

But the way he used it surprised even Anderson.

"I have some doubts," Anderson said, "but Coach Hall hollers at me a lot. That's good for me."

Hall admitted he considered taking Anderson out of the game at one stage. "But he was getting good shots and they weren't stopping him, so we decided to stay with him," Hall said.

CHAPTER 37

Bowie Consoles UK
as Its Dream Dies

BY JOHN McGILL
Special to The Courier-Journal

KNOXVILLE, March 26, 1983 —
Halfway down the long, dark corridor, Joe B. Hall and Frustration went
one-on-one. Clutching his rolled-up
program, the University of Kentucky
coach smacked it against the wall,
threw it to the concrete floor and
kicked with all his might.

On a bench outside the locker
room, where UK players waited glumly for a key to open the door, Dirk
Minniefield sat. His shoulders sagged.
His head drooped. His silence
screamed. Limping by, Sam Bowie
surveyed the scene and turned toward
Minniefield.

"You ain't got nothin' to be
ashamed of, man," Bowie said. "You
played a hell of a game."

He had indeed. So had the rest of
Kentucky's players. But, in a monstrous
display of full-court pressure, Louisville
scored 14 consecutive points to open
an overtime and turn The Dream
Game into a Wildcat nightmare. The
final: Louisville 80, UK 68 in the
N.C.A.A. Mideast Regional final.

In one very real sense, of course, the
margin was a deceit. If it underscored
the megatonnage of Louisville's explo-
siveness, it nevertheless hid the fury, passion and chills of the game's first 40 minutes — which ended with a swishing,
12-foot baseline shot by UK's Jim Master at the buzzer to force the overtime.
"It typified the game," said Master.

*Unable to play due to injuries, Sam Bowie was forced to watch from the
Wildcats' bench during this emotional loss.*

And those first 40 minutes?

"I hope that's what everybody remembers," said Master, "because that was a great game."

Master, who logged more court time (40 minutes) than any other UK player, hit 9 of 13 floor shots and shared team scoring honors with Melvin Turpin. Each had 18 points. Minniefield, meanwhile has 12 points and five assists. Derrick Hord, his shot resurrected in the first half, scored nine. And UK, which led by 13 points in the first half, came back from a five-point deficit in the final minutes of regulation.

All of that had the Stokely Athletics Center crowd of 12,489 in a lather. But when the overtime began and the Louisville press generated maximum duress, Kentucky withered. On its first seven possessions, UK suffered five steals. The two times it survived the heat, UK suffered missed shots.

"They were all over the floor," said Kentucky guard Dickey Beal. "They were just everywhere. Even Louisville's forwards were picking up guards, and you don't see that from many teams. Plus, they play it so well. In practice we had worked on them denying passes by having players making cuts. They covered them as if they had been at our practice. It was unbelievable."

"It was like," said Master, "a calvary charge."

"Our press works in mysterious ways," said Louisville's Scooter McCray. Then, shifting to a grin and a spooky falsetto: "Whooooooooooo."

Ironically, UK had sailed through great gulps of the game without taking any direct hits by the press — shredding it, in fact, on some occasions.

"When we were up by 13 (23-10 with 10:16 left in

THE LINE-UPS

KENTUCKY (68)

	FG	FT	Pts.
Hord	4	1	9
Hurt	3	1	7
Turpin	8	2	18
Minniefield	6	0	12
Master	9	0	18
Beal	0	0	0
Harden	0	0	0
Bearup	1	0	2
Walker	1	0	2
Totals	**32**	**4**	**68**

LOUISVILLE (80)

	FG	FT	Pts.
S. McCray	3	1	7
R. McCray	7	1	15
C. Jones	4	4	12
Gordon	11	2	24
Wagner	7	4	18
Valentine	0	0	0
West	0	0	0
Hall	0	0	0
Thompson	2	0	4
Totals	**34**	**12**	**80**

the first half), I felt darn good," said Master. "I really felt if we lost, we'd more or less have to give it away."

Pause.

"But I don't think we did. Louisville's got a come-from-behind team. And they're sort of unique. I don't see any other team doing it (the press) as well as they do. And they're so fluid with it. At times we ran through it like it wasn't there. But maybe it just builds on you. Then they get that enthusiasm going."

"And the McCray boys (Scooter and Rodney) are two of the finest forwards you'll find in America. The big difference I noticed was how well the whole team jumps. I'd heard they were the best, and I gotta go with it. Those son of a guns jump better than anybody I've ever seen."

"It's definitely the leapingest team I've ever seen," said UK forward Bret Bearup. "I've never played a team that can jump like that."

Louisville was credited with only five blocked shots, but its continual hovering and harassing around the rim obviously took a toll on UK — particularly in crucial situations. One in particular.

With the score tied, 60-60, UK got the ball when Milt Wagner made a bad pass out of bounds with 2:25 to go in regulation. Kentucky decided to stall for a final shot, calling time-outs at 1:48 and 49 seconds remaining to map its strategy.

With about 20 seconds left, Minniefield — dribbling on the wing — saw a wide-open route to the basket. He took it. But as he went up with a lay-up, Louisville's Charles Jones soared to tap the ball away. Lancaster Gordon hit a fast-break bank shot to make it 62-60 with 11 seconds left, and although Master saved UK with his heart-throb shot, Minniefield knew his miss had destroyed a golden chance

Jim Master led the Wildcats in scoring against Louisville with 18 points, including the 12-foot baseline shot that sent the game into overtime.

later it's going to get you. I definitely think they're the best team in the country."

There was one difference in this UK squad and the ones that had gone 1-3 the past three years in the N.C.A.A. Tournament, including first-round losses in the last two. For the senior trio of Hord, Hurt and Minniefield — whose freshman dream of Final Fourdom never materialized — there was some consolation in making the Mideast Regional title game, of beating Indiana in the semi-finals and of taking this one into overtime.

"It's all over with now," Hord said. "But we did give the effort. And we did accomplish things for a while."

"It (the final margin) hurts a little bit, but it wasn't how the game went," said Hurt. "People who saw it realized how well the teams played. We both played well."

"Maybe if my shot had rolled in, things would be different," said Minniefield. "But those are just the breaks. I've gotta keep on truckin'. I feel we accomplished something. We made it all the way to the door. We just didn't knock it down. So there's nothing to be ashamed of. I gave it all I had for four years."

Said Hall: "It is a real sign of character when a ball team can come back like Louisville did. But I'm proud of our team."

After his press conference, Hall mad a brief visit to the Louisville locker room. He shook Scooter McCray's hand and then turned to another player. "Best of luck, Rod," said Hall.

One problem. The player he was talking to was Wagner, not Rodney McCray.

For UK, Hall's error in an otherwise nice gesture mirrored his team, which had played well only to trip in the end.

for UK to have gone ahead and given Louisville the pressure of making a last-second shot to tie.

"I think Jones got a piece of the ball and it was a judgment call (on whether it was goaltending)," Minniefield said, "but I thought I probably should have dunked it. If I had it to do again, I would have dunked it. I know that."

For all the sadness and misgivings, Minniefield likewise had praise for Louisville.

"They're quick enough to play man-to-man and they can change their fronts with the press. They can zone it and they can play it hot," he said. "Sooner or

After Dream Game I, Joe B. Hall congratulates winning Louisville coach Denny Crum.

CHAPTER 38

Cats Rumble, Cards Crumble in Dream Game II

By Mike Sullivan
Special to The Courier-Journal

LEXINGTON, Nov. 26, 1983 — Say pilgrim, did anyone get the license number of that big blue Cardinal crusher? Without a doubt, the University of Kentucky was a movin' machine in its 65-44 demolition of Louisville last night.

As an overflow Rupp Arena crowd of 24,012 set the air on fire with noise, UK filled the floor with its tank-sized bodies.

It filled the air with dunks and blocked shots. And it filled the statistics sheet with — holy role reversal — steals. "I don't know how many steals they gave me (he was credited with three), but I felt like I got my hand on a lot of balls tonight," said Sam Bowie, Kentucky's 7-foot-1 forward. "You get used to what a team is doing and you start to anticipate things."

Given UK's history of gaudy December showings in Rupp Arena, it was probably logical to anticipate a measure of revenge for that 80-68 overtime loss to Louisville in the N.C.A.A. Tournament last March.

What was more difficult to anticipate — but what came to pass as these teams opened the season with their first regularly scheduled game since 1922 — was the following:

The Man-to-Man Menace. Kentucky, allegedly too slow to prosper defensively in anything but a zone, played Louisville head-up. UK limited the Cardinals to a 35.6 field-goal percentage (21 of 59) while forcing 20 turnovers — 12 of those on steals — and block-

Kenny (Sky) Walker, a masterful shot-blocker, scored 13 points in the Wildcats' revenge victory over the Cardinals.

ing seven shots (Bowie had five).

"The only time we played zone was on out-of-bounds plays," said guard Jim Master, the game's leading scorer with 19 points.

The Killer Instinct Issue. Wildcat coach Joe B. Hall often finds that quality missing in his teams, and he many have set a record this year by complaining about it in the preseason. But Kentucky, which put the game away by outscoring Louisville, 13-0, over a 3-minute span late in the first half, was definitely in an overkill mode.

Opening the final period with a 35-20 lead, the Wildcats ran off 20 points to only six by the visitors to hold a shocking 29-point lead (55-26) with 10:49 left to play. The final 21-point margin was the second worst that any Denny Crum-coached Louisville team has suffered. The worst was an 86-64 loss to North Carolina on Dec. 29, 1980.

"We wanted to come out after halftime and pick up where we had left off," said sophomore forward Kenny (Sky) Walker, who had 13 points, three rebounds and three steals. "Coach Kelly (first-year assistant Lake Kelly) has really done a good job of teaching us some fundamental man-to-man."

When the damage was added up, 6-foot-11 center Melvin Turpin had 16 points and nine rebounds for Kentucky, which shot only 39.6 percent from the field (19 of 48) but also took a startling total of 36 free throws and sank 27 of them.

Bowie had seven points and a game-high 10 rebounds and dished out five assists to go with his five blocks and three steals. A pair of freshmen, 6-foot-7 Winston Bennett (two points, seven rebounds) and 6-foot-3 James Blackmon (six points, four assists, three steals) were effective off the bench, especially when Louisville was fading from a modest 22-16 deficit over the final 5:49 of the first half.

"Bennett seems to be a catalyst for this team," Hall said. "I don't know if I've ever had a freshman who had that much leadership influence on a team. I've got to single out a great defensive effort. Our 1978 (N.C.A.A. championship) team played excellent defense, and this bunch seems to have the same chem-

THE LINE-UPS

KENTUCKY (65)

	FG	FT	Pts.
Bowie	0	7	7
Walker	6	1	13
Turpin	5	6	16
Master	5	9	19
Harden	0	0	0
Blackmon	3	0	6
Beal	0	2	2
Andrews	0	0	0
Bearup	0	0	0
Bennett	0	2	2
Heitz	0	0	0
McKinley	0	0	0
Totals	**19**	**27**	**65**

LOUISVILLE (44)

	FG	FT	Pts.
Forrest	3	0	6
Thompson	2	0	4
C. Jones	2	2	6
Gordon	4	0	8
Wagner	2	0	4
Valentine	0	0	0
Jeter	0	0	0
Sumpter	0	0	0
Hall	3	0	6
Mitchell	0	0	0
McSwain	5	0	10
Totals	**21**	**2**	**44**

istry. We were dominating inside and our guards were pressuring them outside. Sam was a factor in our full-court offense against their press, and his blocked shots were an intimidating factor."

Bowie, in fact, might have been the single most noteworthy sidelight to Kentucky's many-splendored show. He had been out of competition for two full seasons because of a stress fracture, and he had looked both tentative and lacking in stamina in Tuesday's exhibition game against The Netherlands.

While logging 33 of the game's 40 minutes last night, he was neither. But he did help break down Louisville's half-court defense with his adroit passing.

"That's a role I enjoy, because the guys seem to appreciate it a lot," Bowie said. "I can't remember the last time I didn't score in double figures, but this team is filled with guys who went out and got 30 a night in high school. I'm not the only one making sacrifices."

The only player scoring in double figures for Louisville was a freshman substitute, 6-foot-7 forward Mark McSwain, who hit all five of his shots from the field while scoring 10 points. Guards Lancaster Gordon and Milt Wagner, who combined to average nearly 29 points a game last season, scored only eight and four, respectively, while hitting a combined 6 of 21 from the field.

"To tell you the truth, I was most disappointed in our three returning starters (Gordon and Wagner and center Charles Jones)," Crum said. "They tried to take it all on themselves and do too much. They went one-on-one instead of being patient."

"I'm not sure, considering the relative talent levels and physical size, that we'll ever be able to beat Kentucky this year. But our young people are going to have to play every game and keep learning. Kentucky's defensive pressure was excellent, but we have options that we go to against pressure and overplay. We didn't use them, but give Kentucky the credit."

During its decisive run late in the first half, UK got a pair of inside baskets from Turpin and Walker — each coming on a Bowie lob — and two consecutive steals from Blackmon, who stripped Louisville sophomore Jeff Hall in the backcourt on the second one and followed each theft with a lay-up.

"I thought we complemented each other really well," Master said. "We played a great inside-outside game, I thought."

Gordon said he wasn't greatly surprised to see Kentucky play the man-to-man.

"If you had a couple of 7-footers, wouldn't you pressure the outside jump shot and force everything in to Bowie and Turpin?" Gordon asked. "As a team, we weren't where we should have been, but I think everyone learned something. Kentucky is more experienced and playing at home, so you had to expect something like that, but I don't think anybody's unbeatable."

The game included one sequence in which Turpin, feeling he had been fouled on a shot, faced Gordon before running upcourt and shook his fist at him angrily.

"He pushed me or hit me and I said some words to him," Turpin said. "Another one said something and I said, 'Come on if you want to.' Then the ref talked to me and I said, 'Fine, just tell him to get off my back.' I'm not the kind to take nothing. If they want a brawl, I'm the man to do it."

Gordon said he didn't remember much about the play, noting, "Let me watch the film and I'll tell you about it."

Melvin Turpin goes airborne to score 2 of his 16 points against Louisville.

CHAPTER 39

Wildcats Stop Akeem & Cougars

BY BILL WERONKA
Special to The Courier-Journal

LEXINGTON, Jan. 22, 1984 — It was supposed to be a fun game — the nation's No. 3 and No. 4 college basketball teams running, dunking, blocking. It was supposed to be a game of giants playing in the stratosphere — Akeem the Dream vs. The Twin Towers.

It was all of that and more as third-ranked Kentucky won the nationally televised playground battle in Rupp Arena yesterday, beating fourth-ranked Houston, 74-67. However, there was another battle going on at ground level, far below the skirmish in the sky.

"After they fell behind, 11-1, they started executing better," Houston coach Guy Lewis said of the Wildcats. "Then they put that little guard in there that had been starting but didn't. He turned it around."

That little guard was 6-foot-1 sophomore Roger Harden, who found out five minutes before the game that 6-foot-3 freshman James Blackmon was replacing him in the starting line-up.

"Naw, that didn't bother me," Harden said. "Coach (Joe B.) Hall just has to do what he has to do."

What Hall ended up having to do was replace Blackmon four minutes into the game after his four turnovers and tentative play helped the Cougars jump to that 11-1 lead.

"Eleven to one — I was thinking

UK's Twin Towers — Melvin Turpin (54) and Sam Bowie (31) — were a roadblock in Akeem Olajuwon's scoring plans.

disaster. I didn't know what had happened," said UK forward Kenny Walker, who led the Wildcats with 20 points and hauled down 10 rebounds.

"I was thinking blowout," said 6-foot-11 center Melvin Turpin, who scored 19 points and grabbed 11 rebounds.

Harden was thinking about only one thing, and it wasn't panic.

"I just wanted to get the squad organized," said Harden, who scored six points on key jumpers and handed out six assists, five during a crucial first-half comeback. "The press was hurting us bad. My biggest asset on the club is knowing where to put the ball against the press. Coach Hall wanted to attack more, get it across and get them in foul trouble."

So, as the sky battle increased in fury, Harden was finding out that "there's always room for the little guy in basketball. When the press is bothering us, it's my job to do something about it. I just did what I'm supposed to do. I got us organized and breaking.

"I did spend a lot of time looking up, though."

One of the players he was looking up at was his roommate, 7-foot-1 Sam Bowie, who was having his best game of the year.

UK controlled the boards, 51-45, and Bowie's 18 rebounds were the big reason. "This is my best game since coming back, at least on the boards," Bowie said. "We knew one of the keys to beating Houston was blocking out on the boards and rebounding with them. I knew I had to do that."

Bowie noticed how his roommate got things going, and it didn't surprise him a bit.

"He's the quarterback of our squad," Bowie said. "When you see me get a blocked shot, that's probably because Roger Harden told me to get in position."

It took UK five minutes to get its first field goal. But after Turpin dropped in a short jumper, the Wildcats

THE LINE-UPS

KENTUCKY (74)

	FG	FT	Pts.
Walker	7	6	20
Bowie	4	0	8
Turpin	8	3	19
Blackmon	4	1	9
Master	0	0	0
Beal	0	1	1
Harden	3	0	6
Bennett	1	9	11
Totals	**27**	**20**	**74**

HOUSTON (67)

	FG	FT	Pts.
Young	8	3	19
Winslow	2	0	4
Olajuwon	6	2	14
Franklin	8	8	24
Gettys	0	0	0
Giles	1	2	4
Thomas	0	0	0
Dickens	1	0	2
Anderson	0	0	0
Totals	**26**	**15**	**67**

began turning the game around, shooting 58.3 percent for the half and limiting Houston to 40.6 percent.

Bowie got one of his two blocks and Walker converted at the other end when 7-foot Akeem Olajuwon's block was ruled goaltending. The two big men began UK's 12-6 run that cut the Houston lead to four. The Wildcats finally tied it at 27 when Bowie tapped in a rebound with 3:11 left. They missed the opportunities to build the lead by missing free throws and contributing their total of 18 first-half turnovers, but somehow led, 35-31, at the half.

"With all the mistakes we made, we were lucky to be up at the half," Bowie said. "Coach Hall diagnosed very well what we needed to do at halftime. Houston had forced the action with the press and left Olajuwon back, which is sort of like six people back there. We needed to force the action."

That is what Kentucky began

Winston Bennett, a 6-foot-7 freshman, tossed in 11 points.

Rupp Arena, which opened in Fall 1976 with a seating capacity of 23,000, is the finest basketball palace in the country.

doing in the second half, starting Dickey Beal for Harden and Blackmon for Jim Master, who was 0 for 4 from the field. Still, the Cougars trailed only 46-44 five minutes into the second half, as point guard Alvin Franklin created offense by driving inside.

Then Olajuwon picked up his fourth foul and UK went on a tear, outscoring the Cougars, 15-7, to take a 61-51 lead with 7:36 remaining. Olajuwon, who played a strong game with 14 points, 12 rebounds and five blocks, fouled out with 6:14 left, and the Wildcats seemed to let down.

"I guess we did when he sat down on the bench," Walker said. "They didn't, though."

Franklin, who finished with 24 points, certainly didn't. He led his team back to within three, but the Cougars' chances died with missed free throws and other scoring opportunities. Houston's 6-foot-8 forward Michael Young finished with 19 points and nine rebounds, but he had to battle Walker and 6-foot-7 freshman Winston Bennett at every turn. He hit only 8 of 25 from the field.

"If I went around a pick, someone else would always pick me up," Young said. "One of the main things was they outrebounded us. That was basic."

Hall expressed pleasure at his team's performance.

"As I said earlier, I thought that it would be the kind of game we needed, and it turned out to be just that," Hall said. "It was a good game to get out and run. There was a lot of action and a lot of great plays. I think our players enjoyed the game. To come back like we did took a lot of poise. I thought we played with a lot of aggressiveness. We really came through the way a good team should."

Lewis said it "was about as physical as you can play college basketball." But Lewis and most of the UK players said it was the odds that beat Olajuwon and Houston.

"If you've got two 7-footers against one 7-footer, the intimidation should work out about two-to-one," Lewis said. "That's about the way it worked out."

"I just had to make adjustments," Olajuwon said.

142

Melvin Turpin, who scored 19 points for the Wildcats, listens to UK coach Joe B. Hall's strategy.

"I would like to play them again on neutral ground."

Turpin and Bowie were glad the odds were in their favor.

"That's the hardest game I've played this year," Turpin said. "Olajuwon is strong. I've got nothing bad to say about the young man. We didn't change nothing for him and he didn't change nothing for us."

Bowie at first said the combination of Turpin and himself did make Olajuwon change his tactics, but then wasn't so sure.

"That's asking a whole lot of him, playing both of us," Bowie said. "Akeem was concerned by Melvin and myself — but looking at his stats, I'm not sure how much. He's as good a player as he's built up to be, and maybe a little bit more. He doesn't play like your average 7-footer. He jumps like a 6-2 or 6-3 guy."

CHAPTER 40

UK Grabs S.E.C. Tournament Crown

BY BILL WERONKA
Special to The Courier-Journal

NASHVILLE, March 10, 1984 — The sigh of relief escaped from Kentucky coach Joe B. Hall like air rushing from a balloon.

"Whew!" he exclaimed, and for a moment slumped every so slightly to let the tension and excitement subside. Then quietly, he added, "Finally."

Yes, finally, the Southeastern Conference Tournament trophy was handed to Kentucky after a 31-year drought after Kenny Walker's shot at the buzzer bounced on the rim and fell in to give the Wildcats a 51-49 victory over Auburn yesterday afternoon.

It was UK's first championship since the renewal of the tournament in 1979, and made UK (26-4) the sixth different champion in that period. It was also the first time the regular-season champ has won the tournament in those six seasons.

Before Hall could sigh, though, he had to experience the moment. And his face was frozen and drained of color as Walker moved off a screen and put up the winning jump shot. It was as Hall had set it up, almost.

With 14 seconds left and the score tied, the plan was for point guard Dickey Beal to inbound the ball to Jim Master, who would give it back to Beal. Then Beal would wait for Master and Melvin Turpin to set a screen for Walker.

That's the way it worked, except Beal never touched the ball after throwing it in. Master had to take over

Kenny (Sky) Walker leaps above the Auburn defense to shoot his game-winning basket at the buzzer.

Beal's role and vice versa.

"I think that was as satisfying a situation as getting the win," Hall said, referring to Master's and Beal's switching roles. "It was a great thinking job. You can't practice that. They did it on their own, used their own judgement and executed it perfectly. Master deserves a lot of credit. He probably pulled the play of the night. He and Dickey are roommates, and I guess they think alike."

Beal was being overplayed after tossing the inbounds pass, and that's when Master figured a change was in the wind.

"Of course, I wanted to get the ball back to Dickey," said Master. "After that I guess it was instinct, and maybe fear, too. I kept holding it and holding it, trying to get it back to him. But once I put the dribble down, I saw Dickey cut in and then I guess it was instinct after that."

Master passed to Walker at the top of the key and the 6-foot-9 forward moved in and put up a 15-foot jumper over the screen that kept out Auburn's Chuck Person.

"I didn't want to fight through the screen," said Person, who bounced back from a knee injury Friday to score 14 points and grab seven rebounds. "With what seemed like 15,000 Kentucky fans out there, I knew they would call a foul. I saw it bounce, but I guess we didn't get our third bounce of the tournament."

Person was referring to the two previous Auburn games in which last-second shots by Vanderbilt and Tennessee bounced off the rim.

And what did Walker think of the shot and bounce?

"I just thought it was going in," he said. "When it left my hand it felt real good," Walker said. "I saw it hit the rim, but I guess I was lucky enough for it to go in. You've got to be lucky, and last night and today we proved that."

Friday night, in UK's 48-46 victory over Alabama, the situation was the same. Only that time, Beal took the lead, missed his shot, but was fouled and hit the decisive free throws. Hall said he didn't want to try that again because Auburn probably would be looking for it.

Hall was right, said Auburn coach Sonny Smith.

"Yeah, he (Beal) had taken the shot in the same sit-

THE LINE-UPS

KENTUCKY (51)

	FG	FT	Pts.
Bowie	3	0	6
Walker	6	0	12
Turpin	6	1	13
Master	5	0	10
Beal	3	0	6
Blackmon	1	0	2
Bearup	0	0	0
Bennett	1	0	2
Totals	**25**	**1**	**51**

AUBURN (49)

	FG	FT	Pts.
Person	7	0	14
Turner	4	1	9
Barkley	5	4	14
White	3	0	6
Ford	1	0	2
Daniels	0	0	0
Strickland	2	0	4
Totals	**22**	**5**	**49**

uation last night," Smith said. "I figured they would do that or get the lob in to Turpin or Bowie."

But it went to Walker, the man who couldn't buy a basket Friday night (1 of 11) but hit 6 or 7, scoring 12 points, and grabbed nine rebounds yesterday.

"Kenny never has a bad night, so his going 1 of 11 is unbelievable," Hall said. "He made up for it tonight."

Walker said he had joked with his roommate after Friday's game.

"I told him he might have to take me to a repair shop to fix my jumper," Walker said. "But, really, you just have to forget about those games. I know where I fit in the offense, and I just have to remember not to force anything."

What got lost in the shuffle of final-second madness was the play that set up the play.

With 4:06 to go, Kentucky was down, 49-47, and Auburn had the ball. But Master's pestering of Person paid off. Person lost the handle and in the scuffle was called for stepping out of bounds. Kentucky went down the floor and Beal fed Sam Bowie an alley-oop pass for the tying dunk, and the 14th tie of the half, with 2:22 remaining.

Following a time-out, 6-foot-7 freshman Winston Bennett came in to play, slapping away a pass intended for Person and feeding a breakaway pass to Beal. But Beal missed the lay-up, Walker rebounded, and it was time to play keep-away to find out how Auburn planned to react.

"When they used the half-court trap on Dickey (at 1:05 left), we knew and called a time-out," Hall said. "Charles Barkley (the tournament m.v.p.) does a good job zoning the basket and we didn't want to attack him. We made the decision to hold the ball."

The decision proved the right one to secure the Wildcats the S.E.C. tournament title. That, coupled with the regular-season title, virtually assures them the No. 1 seed in the N.C.A.A. Mideast Regional.

the ball to Auburn seven times, and six times with a chance to increase its lead. But Auburn's shots didn't fall or the War Eagles turned the ball over.

Instead of fighting from behind, UK stayed even and went ahead at the half, 30-27, when Beal hit a jumper at the buzzer.

"In the second half we were patient and shot the ball well for the most part, but we had two critical turnovers late in the game," Smith said. "This is a difficult game to be on the losing side of. We did the things you have to do to win. It's a shame but they (UK) did too."

The game was tied 12 times and there were 18 lead changes, with neither team ever leading by more than four points. Barkley scored 14 points for Auburn. Turpin led UK with 13.

Smith has been a watcher of the Wildcats all year, and said he thinks perhaps they are playing with more emotion now.

"They didn't against Alabama, but the got with it today. They had a lot of enthusiasm, considering they played three straight nights. But I think Beal playing so well is the main difference. When you get leadership like that, you play harder and everything else falls into place."

Jim Master, who had 10 points, was UK's key playmaker against Auburn.

Nothing, however, was assured in the game until Walker's shot fell through the net, which he later cut down.

Smith thought his War Eagles lost the game much earlier than that.

"Our inability to shoot the ball in the first half was a factor," he said. "In fact, the key to the game might have been the fact that we shot just 33 percent in the first half."

Many of those misses came midway through the period when Auburn (20-10) could have capitalized on a Kentucky drought.

The Wildcats went five minutes without a field goal, struggling against the 3-2 zone. Master's shooting kept them close early, but when that failed briefly, UK gave

thing else falls into place."

Beal was not claiming too much of the credit. But, just as his time has come late in the season, he feels it is UK's time, too.

"We've been in the top 10 my last three years and haven't done anything," he said. "But winning games like this makes a difference. We've got that attitude that North Carolina State had last year."

Beal might have been a bit ahead of himself, because it should be remembered that N.C. State won the N.C.A.A. title last year.

"It will take five more victories for Kentucky to prove Beal prophetic and not presumptuous.

CHAPTER 41

The Final Force

By Billy Reed
Special to The Courier-Journal

Lexington, March 24, 1984 — In the midst of the madness, as delirious fans clawed at them and the noise cascaded from the rafters of Rupp Arena, the University of Kentucky players formed a knot at midcourt and thanked each other.

It was their moment, after all, and it was touching to see the smiles and hugs. By beating Illinois, 54-51, yesterday in the final of the N.C.A.A. Mideast Regional, Sam Bowie, Dickey Beal & Co. did more than just earn a berth in next Saturday's Final Four in Seattle.

They put the Wildcats back where they are accustomed to being, which is at the top of the college game. Now, after six long and frustrating years, the Big Blue is no longer the Big Blew.

"It's an awesome feeling," said Beal, the 5-foot-10 senior from Covington. "Making the Final Four has been a goal of ours for a long time. It makes all the hurt and pain and hard practices worth it. But this victory is not just ours — it's everybody's."

Since winning the N.C.A.A. title in 1978, the Wildcats and their followers have had to swallow one bitter pill after another. Upset tournament losses at home in 1979 and 1980 to end the season. Upset tournament losses to lesser teams (where did you go, Middle Tennessee State?) in 1981 and 1982.

And last year, of course, The Game against Louisville in Knoxville for the Mideast championship. The Cats played well for 40 minutes, but collapsed in overtime. The Cards of Denny Crum took an 80-68

Dickey Beal drives for a lay-up against Illinois. Beal was the Wildcats' emotional leader in their journey back to the Final Four.

victory, the trip to Albuquerque for the Final Four, and bragging rights in the state.

But now, a year later, The Empire has struck back.

"I'm on Cloud 10," said Bowie, the 7-foot-1 senior from Lebanon, Pa., who was celestial yesterday with 14 rebounds and 11 points.

This Saturday the Cats will meet the winner of today's West Regional final.

Illinois coach Lou Henson yesterday said he liked UK's chances to win its sixth N.C.A.A. title and second in the Hall era that began in 1972-73.

"Kentucky's a super team," Henson said. "They're well-coached, they play hard, and we wish them well in Seattle."

But regardless of what happens in the Kingdome, this has been a marvelous season for Hall and his team no matter how you measure it: a 29-4 record, the championship of the Southeastern Conference regular season and tournament, and the N.C.A.A. Mideast Regional title.

Of course, UK was expected to do all those things, but as North Carolina coach Dean Smith no doubt would testify today, it's not always so easy to fulfill the great expectations that are born of great talent.

The seeds for this Final Four team were planted by Hall back in 1979, when he landed Bowie to go with a freshman class that included Derrick Hord, Charles Hurt and Dirk Minniefield.

However, after showing extraordinary promise and growth as a freshman and sophomore, Bowie came down with a hairline fracture in his left shin — an injury that, mysteriously, required him to miss two complete seasons.

The events of this season indicate how good UK might have been in those seasons with a healthy Bowie to go with 6-foot-11 Melvin Turpin. Maybe the Cats would have been in the Final Four both years, and maybe they wouldn't, but you can count on this: They wouldn't have lost to Middle Tennessee in 1982.

This season, finally, Bowie was able to come back. And if his play — especially on offense — wasn't always quite what he wanted it to be, he still was good enough to instill a new sense of confidence in his teammates.

He no doubt would be UK's

THE LINE-UPS

KENTUCKY (54)

	FG	FT	Pts.
Walker	3	0	6
Bowie	3	5	11
Turpin	6	1	13
Beal	3	3	9
Master	3	0	6
Blackmon	0	0	0
Bearup	0	1	1
Bennett	3	2	8
Totals	**21**	**12**	**54**

ILLINOIS (51)

	FG	FT	Pts.
Winters	3	1	7
Altenberger	5	3	13
Montgomery	2	0	4
Richardson	8	0	16
Douglas	3	1	7
Wysinger	0	0	0
Meents	2	0	4
Totals	**23**	**5**	**51**

Comeback Player of the Year were it not for Beal, the Cat-a-lyst whose dribbling, ballhandling, passing and outside shooting have turned this team from a good one into an outstanding one.

Hampered since the end of last season by a knee injury, Beal reached the point this season where he was ready to quit. But Hall, understanding the difference a healthy Beal would make, prodded and nudged him into sticking with it.

He came off the bench against Auburn on Saturday, Feb. 11, to spark UK to a 20-point win. After only one more game, Hall put him in the starting lineup at point guard in place of sophomore Roger Harden.

From that time to this, the Wildcats have lost only once — to Tennessee at Knoxville on Monday, Feb. 27. That led Hall to crack down in practices. The coach simply would not permit this team to fall short of its potential.

"All the tough practices were no fun while they were going on," said 6-foot-8 sophomore forward Kenny Walker, "but winning this makes it all worthwhile."

After closing the regular season with homecourt wins over Ole Miss and L.S.U., the Wildcats went to Nashville for the S.E.C. Tournament — and won the trophy for the first time since the event was revived in 1979.

After the victory over Auburn in the S.E.C. title game, Beal said he thought it would make a big difference for UK to go into the N.C.A.A. on a winning note.

Let the record show that he was correct.

In their opening N.C.A.A. game last Saturday in Birmingham, the Cats blew out Brigham Young to earn the trip back home. Then, on Thursday night, they had the poise to overcome an incredibly courageous performance by Louisville.

It's pointless to speculate about what might have been had the Mideast been played somewhere other

Sam Bowie added 11 points in UK's win over the Illini during his remarkable comeback season.

Melvin Turpin lunges toward the Illini's basket.

two team fouls — meaning that the Wildcats could give up a few at the end without being penalized.

Also, with UK leading, 52-50, at the 14-second mark, Henson felt that Beal should have been called for traveling when Illinois had him double-teamed and trapped near midcourt.

Instead, the Illini's Bruce Douglas was whistled for hacking Beal on the arms. The UK guard made both free throws for a 54-50 lead that provided the Cats with the cushion they needed.

It was an excellent defensive game.

While the Illinois man-to-man did a good job of containing UK's inside game, the Cats used both a man-to-man and a 2-3 zone to handle the intricate Illini offense built around perpetual motion and picks.

It also was a hard-fought game in which, at one time or another, UK's Walker, Bowie and Beal all had to leave, momentarily, because of injuries.

In Beal's case, he made the mistake of venturing under the basket during a rebounding scuffle — a No Man's Land for a player of his size. He took an elbow to the nose from Bowie, of all people, and had to go to the bench.

"One of the few times I go under the basket — and I get knocked out," Beal said later, smiling ruefully. "You're not going to see me go under there anymore."

But, of course, he came back to lead UK to its most important win in years.

After the game, when it was announced that Beal had been named the Mideast's Most Valuable Player, Walker and Turpin hoisted him onto their shoulders.

The little man had a smile that stretched from here to Seattle. At that moment, in every place around the country where there are fans who bleed Blue, there had to be hearts full of joy.

The Empire, finally, had struck back.

than Rupp. Perhaps UK might have lost to Louisville or Illinois.

Then again, without having to deliver before the most demanding fans in basketball, perhaps the Wildcats would have played even better.

"At a neutral site," said Illinois center George Montgomery, "it might have gone our way. I guess it all depends on what kind of referees we have."

The Illini weren't crybabies about it, but Henson indicated that he definitely thought the officiating hurt his team yesterday. For one thing, going into the last couple of minutes of the second half, UK had only

CHAPTER 42

The 1983-84 Wildcats won 29 game, lost 4 and advanced to the Final Four.

Georgetown Rally Overcomes Wildcats

BY PETER ALFANO
Special to The New York Times

SEATTLE, March 31, 1984 — Sometimes, their best quality is lost in the controversy that surrounds them and gives the impression that the Georgetown Hoyas win simply by huffing and puffing and bullying their opponents. But the Hoyas are more than bluster, as they proved again today. They are relentless, especially on defense, a part of the game that is an afterthought for some teams but is Georgetown's life-support system.

The defense led a second-half comeback for a 53-40 victory from Kentucky today as the Hoyas earned a berth in the national championship game Monday night against Houston at the Kingdome.

At halftime it did not look as if the Hoyas would get that far. They trailed by 7 points, and Patrick Ewing, the 7-foot junior center, had missed the last 8 minutes 52 seconds of the half because he had drawn his third foul. John Thompson, a big man who scowls at officials and carries a white towel over his shoulder to wipe the sweat from his face during a game, admitted that he was even more nervous than usual.

"Patrick was out and I had to keep reminding our guards, 'Be patient, Patrick's on the bench,'" Thompson said. "When we got to be 10 points down, I thought about going into a delay game and trying again in the second half with the big fella."

But when most teams rely on their scorers to get back into a game, Georgetown counts on tightening its grip defensively, forcing turnovers and poor shots.

UK's Melvin Turpin (54) keeps Georgetown's Patrick Ewing in check. He limited the Hoyas' center to just 8 points.

What it did to Kentucky in the second half today was almost sacrilegious, given the proud tradition of the school that treats basketball as if it invented the sport. Georgetown overwhelmed the Wildcats with a 12-point outburst at the start of the second half and kept them scoreless for the first 9 minutes 56 seconds.

"We like to tease our enemies, make them happy and think they will blow us out," said Thompson after the game, no longer sounding nervous. "Then we come back."

The key to the victory was a pressing defense that smothered Kentucky, forcing hurried shots, 15 turnovers, and prompted Joe B. Hall, the Wildcats' coach, to toss his rolled-up program over his shoulder in exasperation with four minutes to play.

Kentucky made only 24.5 percent of its shots overall, and incredibly, hit only 3 of 33 attempts in the second half when none of its starters made a field goal. The 40 points were the fewest by any team in the Final Four since 1949 when Kentucky defeated Oklahoma State, 46-36, in the championship game. Today's performance had Hall groping for answers.

"What happened was totally beyond me," he said. "I've never seen a team shoot like we did today. There had to be some electronic device sending out sounds around the basket."

Dickey Beal, the Kentucky point guard, said it was a combination of Georgetown's defense and his team missing open shots. "It just wasn't like us out there," he said. "But credit their defense. They disguised it well and took us out of our defense."

With 3:04 to play in the first half, Kentucky was in control, leading by 27-15. Ewing was on the bench with three fouls and Thompson was tempted to send him back before the game was out of reach. Instead, he implored his players on defense, substituting liberally and cutting the deficit at halftime.

THE LINE-UPS

KENTUCKY (40)

	FG	FT	Pts.
Bowie	3	4	10
Walker	1	2	4
Turpin	2	1	5
Beal	2	2	6
Master	2	2	6
Bennett	1	0	2
Blackmon	2	1	5
Bearup	0	2	2
Harden	0	0	0
Totals	13	14	40

GEORGETOWN (53)

	FG	FT	Pts.
Wingate	5	1	11
Dalton	0	0	0
Ewing	4	0	8
Brown	0	0	0
Jackson	4	4	12
Smith	2	1	5
Martin	1	0	2
Graham	4	0	8
Williams	1	0	2
Broadnax	2	1	5
Totals	23	7	53

Perhaps Kentucky was still admiring its handiwork when the second half started. The Wildcats had been dominant inside as Sam Bowie and Melvin Turpin swatted shots and neutralized the Georgetown power game. Bowie had even stood up to the aggressive play of Ewing and forward Michael Graham in minor scuffles under the basket. And Beal, Jim Master and James Blackmon, the guards, were handling the ball well.

But if Kentucky was elated, Georgetown was not depressed by the score either. "We knew we had been awful," said Hoyas guard Michael Jackson. "And we knew that in the second half, Patrick would be back in there and that we could spread our defense out to the perimeter.

Georgetown's comeback was so swift that Hall could not counter it until his team had fallen behind. David Wingate opened the half with a jumper and Gene Smith followed with a lay-up. Then Jackson scored from outside, and the Hoyas took the lead for the first time with 17:07 remaining when Ewing tapped in a missed shot.

Graham, whose inspired defensive play and rebounding were given a major share of the credit for the comeback, made a lay-up, and Horace Broadnax followed with another before Winston Bennett scored Kentucky's first points of the half with 10:04 to play.

But it was just an interruption in the surge. The Hoyas continued to pressure Kentucky, forcing Bowie and Turpin to shoot long range jumpers instead of maneuvering inside for easier baskets. Hall was also upset that Turpin did not challenge Ewing, trying to draw a fourth and fifth foul. But it might not have been as easy as it looked from the bench.

"We play pretty good defense," Jackson said. "I've played against our defense in practice and it gets pretty rough."

As UK fans celebrate their trip to the 1984 Final Four, little did they realize that a return would be nearly a decade away.

CHAPTER 43

Redmen of St. John's Defeat Kentucky, 86-70

BY WILLIAM C. RHODEN
Special to The New York Times

DENVER, March 22, 1985 — Playing one of its most physical games of the season, St. John's moved a step closer to the Final Four tonight, defeating Kentucky, 86-70, in a West Regional semi-final.

The Redmen, relentlessly exploiting the Wildcats' weaknesses in the middle, simply took over the offensive boards in the second half and ended the Wildcats' brief reign as the Regional's Cinderella team.

After the game, Joe B. Hall ended his 13-year career as Kentucky coach, announcing his resignation.

Chris Mullin, scoring at will from the outside, and adding a few punches to the middle, scored a game-high 30 points and made 7 assists and grabbed 10 rebounds.

Walter Berry added 22 points and had a game-high 11 rebounds as the Redmen earned a berth in the Regional final Sunday against North Carolina State. The Wolfpack beat Alabama, 61-55, in the first game here tonight.

Mark Jackson, a reserve guard, played one of his best games, scoring 12 points and adding 4 assists.

Bill Wennington added 10 points, 2 assists, but only 3 rebounds.

"I think we played excellent defense in the second half," said Lou Carnesecca, the Redmen coach, "and we hit the offensive boards."

Roger Harden, the Wildcats' chief playmaker, scored 13 points for UK against St. John's.

"I think our guys did a helluva job off the bench," added Carnesecca, singling out Willie Glass and Jackson. "They gave us the lift we needed."

The Redmen could not stop Kenny Walker, Kentucky's 6-foot-8 all-American, who scored 23 points even though he was hampered for most of the game by a swollen right eye.

The Redmen outrebounded the Wildcats, 36-27 — including 26-14 in the second half.

Both teams shot 63 percent in the first half. St. John's finished with 53.6 percent and Kentucky with 52.5

"That was the key," said Hall after the game. "They did a great job of going to the boards against our zone."

St. John's led at the half by 38-39 and by only 49-47 with 15:20 left. Then Wennington hit a hook shot and Glass went flying across the lane to rebound and slam it home for a 53-47 lead. Soon after, Glass rose over 240-pound Wildcat center Bret Bearup for a tip-in and a 57-51 lead.

The Wildcats started quickly in the opening half and created problems for St. John's.

The Redmen were damaged by the outside shooting of Roger Harden and Troy McKinley, who combined for 19 points in the first 20 minutes. With 11:16 left in the half, Kentucky led, 18-13. But then St. John's came back, taking a 39-38 lead in what was one of the most physical halves the Redmen have played all season, even rivaling the games against Patrick Ewing and Georgetown.

THE LINE-UPS

KENTUCKY (70)

	FG	FT	Pts.
Bennett	2	2	6
Walker	10	3	23
Bearup	1	0	2
Davender	5	1	11
Harden	6	1	13
Byrd	0	0	0
Blackmon	0	0	0
Andrews	0	0	0
Ziegler	0	0	0
McKinley	4	0	8
Madison	2	1	5
Lock	0	0	0
Jenkins	1	0	2
Totals	**31**	**8**	**70**

ST. JOHN'S (86)

	FG	FT	Pts.
Berry	7	8	22
Glass	4	2	10
Wennington	4	2	10
Mullin	11	8	30
Moses	0	0	0
Jackson	3	6	12
Jones	0	0	0
Stewart	1	0	2
Totals	**30**	**26**	**86**

Midway through the half, Mike Moses, the Redmen point guard, ran into a brutal pick set by Walker and was forced to leave the game.

Moments after the Moses mishap, Mullin decked Bearup, who was setting a pick.

At another point, Mullin, who had been helping out on Walker, came around from the back while Walker was holding the ball and took a swipe at it. Instead of the basketball, all Mullin got was Walker's right eye.

Walker recoiled in pain and spent the next three minutes on the bench.

When he returned, with 8:12 left, St. John's had closed the game to 22-19.

The problem of how to contain Walker had preoccupied the Redmen all week. Glass, the 6-foot-6 sophomore, started out on Walker with help from Wennington and Mullin. Walker scored 8 points in the half.

In Walker's absence, the Redmen established a strong inside presence. With Walker back in the lineup, his eye swollen shut, the Redmen continued their comeback.

After Winston Bennett hit a jumper to make it 24-19, Mullin, who hit 6 of 11 shots for 15 points in the half, connected over Walker to make it 24-21.

Walker scored on a goaltending call by Berry. After the teams exchanged misses, Berry hit and drew the foul, but missed the foul shot.

After another Kentucky foul, Wennington slammed home a miss by Berry to make it 26-25 with 6:23 left.

Dramatic Sign-Off For Hall

BY WILLIAM C. RHODEN
The New York Times

After a season of speculation and 13 seasons of enduring one of the most pressurized positions in sport, Joe B. Hall, the basketball coach at the University of Kentucky, announced his resignation tonight after his team's loss to St. John's in the West Regional semifinal.

Immediately following the game, he apologetically refused to answer questions about the speculation that had circulated through McNichols Sports Arena all evening. But after his post-game press conference was completed, Hall made his announcement on his radio broadcast on the Kentucky network.

"When I accepted this position 13 years ago," Hall said, reading from a typed statement he prepared for the broadcast, "I knew in my mind I would not coach beyond my middle fifties. I really have not had the time during the past 13 years to spend with my family that I wanted to have. I intend to have that time in the years ahead."

Hall, who is 56, later said that he had not told the Wildcat players of his decision. Dr. Otis A. Singletary, the university president who sat near Hall during the announcement, said that a search committee would begin work to select a replacement, and that candidates had not yet been submitted.

When asked if he would offer suggestions to the committee, Hall said, "I'll do what they like, but I don't want to interfere."

Hall, the 18th coach in Kentucky history, succeeded the late Adolph Rupp for the 1972-73 season. His final Wildcat team completed its season with an 18-13 record, tying a school record for most losses. In 13 seasons, his Kentucky teams had a record of 297-100.

The 1978 Wildcats won the national championship for the fifth time in the school history, but the only time in Hall's tenure.

At Kentucky, anything less was not considered acceptable. Ironically, his final Kentucky team had completed its season in the role of the underdog, with a record of 16-12, the worst of the at-large teams in the N.C.A.A. tournament.

The Wildcats, after hearing that they did not belong in the field, defeated Washington and Nevada-Las Vegas last week to reach the game tonight, and Hall seemed relaxed along the way.

While Hall has been booed at home games, he did not voice any complaints tonight. "I've done what I like to do," he said after completing his statement. "I've done it where I wanted to do it, with the people I wanted to do it with."

Hall said he had received several offers to enter private business, and would take some time to decide. "I'm going to fish for a while," he said. "After that, I don't know."

After retiring from coaching, Joe B. Hall teamed with ABC-TV's Al Michaels as an analyst on college games.

Following his retirement, Kentucky coach Joe B. Hall was honored when a banner bearing his name was raised to the rafters in Rupp Arena.

CHAPTER 44

Dream Game? Call This One The Cream Game

BY JIM TERHUNE
Special to The Courier-Journal

LOUISVILLE, Dec. 27, 1986 — Some months ago, Ed Davender nicknamed Rex Chapman "Rosey." As in "Roosevelt" Chapman. As in, "Here's one of the brethren coming off the brickyards of the inner city who can flick the switch on a spin-dribble 18-footer as smoothly as he can turn up the volume on a ghetto-blaster."

Davender and his University of Kentucky teammates knew by the end of the summer pickup games that they had been joined by a freshman who transcended the stereotypes of the college basketball world that say: The black player can jump, is quick and has the moves; the white player can muscle and fire the deep jump shot.

Yesterday in an 85-51 victory over Louisville at Freedom Hall, Chapman twisted, leaned, tumbled, and jammed his way to 26 points. He gunned home 5 of 8 three-point field goals, two of them launched not from the N.C.A.A.'s 19-foot-9 arc but from the National Basketball Association's 23-9.

With Richard Madison spending only 29 minutes to grab 17 rebounds, each snatch sounding like the report from a rifle; with James Blackmon (1 for 5 going in) hitting all three of his three-pointers; with Davender getting 16 points and five assists; and with Rob Lock not only helping to unbalance Pervis Ellison into 2-for-8 shooting but also driving the baseline for a thunder dunk, UK did something no one this side of a mental hos-

Rex Chapman twisted, leaned, tumbled and jammed his way to 26 points in the Wildcats' 85-51 rout of arch-rival Louisville.

pital could have expected.

It trounced defending national champion Louisville on its own court by 34 points. Never in the 15-season Denny Crum reign has anything like this happened.

Never in the history of Freedom Hall. Never at home in the last 46 years.

Louisville's worst previous loss under Crum was 22 points (North Carolina, 1980). Its worst loss under Crum at home was 20 points (Virginia Tech, 1985). Its worst loss to UK was by the same margin, 34 (in an Olympic Trials match in 1948).

Never had it lost by this margin in its 30 seasons at Freedom Hall. Never had it lost by this margin on any home court since Jan. 29, 1940, when Evansville won, 80-43.

One has to go back to a 99-59 pasting at Xavier on Feb. 13, 1956, to find a worse defeat anywhere.

"Things snowball," said Crum. "A team gets so much momentum up that whatever you try fails to work."

"We don't play that well every day," said Kentucky coach Eddie Sutton. "We're not 34 points better than Louisville. I think everybody knows that."

"We have confidence and knowledge in our personnel," said UK assistant Dwane Casey. "We didn't come in here thinking we'd rub Louisville's nose in it. No one with a sane mind would think that."

But, said Lock, "It's such an awesome feeling because some are saying it's the greatest victory in UK basketball ever. They expected it with teams like the Twin Towers and others. I can't describe how I felt when we were up by 20 with 15 minutes to go. The full effect won't sink in until later."

Because of the emotional pitch of the rivalry and the location of the game, Louisville was a slim favorite going in. Now it owns a 4-6 record to Kentucky's 6-1.

"If anything, I think this makes our fans believers," said Sutton. "They've been talking about waiting until next year. I like this year."

Jumpers by Kenny Payne and Tony Kimbro got Louisville off to a 4-0 lead and the game teeter-tottered to a 14-12 UK advantage.

THE LINE-UPS

KENTUCKY (85)

	FG	FT	Pts.
Chapman	10	1	26
Blackmon	4	0	11
Davender	5	5	16
Lock	4	1	9
Thomas	2	2	6
Miller	3	0	8
Bruce	0	0	0
Shigg	0	0	0
Madison	4	1	9
Jenkins	0	0	0
Totals	**32**	**10**	**85**

LOUISVILLE (51)

	FG	FT	Pts.
Payne	3	0	7
Crook	1	4	6
Ellison	2	0	4
Hawley	1	0	2
Kimbro	4	2	10
Williams	0	0	0
McSwain	1	0	2
West	0	0	0
Marshall	1	0	2
Abram	4	0	8
Spencer	4	2	10
Totals	**21**	**8**	**51**

Chapman offered the first peek at his artistry with 4:43 left in the half. He already had hit 3 three-pointers when he appeared above the crowd to intercept a front-to-backcourt pass from Ellison and began a right-hand drive to the other end. As he lifted off toward the basket for the expected dunk, Keith Williams got in the way. Chapman adjusted his thoughts and finger-rolled it in.

That made it 29-18 UK and put the visitors on the brink of a breakaway. But it was early and Louisville stomped back. A jumper by Kimbro, a lay-up by Ellison and two free throws by Herbert Crook cut a 36-22 UK lead to 36-28.

Thirty-four seconds remained in the half. Perhaps Louisville could get a steal, a field goal and ...

Chapman dribbled lonesomely in the backcourt. He held up one finger, then four. That meant the 1-4 offense. Hit the baseline, guys, and I'll see what I can do.

"I try to lose whoever's guarding me," Chapman said. "If I don't, I dish it off."

He was eyeball to eyeball with Craig Hawley. At the top of the key, he dribbled behind his back to the right. He reverse spin-dribbled to his left, entering the free-throw circle and left Hawley on his right hip. Crook jumped up to help. The clock ticked toward 5 seconds remaining. Chapman jumped at a 45-degree angle to his left as Crook went up with him and Hawley leaned in from the other side.

Chapman shot, fell and did a somersault. The shot swished.

Fouled? "I thought so," said Chapman.

Were any of these creations new? "I've done them all before," Chapman said.

Was that a shock to Crook? "I believe anything he shoots," said the 6-foot-7 forward. "He was like that in high school. Even though he's only a freshman, he's

Ed Davender (15) challenges a Louisville player with his 2-pointer. He finished with 16 points.

A jubilant Wildcat bench enjoys the stunning victory over the Cardinals.

got to be one of the top guards in the country."

So it was 38-28 at intermission. Kentucky went on from there, its barnacle-like defense combining with Louisville's crooked shooting eye to send UK on a 10-0 run at the start of the second half.

It was 48-28 with so much time (15:33) still to go, and UK still went off with it. Chapman was rejected by Ellison but dunked on Payne and slapped three hard medium-fives with Irving Thomas at midcourt... Blackmon drilled 2 three-pointers in 86 seconds... The blocky Lock delivered his baseline move, then a dunk to make the final score the game's widest margin.

"The whole side of the court was open," Lock said of his 15-foot drive with 45 seconds left. "I took a dribble, then stopped, looked and nobody moved because I never do something like that." He grinned. "So I went on."

A 34-point margin?

"The credit goes to the coaches," Chapman said as he waited in the Louisville training room for a public interview. "We'd go into the huddle and it seemed like we were ready to relax. They told us to keep up the intensity and they really kept us up. I just knew this would be a close game. The way it happened, it will stick in our minds. But our season will go on, theirs will go on, and we'll both get better."

Sutton, with Chapman, shook the hand of Louisville assistant coach Wade Houston and looked at Kimbro,

on one of the tables. "I hope we meet for the national championship in New Orleans," he said.

UK hit 11 of 17 three-point shots — 65 percent compared with its 39 percent entering the game.

"That spells trouble," said guard Derrick Miller, who added 2 of 3 to the total. It shot 54.2 percent to Louisville's 36.2 percent (including 1 of 8 three-pointeres) and outrebounded Louisville, 41-33 — the 6-3 Davender getting eight and Lock seven. Kimbro and Felton Spencer led Louisville scorers with 10 points.

UK received about 50 tickets for the game and the crowd sounded like a 19,463-50 domination at first. But by the end it almost had turned around, the "Go Big Blue" chant drowning out those who were trying to remain vocal for Louisville.

"We're all friends out there," said Chapman. "Keith Williams would come in and we'd kind of talk back and forth. I don't know what I was thinking about, trying to dunk on Pervis and I got it knocked down my throat. Then I got one on Kenny. That's the way it is. Richard Madison played great. We room together on road trips, and we were so keyed up last night we couldn't go to sleep."

Chapman grimaced. "I had to listen to him play the same tape three times." What tape? "Fat Boys."

Fat Boys is a rap group. That doesn't fit Rosey's image. Or does it?

A Red Sea Turns into a Dead Sea

BY RICK BOZICH
The Courier-Journal

Never has Freedom Hall seemed so quiet. No rousing cheers from the balcony corners. No blasts of musical energy from the University of Louisville pep band. Cheerleaders sat, players slumped, the unfaithful exited.

Even Denny Crum was suddenly stoic. Blinking in silence, the Louisville coach watched as blue-and-white pompons bobbed around him and University of Kentucky coach Eddie Sutton formed a one-man receiving line in front of the Wildcats bench.

Joyous, Sutton walked three steps onto the court and presented a hug and pat on the behind to everybody dressed in blue. An arena that once rocked with noise created by crazies dressed in red turned suddenly — and thoroughly — quiet yesterday. Was this Blue Heaven?

No, call it Three-Point Heaven instead. And call it the most wonderful thing the University of Kentucky basketball team has ever seen.

"A perfect game?" asked Winston Bennett, the injured Wildcat who grew up in Louisville. "I don't know about that." Then a huge smile rippled across Bennett's solemn face. "But it was close enough, wasn't it?"

Indeed, indeed. Which is why this was a basketball game that was never close at all. Kentucky defeated Louisville, 85-51, and never had one team looked so relentless in its domination, so complete in its approach.

"Wonderful," said UK president Dr. Otis Singletary. Aglow in victory, Singletary's eyes danced as he made his way into the UK locker room.

"Wonderful," said Singletary, smiling again.

"Hard to believe," said Dr. Donald Swain, Singletary's counterpart at Louisville.

"The best Christmas present a UK fan living in Louisville could ask for," said Winston Bennett II, father of the injured UK forward. And the elder Bennett proved that by distributing hugs throughout the Wildcats' locker room.

"Discouraging," said Mike Abram, a Louisville guard.

"Boys," said Tommy Kron, "I live in Louisville and you don't know how much I appreciate this." The visit from Kron, one of the starting players from Adolph Rupp's fabulous 1966 Rupp's Runts squad, was particularly appropriate yesterday.

Kentucky proved several things in this blowout. One thing was that a talented, aggressive, small team, playing relentlessly, can overwhelm a tentative, taller team, playing perplexed.

You look at Kentucky and you see Winston Bennett in street clothes and Cedric Jenkins with a tender foot, and you fear that this group won't beat any team that is strong around the basket. Figure again.

What Kentucky has is a solid collection of skilled players who aren't that tall, and aren't that concerned about it, either. Coaches, fans and critics look for security in large bodies. This year, more than most years, they will be betrayed. One reason is the three-point field goal.

Kentucky coach Eddie Sutton might not love the three-point field goal. But what Sutton does love is winning. And it is that love of success that has persuaded Sutton to make the three-pointer as much a part of the Kentucky offense as lay-ups and backdoor lobs.

"We work very hard on the three-point shot," said Sutton. "We're struggling a little bit with our frontcourt play. So we've probably experimented with the shot a little more than most teams in the country. But we've got some designed plays that we run with it."

Designed plays with designed instructions: Take it and bury it. "When we saw Louisville go to that zone defense, we started looking at each other and smiling," said Derrick Miller, the UK freshman who buried 2 three-pointers in the first half. "That was just what we wanted to see." You know it.

Eventually, the Louisville players knew it, too. "The three-pointer kills you," said Abram. "You think you're playing well and gaining ground, and then you look at the scoreboard and you're down 10 or 11 points when you think you should be down five or six."

Once, after Rex Chapman drilled his first three-pointers, Mr. Everything soared for a three-point shot from beyond the N.B.A. distance of 23 feet 9 inches. The ball sailed off the rim wide right. At the next break Sutton called Chapman to the Wildcats' bench.

A scolding, perhaps? "He said I shot it too quick," said Chapman. Not too far? "No," said Chapman. "Just too quick. Coach just told us to take it to them."

So Chapman, the appropriately numbered (3) freshman, took it to, through, over, around and above Louisville for 26 points, including 15 on three-point field goals.

Understand this about the three-pointer. It does more than make points multiply on the scoreboard quicker. It discourages defenders who think they've forced a shooter into a bad shot. And it encourages offensive players who think they'll never miss.

That describes Kentucky's shooters yesterday. Ed Davender hit his first three-pointer. So did James Blackmon. Chapman hit his first three. Miller missed one, then hit two straight. When Miller hit his sec-

ond, Kentucky, which made 7 of 10 three-pointers in the first half, was ahead, 32-20.

By game's end Kentucky was 11 for 17 from beyond the 19-foot-9 line. And Louisville was 1 for 8. To understand what the shot means to each team, make a note of this: Kentucky made as many three-pointers in the second half — four — as Louisville has all season.

Kentucky used the three-point goal so effectively that by halftime it had stretched Louisville defense into five different ZIP codes. One result was even the UK frontcourt enjoyed the afternoon, with center Rob Lock and forward Richard Madison outscoring (18-10) and outrebounding (22-11) Louisville's Pervis Ellison and Herbert Crook.

Befuddled, Crum eventually pulled Ellison eight minutes into the second half. It is one reason the all-American did not produce a point in the second half.

No matter, by game's end all Crum or Ellison could do was watch the Wildcats push the margin to a point even readers of *The Cats Pause* could not have dreamed of.

"We thought we could win," said Lock, "but I don't think anybody thought we could win by 30."

Actually the margin was 34, the worst loss a Crum-coached team has ever suffered. And if nobody knows if this was the last time the two teams will play in a regular-season series, everybody knows this:

Never has Freedom Hall seemed so quiet.

CHAPTER 45

Wildcats athletic director C.M. Newton presents Rick Pitino with a UK lapel pin, welcoming him as the school's new basketball coach.

Pitino Feels at Home in Kentucky

BY PETER ALFANO
Special to The New York Times

LEXINGTON, June 1, 1989 — Accompanied by his wife, Joanne, and modest applause, he walked into a conference room brimming with 15 television camera crews, a sportscaster powdering his nose with makeup, a number of newspaper reporters and the 22 members of the University of Kentucky Athletics Association Board of Directors, as well as other university dignitaries.

Dressed in a gray suit, his dark hair neatly in place,

able to pass for a postgraduate student, Richard A. Pitino — as the athletic director C.M. Newton presented him — stepped to the podium and conducted his first news conference as the head coach of the commonwealth's favorite team. In his unmistakable New York accent, Pitino spoke about how happy he was to be back home again in the world of college basketball.

"We missed the college community and dealing with young people," he said. "Every day for the past two years, we've looked back and missed Providence. I almost went back there last year. We're New Yorkers and the New York Knicks are a class organization

After his appointment in 1989, Rick Pitino's goal was to set the Wildcats back on a path toward winning championships and Big Blue glory.

that will win a championship, but emotionally and physically, I needed to get back to college.

"We may speak differently, but I believe people are people anywhere you go and we're all the same. We wanted stability and roots; I want my children to go through the same grammar school and high school, something I didn't have, I hope that Kentucky bas-

ketball and the city of Lexington will be part of our lives for a long time."

Knows His Audience

He might not know all the words of "My Old Kentucky Home," but the 36-year-old Pitino recited the phrases that will quicken the pulses of the fans, alumni and boosters in a basketball-made state that has been devastated by the sanctions imposed on the Kentucky basketball program by the National Collegiate Athletic Association.

Kentucky was placed on probation for three years for recruiting and other violations. The 1989-90 men's basketball budget of $3,128,000 approved today by the board of directors was $716,000 less than last year's total, reflecting the projected loss of income from television appearances and the N.C.A.A. postseason tournament.

"The one thing I can promise is that we will try to prove we can be competitive," Pitino said. "For me, it's been a tradition to say we will win right away. These will be exciting years and we want to see something so rich in tradition be brought back the right way — the way Dr. Roselle and C.M. Newton have done.

"I don't want people here thinking of oil or horses but of Kentucky basketball tickets. I want them to be the most precious thing in life some day."

Pitino's hiring was approved by the board at a 10 a.m. meeting chaired by David Roselle, the school president. It was the fifth item on the agenda, but obviously, the reason for all the news media attention. The local stations interrupted their morning programming to carry the news conference live.

Roselle, who greeted Joanne Pitino with a kiss on the cheek, called her husband a well-known and highly respected coach.

A New Day

Newton made the recommendation that Pitino be hired. "Today begins a new day," he told the board members. "It's the first day in rebuilding the program. I've traveled across the commonwealth carrying the message that what's done is behind us. We face some tough times but I think we named the best head coach in the country. We will have an exciting, aggressive style and a program with class."

Pitino signed a seven-year contract, a package reportedly worth $5 million. According to Roselle, the university president, Pitino's base salary will be $105,000 a year, plus fringe benefits accorded all university employees. The base salary of Eddie Sutton who resigned after last season, was approximately $20,000 less.

The bulk of Pitino's income will be derived from outside sources, such as weekly radio and television programs, endorsements, speaking fees, clinics, a sneaker contract and a summer camp, as well as other perks that might include country club memberships and the use of an automobile.

That is how the major college programs are able to entice highly regarded coaches for as much, and sometimes more, money than professional teams pay.

Pitino joked about the money, saying he would earn $11 million a year. "Counting the supplemental money I made with the Knicks, this is a lateral move economically," he said later. "The difference is the standard of living here and in New York. I got a nice haircut yesterday and it didn't cost $30."

Tainted Reputation

Kentucky has the most storied college basketball tradition in the country, but even during the 42-year reign of Adolph Rupp, the perception was that Kentucky cheated. Newton and Pitino pledged an end to that.

Players here have been treated like celebrities, living in an athletic dormitory, The Wildcat Lodge, beneficiaries of gifts from boosters.

"I want the boosters to show me what great fans they are," Pitino said. "I want them to give donations to the university and they can be my friend. But they will stay away from our practices and our players.

"I also want the players to live like the rest of the student body. Once you leave here, you have to be able to deal with people and you can't prepare for that living off by yourself. These kids will come to Kentucky as students first, then athletes."

Pitino had a 40-minute meeting with his players this morning, encouraging them about the future, asking them to consider staying despite the N.C.A.A. sanctions.

"I gave up a potential championship to come to Kentucky," he said. "I told the players they will need a substitute for the goal of making the N.C.A.A. tournament.

"They will have fun. And I told them to think about their careers and lives. That's more important than the N.C.A.A. tournament."

CHAPTER 46

Richie Farmer and Wildcat coach Rick Pitino discuss strategy during a time-out.

UK Holds Off Advancing L.S.U., 100-95

BY SCOTT FOWLER
Special to The Courier-Journal

LEXINGTON, Feb. 15, 1990 — Richie Farmer nailed six free throws in the final 1 minute 5 seconds, and Kentucky survived 41 points by Chris Jackson to upset Louisiana State, 100-95, last night in an electrifying basketball game played before the largest and probably loudest crowd in Rupp Arena history.

UK built a 23-point lead in the first half over the nation's ninth-ranked team, saw Jackson almost sin-

gle-handedly whittle it to two in the closing moments and then held on for what most of the players called the best victory of their careers.

"It's the biggest game I've ever been associated with and the most exciting win I've ever been part of," said senior guard Derrick Miller, who led the Wildcats with 29 points.

The 24,301 fans shoehorned into Rupp Arena — 13 more than the number who witnessed L.S.U.'s 64-62 victory here last season — agreed. More than half of them stuck around for Wildcat coach Rick Pitino's postgame radio show.

Pulling out this emotional triumph on a night when jerseys honoring former coaches Adolph Rupp and Joe B. Hall were retired also aided the Wildcats in the race for the Southeastern Conference title.

UK (13-10, 9-5 in the S.E.C.) moved within half a game of L.S.U. and Georgia, now tied for first, with its fourth straight victory. The Wildcats, alone in the third place, will face fourth-place in Alabama (8-5) tomorrow in Tuscaloosa.

L.S.U. saw a seven-game winning streak end and fell to 19-5 and 9-4 despite Jackson's heroics. The sophomore all-American, double- and triple-teamed in the final five minutes, nevertheless hit three-pointer after three-pointer to nudge L.S.U. ever closer. Pitino called Jackson's individual performance the finest he has seen.

"We had two or three guys hanging on him, and he still hit threes that I don't think we would have even hit the rim on," Pitino said. "He was spectacular. The amazing thing was this: Despite a performance I had never seen the likes of, we still did all the right things to win the basketball game."

Those things included forcing L.S.U. into 24 turnovers (17 in the first half), getting 7-footer Shaquille O'Neal (21 rebounds, 14 points, six blocks) to foul out with 6:52 left and never cracking under pressure.

"All those 5 a.m. practices in the preseason that we had," said UK point guard Sean Woods, "and Coach would be screaming at us, 'Get up! Get up! L.S.U.'s not practicing now; they're still in dreamland!'

"Guys would be looking at each other saying, 'This guy is crazy.' But it all paid off."

Nothing came of the highly publicized "rematch" between Pitino and L.S.U. coach Dale Brown, who almost got into a fight during L.S.U.'s 94-81 victory last month in Baton Rouge. Both coaches stayed on

THE LINE-UPS

KENTUCKY (100)

	FG	FT	Pts.
Pelphrey	3	3	10
Feldhaus	9	5	24
Hanson	4	2	11
Miller	10	4	29
Woods	4	4	12
Brassow	1	1	4
Farmer	1	8	10
Totals	**32**	**27**	**100**

LOUISIANA STATE (95)

	FG	FT	Pts.
Singleton	0	0	0
O'Neal	6	2	14
Sims	2	3	7
Williamson	3	2	9
Jackson	13	8	41
Roberts	6	1	13
Devall	3	3	9
Boudreaux	0	0	0
Krajewski	1	0	2
Totals	**34**	**19**	**95**

their own half of the floor and shook hands warmly before and after the game.

"But I think the fans got their money's worth anyway," Miller said with a smile. "Don't you?"

Brown was complimentary of UK and said he was happy with his players even though they lost.

"This was a wonderful sign," he said. "We didn't get the victory, but it was the next-best thing ... That was a hell of a comeback we made. We could have wound up with Noriega. UK about pushed us out of the continent early."

The Wildcats sailed to an unlikely 41-18 lead. They harried L.S.U. into turnover after turnover with their press and were helped by the Tigers' ice-cold shooting. L.S.U. made only five of its first 23 shots.

"I didn't think we handled our emotions well in the first 10 minutes," Brown said. "That really kind of got us off track."

The Wildcats trailed only once, 3-0, before reeling off nine straight points. L.S.U. got within 9-8, but UK had another 16-4 burst. Brown spent his first time-out after a Miller three-pointer made it 25-12.

UK continued to pull away, to the delight of the crowd, stretching it to 41-18 on Miller's three-point play with 6:24 left. Then L.S.U. finally got on track, scoring 14 in a row as Jackson started beating the press and either shooting the ball or lobbing it inside to O'Neal or fellow 7-footer Stanley Roberts.

Another trey by Miller plugged that dike, and UK ended up in the locker room with a 48-36 lead. "I told them, 'Don't ask for this game to end,' " Pitino said.

" 'You guys don't have an N.C.A.A. tournament. You have to wish that this type of crowd, this type of atmosphere, this type of game goes on forever.' "

UK played just as aggressively in the second half, maintaining a 12- to 17-point lead for much of the period. L.S.U. scored seven straight points to halve

Deron Feldhaus powers his way to the Kentucky basket. He scored 24 points against the Tigers.

When the 1989-90 season began, there were more coaches, managers and trainers on the UK team than players.

the margin from 88-74 to 88-81 with 3:42 left.

The Wildcats went ahead, 92-83, on two free throws by Woods, but L.S.U. scored six in a row to make it 92-89. Moments later it was 94-92 after a Jackson three-pointer, but Farmer then took over, making two free throws on each of the Wildcats' last three possessions. L.S.U. never had the ball with a chance to tie.

"The pressure didn't bother me a bit," Farmer said. "I liked it."

Cats Don't Go To Lair, Despite Season's Obstacles

BY RICK BOZICH
The Courier-Journal

When the N.C.A.A. handed the University of Kentucky its three-year basketball probation last May, the annual trip to the N.C.A.A. Tournament became impossible. Scratch the Southeastern Conference Tournament, too. And live television appearances for one long, silent winter.

Grinning wildly, the rest of the league knew this was the year to put a solid sleeperhold on the Wildcats. Sorry, S.E.C.

The heartbeat of Kentucky basketball is strong and getting stronger. There was nothing in the N.C.A.A. report outlawing fun, or the pursuit of an S.E.C. regular-season championship.

Kentucky 100, Louisiana State 95.

Richie Farmer, an 83 percent free-throw shooter L.S.U. thought would shiver in his sneakers, did his best Kyle Macy impersonation and sank six free throws in the final 65 seconds to secure success. Two Farmer free throws with eight seconds remaining cued the celebration.

When the buzzer went off, the UK players thundered into an emotional midcourt embrace. People in the student section hugged and swayed, chanting, "S-E-C, S-E-C, S-E-C."

Everybody else was dancing or jumping or screaming, too. This was one of those magical nights when Kentucky could have beaten L.S.U., Missouri or the New York Knicks.

"It was one of those nights that you don't want to end," Kentucky coach Rick Pitino said. "You hope this atmosphere goes on forever."

Look out, S.E.C., for here comes Kentucky, now 9-5 in the league and only a half-game behind L.S.U. and Georgia (each 9-4) in the conference standings.

And the Excitement Meter has never shaken the way it did in Rupp Arena last night. The place was stuffed with more howling bodies — 24,301 — than the place has ever held before. We're talking adrenalin overload, folks. Somebody tell the N.C.A.A. the fun has not stopped in Rupp yet.

Look on the baseline, and there's Mr. Unstoppable, Dan Issel, waving to the crowd. And over there it's Cotton Nash, another former Wildcat great. Then look above the balcony, near section 232 where jerseys are being hung to honor Adolph Rupp and Joe B. Hall, two coaches prominent in building Kentucky's tradition.

"An awesome performance," Hall said, beaming. "Absolutely awesome. The crowd had fun, and Kentucky just played so well together."

Pass the earplugs and Tylenol, please. L.S.U. evidently forgot to come prepared for the moment. The Tigers threw the ball away more in the first 20 minutes — 17 — than Kentucky did the entire game (only 13). Here were John Pelphrey and Farmer forcing Chris Jackson, L.S.U.'s all-Universe guard, into the corner and coming away with the ball. Several times.

Here was L.S.U. struggling to maneuver downcourt through UK's relentless pressure, working for 14 minutes before generating an assist.

And here was Kentucky, relying again on its trademark assortment of three-pointers, run-out lay-ups and slashing backdoor cuts, sprinting to a 41-18 advantage.

Here was Kentucky, with point guard Sean Woods on the bench with foul trouble after 142 seconds, holding together under the direction of Farmer, who refused to turn the ball over the entire night despite the relentless harassment of Jackson and Maurice Williamson.

And here was Derrick Miller leaning forward fearlessly to drill five three-pointers and lift the Wildcats on his narrow shoulders with a team-high 29 points.

"Coach (Dale) Brown told us before the game that the No. 1 thing we had to do was control our emotions," Jackson said. "And we didn't do that. We let the atmosphere get to us."

"If they lose the rest of their games, this will be their championship game," Williamson said. "They'll remember this the rest of the year. They just rode the emotions."

"They were so emotional it was like an avalanche early," Brown said. "We could have wound up with Noriega. They pushed us right out of the continent."

Or to Pluto. Or beyond. But the L.S.U. ship almost touched down on Rupp Arena — and the UK party — again. Never forget that this ship is controlled by Jackson as well as Brown. Swirling downcourt, Jackson ignited a 14-point L.S.U. run that brought the Tigers within 48-36 at halftime.

And in the second half, Jackson played as only Jackson can. That means three-pointer after three-pointer. That means blowing downcourt until he bounced within inches of the magic circle, stopping without checking his feet and lifting off for shots that rarely even brushed the rim. I know it seemed like 81, but Jackson scored 41, including seven threes.

"A performance I've never seen the likes of," said Pitino, blinking. The UK coach put everybody but

Issel, Nash and Bill Curry on the L.S.U. missile. It mattered little.

Average degree of difficulty on Jackson's second-half shots: 9.9. Twice he drilled three-pointers with two UK players yapping in his face. Once he was tumbling out of bounds in the corner.

"I just felt like I had to take over," Jackson said. "Once I got on a roll, I just decided to keep going. We had to do something to get going."

And Kentucky had to do many things to keep going. A pair of Jackson free throws pulled L.S.U. within 88-81 with 3:42 to go. Pitino asked for time, then asked for poised and precise basketball down the stretch.

His players delivered. First a lay-up by Deron Feldhaus, who had 24 gritty points. Then two free throws by Woods. Another Feldhaus lay-up.

And six free throws by Farmer, Mr. Unflappable, sealed it, despite three amazing, incredible, impossible three-pointers by Jackson in the final 2 minutes 45 seconds.

"I don't think my esteem for this basketball team could get an higher," Pitino said. "They are just an amazing group of young men."

And the most amazing stat of the college basketball season remains today's news that Kentucky is only a half-game off the conference lead. Look out, S.E.C.

CHAPTER 47

Richie Farmer clowns with one of the Wildcats' biggest fans, former heavyweight boxing champ Muhammad Ali.

Wildcats Kiss Season and Sanctions Good-bye

BY PAT FORDE
Special to The Courier-Journal

LEXINGTON, March 2, 1991 — What a way to go. The University of Kentucky basketball team let it all hang out last night, perfectly capping a fun-and-gun season with its most explosive showing yet, a 114-93 blitzing of Auburn before a Rupp Arena-record crowd of 24,310.

In the process the Wildcats ended the acrimonious debate about who was the Southeastern Conference's best team on the floor, if not in the official standings,

and announced to the nation that their presence in the N.C.A.A. tournament will be missed.

It was a resounding punctuation to N.C.A.A. probation, a sweet kiss-off to a bitter period in Kentucky basketball history. The 22-6 record, including a 14-4 S.E.C. mark, also could serve as a springboard into next season, when UK is off all sanctions and could be a player in the national title chase.

"This team looked adversity square in the eye and never blinked," said Wildcat coach Rick Pitino, his voice reverberating through the Rupp Arena rafters in a postgame celebration. "...This is truly a 'Special K'

After a slam, Wildcats senior Reggie Hanson hangs around to savor the moment.

...Now we can go beyond the S.E.C. championship and play for real."

When it was all over, the Wildcats showed they know how to celebrate every bit as well as they played this season.

Seniors Reggie Hanson and Johnathan Davis teamed to cut down one net. But they saved the final strand for Pitino, who clipped it to thunderous applause.

An entire fashion store's worth of hat's saying "Kentucky #1 S.E.C. Basketball" and T-shirts reading "#1 S.E.C. Basketball/Back on Top" were handed out to the team.

(The word "champions" was noticeably absent, in accordance with S.E.C. bylaws prohibiting a team on probation from winning the official title. Ironically, it was the same "#" symbol found on the hats and shirts that the S.E.C. used to brand UK in its official releases, denoting its ineligibility for the title.)

Then a 20-foot-high blue banner proclaiming "S.E.C. #1 1991" was paraded onto the court as at

least 23,000 fans stayed in their seats for the postgame awards ceremony. The Wildcats obviously are every bit as proud of this unofficial title as they are of the

THE LINE-UPS

AUBURN (93)

	FG	FT	Pts.
Patrick	3	2	9
Brandt	5	3	13
Arnold	1	2	4
Galton	3	2	8
Battle	6	9	21
Caylor	6	1	13
Person	7	5	20
Wrencher	1	2	5
Smith	0	0	0
Joyce	0	0	0
Totals	**32**	**31**	**93**

KENTUCKY (114)

	FG	FT	Pts.
Pelphrey	4	2	12
Mashburn	6	5	21
Hanson	3	5	11
Woods	3	1	8
Farmer	5	7	20
Feldhaus	2	2	7
Brassow	5	0	13
Davis	2	1	5
Braddy	3	3	11
Toomer	1	4	6
Martinez	0	0	0
Thomas	0	0	0
Bearup	0	0	0
Totals	**34**	**30**	**114**

A coach with many emotions, Pitino voices his opinion about a referee's call.

John Pelphrey bombs one from long distance.

The S.E.C.'s best record was locked up with the help of Louisiana State's 76-73 loss at Mississippi State yesterday afternoon. And although Pitino magnanimously — or perhaps facetiously — said Friday that UK "wouldn't mind sharing" the unofficial title, there was no doubt the Cats were happy to take the top spot all alone. In fact, a couple of players found the press-room televisions to watch the L.S.U.-Mississippi State game.

As if they needed any more motivation for an explosion.

"A lot of guys came out after Mississippi State won, and that just pumped everybody up even more," Hanson said.

"We talked before the game about all the upsets in college basketball and that nothing is taken for granted," Pitino said. "All we had to do is one thing, and that's do what we did every game for two years: just play hard. That's it, and there will be no upset. You will be S.E.C. champions all by yourselves.

"We told the guys no matter whose opinion is right or wrong, valid or invalid, it's all irrelevant. Championships are won and lost on the court, and that's what we did this season."

About the only thing the second edition of Pitino's Bombino's hadn't accomplished was hitting the 100-point mark, and they busted that with ease last night. After ringing up 65 in the first half, the century mark was a mere formality, and the point total was the Cats' highest since they scored 126 against South Carolina in 1979.

The primary weapon — surprise, surprise — was the three-point field goal. The Cats let fly with 34 of them and hit 16, or 47.1 percent. Not bad for a team entering the game hitting just better than 33 percent of its threes.

36 official ones already earned.

Athletic director C.M. Newton announced that rings are in the works inscribed with the same "Back on Top."

Newton announced that the Cats will "celebrate being back on top in an old-fashion way." The team will parade through downtown Lexington atop fire engines Tuesday afternoon.

After the parade, at 4 p.m., the team will return to Memorial Coliseum for what Newton described as "the dadgumdest pep rally they've ever seen."

"It was offense tonight," Pitino said. "Normally it was defense."

Hanson and Davis went out in style as well. Hanson, in a subpar overall game, hit the free throw that pushed UK to the century mark. Davis, who had scored one point all season, finished with five points, four rebounds and four blocks.

Before the game the two were treated to the traditional UK senior sendoff; a run through a paper hoop, a thundershower of applause and an elongated singing of "My Old Kentucky Home."

The eyes were barely dabbed dry before the bombardment began. Auburn didn't get on the board until 2:54 had elapsed, and by then the score was 8-0.

The lead grew like fungus after that — from 10 (17-7) to 15 (29-14) to 20 (49-29) before peaking out at 25 (63-38). At halftime the score was 65-43. Things rolled so easily that Davis tripled his season scoring output with three first-half points.

UK's halftime point total was easily its highest of the season and was only 10 points below the school record set against Georgia in 1956. Seven Wildcats cashed three-pointers in the period as UK hit 10 of 19 from beyond the arc.

The Cats toyed with the Tigers through a ragged final 20 minutes, awaiting the celebration.

Yo, Rick Pitino, Thanks For Another Magic Show

BY RICK BOZICH
The Courier-Journal

Yo, Rick. Aren't you glad you took the job? That's right, Pitino. You.

Yo, Rick, confess. Wasn't this season — the one you finished by securing the Southeastern Conference champ ... er ... *the S.E.C.'s best record by dropping Auburn, 114-93, last night — the most stirring run you've had since somebody introduced you to Armani?

What shaped up as a 16-12 team finishes 22-6. Another U Can't Touch This S.E.C. home record. Outcoaching and outdressing Digger in the Hoosier Dome. Payback against Kansas. Turning Freedom Hall into Three-dom Hall. Showing Wimp he's not the only guy who can pick up clothes at flea markets.

And there you were last night snipping away the final three strands of net, shaking your prize at the record 24,310 folks stuffed into Rupp Arena and letting everybody from Gainesville to Nashville know Kentucky's 14-4 record was the best in the S.E.C.

I know you don't play the Iffin' Game, but if you change a few wiggles of the basketball, we're talking 25-3. You look at Jeff Sagarin's computer rankings and we're talking a No. 3 N.C.A.A. seed if you guys weren't on probation.

Even members of the Committee of 101 feared you'd need five years to generate a 22-victory season. You did it in two. No wonder they're giving you and your players a parade through Lexington Tuesday.

Bravo, Pitino, bravo.

Yo, Rick. That's Coach of the Year material, especially when you check the National Basketball Association files and notice the only one of your guys they're keeping notes on is a freshman, Jamal Mashburn.

I mean you had Reggie Hanson playing like Reggie Miller and strutting around the way Reggie Jackson did. Until you showed up, Hanson's No. 1 col-

lege hoops achievement was being Rex Chapman's best friend.

So you turned John Pelphrey into the Practice Player Poster Boy across the Commonwealth. You inspired Deron Feldhaus to drop fearless finger rolls over Shaquille O'Neal. You found a way for Richie Farmer to handle the University of Louisville the way he handled Louisville Ballard. You've done more for Sean Woods than you did for Mark Jackson.

Yo, Rick, you're the Magic Man. And I'm not just talking about conference championships and coaching moves and beating Alabama, Louisiana State and Louisville. I'm talking about the adrenaline transplant you've performed in Rupp Arena.

Yo, Rick, until you showed up, going to Rupp was as stimulating as going to a zoning board meeting. The folks who sat in the first four rows acted as if somebody had sprinkled formaldehyde in their bourbon. Nobody was certain if they had hands. Everybody was certain that they did not have vocal cords.

Now you walk into Rupp and you can see Arthur Hancock swaying, Joe B. Hall grinning and assorted other members of the horse-and-coal set chanting, "Threeeeeeeeee."

He might not admit it, but I'm sure I saw C.M. Newton yelling, "A little bit louder now, a little bit louder now," the other night.

Yo, Rick, the only thing that's got the folks a little uneasy is the news that leaked out of Madison Square Gah-den Friday. I'm sure you've heard it. Knicks general manager Al Bianchi, the guy who thought you were borderline cocky, was handed a one-way ticket to Joisey. Somebody finally noticed that the Knicks were 52-30 before you headed for Lexington, and this season they'll be lucky to win 38 games. They can't even fill the place for the Celtics.

Peter Vecsey, that guy who used to write for The New York Post and now writes for USA Today, would rip his mother if he thought it would make a clever one-liner. Even he's admitting you could coach a soft breeze into a hurricane.

Yo, Rick. Don't let any stories get started that you're going back to rescue the Knicks. Let John Thompson do it. He's ready to leave Georgetown, and Patrick Ewing's ready for him to come to Manhattan.

I'm sure you miss Barney's, Elaine's, Runyon's, Bloomies, the Hard Rock, Shea Stadium, Marv Albert, Warner Wolf and all that other fun stuff in Fun City. But as of last night's game, UK has served its time for the N.C.A.A. sanctions. Next season it's your turn to chase Tark and The General and Nolan Richardson. Or maybe it's their turn to chase you.

Think of it this way. In New Yawk you've got to deal with a nut on every street corner. At Kentucky all you've got to deal with is Dale Brown. In New Yawk they write your name on subway walls. In Lexington they write it on menus and endorsement contracts. At your current rate, Rick, you could buy Bloomies and move it to Vine Street.

Yo, Rick you made a gloomy situation sweeter than a Sunday afternoon walk through Central Park. Now it's your turn to collect.

Yo, Rick, I don't think you'll let the expectations get as suffocating as they were before you arrived. The healthiest thing you've done is lift some of the hype off your players and place it directly upon your Armani-covered shoulders.

If you understand anything, it's how to get a team to play hard and with enthusiasm. Nobody talks about January slumps or burnout around Lexington anymore.

Yo, Rick, next season you've got about 82 percent of your points coming back, plus four recruits, plus Travis Ford, plus the motivation of chasing some fun in the N.C.A.A. You won't have to suffer any silly debates about conference asterisks. You can just coach, baby.

Yo, Rick. Aren't you glad you took the job?

CHAPTER 48

"The Unforgettables" – Richie Farmer, Deron Feldhaus, John Pelphrey and Sean Woods – and Jamal Mashburn led the 1991-92 Wildcats to their first S.E.C. championship in six seasons – and perhaps the most important in UK's storied history.

UK Makes Its Own Breaks to Win Title

By Pat Forde
Special to The Courier-Journal

BIRMINGHAM, March 15, 1992 — You could say the Kentucky Wildcats got all the breaks in this Southeastern Conference Tournament.

They played the early game every day. They played Louisiana State without Shaquille O'Neal. They didn't have to play Arkansas. They played Alabama after it had gone down to the wire in each of its games, including a classic one-point victory over the Razorbacks on Saturday.

But when title time arrived, when the prize was in sight yesterday afternoon in Birmingham Civic Center, Kentucky needed no breaks. Looking like they could have beaten anybody under any circumstances, the Cats played an awesome final 17 minutes to crush the Crimson Tide, 80-54.

They went from seven down to cutting nets in a blink of an eye — which in hindsight seems about the length of time N.C.A.A. probation affected born-again UK.

"This is special because of everything we've been through," Wildcat coach Rick Pitino said. "Especially after last year, having the best record and not being recognized, it has a special meaning.

"For Kentucky, winning a conference championship may not be that big a deal because they've won so many, but for this team, with what we have athletically, it is a tremendous deal for us."

No doubt. They trophy will be just another chunk of wood and gold in UK's extra-large display case, but the school's 16th S.E.C. Tournament championship will be remembered as a special one.

Just three years after the program went bankrupt, Kentucky is back in the business of winning championships. Next stop for ninth-ranked UK (26-6) is Worcester, Mass., for a first-round N.C.A.A. Tournament game against Colonial Athletic Association champion Old Dominion (15-14).

"This is one of the greatest weeks I've ever been a part of as a basketball player," fifth-year senior John Pelphrey said. Pelphrey, an all-tournament team selection along with m.v.p. Jamal Mashburn, showed how happy he was after the game by picking up fellow senior Richie Farmer and squeezing the stuffing out of him.

Actually the celebration had begun well before the game ended, because the game was over well before the final horn. Alabama, having taken the lead, 38-31, and gotten the crowd of 17,379 roaring, suddenly lost it. Kentucky squeezed, and the Crimson Tide folded.

Alabama scored 16 points in the final seventeen minutes 30 seconds, Kentucky scored 49.

"We got into the finals of the Southeastern Conference Tournament, and we got blitzed," was Alabama coach Wimp Sanderson's blunt assessment.

Blitzed mostly by Mashburn, who single-handedly kept UK in the game at the beginning of both halves. He scored eight of the Cats' first 10 points as Alabama got out to a 13-10 lead, then scored the Cats' first seven after intermission to begin their rally. He finished with 28 points, and 13 rebounds.

After that, everyone in blue and white got involved, and the Tide's will dissolved.

James (Hollywood) Robinson continued a pyrotechnic tournament by scoring 17 in the first half. But in the second half, Hollywood played like Cawood, going 2 for 7 against tough defense from Dale Brown. He, Robert Horry and Latrell Sprewell — Sanderson's three-headed offense — made 16 of Alabama's 23 turnovers and shot 5 for 18 in the second half.

THE LINE-UPS

KENTUCKY (80)

	FG	FT	Pts.
Pelphrey	4	0	9
Mashburn	12	3	28
Martinez	2	8	12
Woods	0	3	3
Farmer	3	1	8
Feldhaus	3	0	6
Timberlake	1	0	2
Ford	2	0	6
Brown	3	0	6
Braddy	0	0	0
Totals	30	15	80

ALABAMA (54)

	FG	FT	Pts.
Horry	5	1	11
Sprewell	2	2	6
Moore	4	5	13
Washington	0	0	0
Robinson	9	1	22
Caffey	0	0	0
Rice	0	0	0
Rich	0	2	2
Totals	20	11	54

The Tide kept the effects of the draining Arkansas game hidden to that point, but all of a sudden Kentucky's pressure knocked the legs out from underneath them.

"I really do think the kids got a little tired," Sanderson said.

"They folded," UK point guard Sean Woods said. "We had a little break (waiting to throw the ball inbounds), and their point guard (Elliott Washington) told me, 'Hey, they're quitting on me.'"

Quitting time for Horry, the Tide's center, came at the 12:36 mark. Things already were going badly at that point, Kentucky having taken a 51-44 lead, but Horry made them markedly worse with yet another outburst against the Cats.

He drove for a lay-up and Pelphrey attempted to step in and take a charge. Horry missed the lay-up, and there was no call, other than the ball going out of bounds off UK. Horry grabbed the ball and slammed it off the floor, inches from a prone Pelphrey's head, and official John Clougherty applied a technical foul.

"All of a sudden the ball was coming at my face," Pelphrey said.

Kentucky responded by scoring 10 straight, and Horry responded by scoring one more point the rest of the way and being called for an intentional foul when he elbowed Gimel Martinez in the mouth.

With that Horry scored a hat trick in the altercation department against UK. He was ejected for fighting with Reggie Hanson in 1989-90, then was ejected last month in Lexington after being called for two technical fouls, the first of which sprang from an altercation with Martinez.

"I really don't know why," said Martinez, talking around a hugely swollen upper lip, about Horry's bad vibes from the Cats. "I think he gets a little frustrated and gets off his game a little bit."

Horry, who had been having a big tournament until

Jamal Mashburn was the game's leading scorer with 28 points and the S.E.C. Tournament's m.v.p.

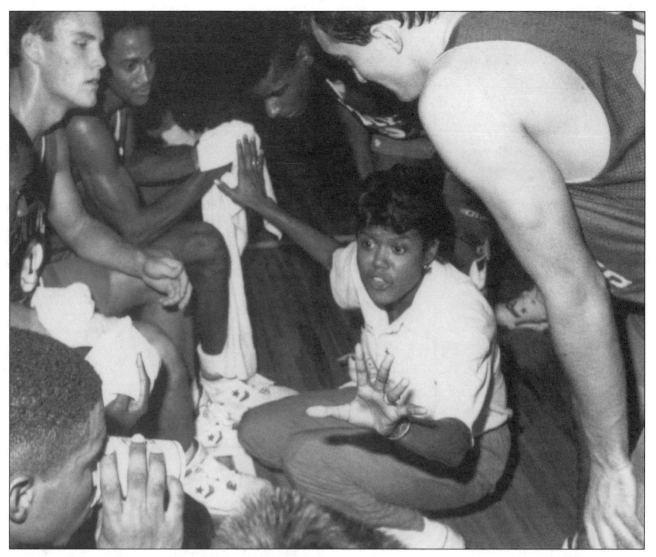

Bernadette Locke, who joined Rick Pitino's staff in June 1990, became one of the first females ever to serve as an assistant coach of a Division I-A men's basketball team.

this, readily took the blame afterward.

"The key to our ballgame tonight was me losing my composure," Horry said. "It was just something I did. I guess I kind of lost it for our team when they needed me the most."

Sanderson stuck up for Horry, saying, "It probably hurts us some, but I've lost mine before, too."

Mashburn Gift-wraps Tourney for Seniors

BY RICK BOZICH
The Courier-Journal

The first one to climb the ladder to cut down the nets of the Southeastern Conference Tournament was Jamal Mashburn. Who else? And why not? Nobody has beaten Mashburn to the glass for three full days.

So Mashburn moved strongly to the top of the ladder and took one, two, three, four, five, six sharp cuts at the net. For the first time since he entered the Birmingham Civic Center on Friday, Mashburn did not finish a job. He handed the scissors to Sean Woods and tried to dissolve into the crowd around the Wildcats' bench.

Forget dissolving. Mashburn's luminous smile betrayed him. Two of Mashburn's teammates — his S.E.C. champion teammates — Woods and Gimel Martinez, worked the scissors, too. And when the net finally came down, Martinez handed it to Mashburn, who shook his prize toward the sky and then dropped it over his head, around his thick neck.

"We're back," Mashburn said.

The scoreboard roared confirmation: Kentucky 80, Alabama 54.

"I told my teammates before the season that a conference championship was the present that I was going to give them because I can't give them any money," Mashburn said, smiling.

What Mashburn gave the Wildcats yesterday was 28 points and 13 rebounds in 38 minutes of Mash-terful basketball. For two months the argument raged about who deserved recognition as the S.E.C.'s finest forward — Alabama's Robert Horry or Mashburn.

Yesterday Mashburn closed the case. The S.E.C. Tournament m.v.p. plaque he lifted proudly with his right hand announced that. Mashburn did it by scoring every way a player can score — with muscle and resolve, with finesse and grace, and with daring and confidence. He showed Alabama finger rolls, sweep-

The Unforgettables: (top to bottom) John Pelphrey, Deron Feldhaus, Sean Woods and Richie Farmer.

Jamal Mashburn enjoys a few snips at cutting the S.E.C. Championship Game's victory net.

ing drives, Globetrotter ball-handling, sweet work from the perimeter and rugged jams.

Seeing this, Alabama coach Wimp Sanderson shuffled defenders against him. He tried height — wiry 6-foot-9 center Cedric Moore. He tried experience — Horry, the flashy 6-foot-9 senior. He tried beef — 230 pound freshman Jason Caffey.

Eventually Sanderson tried the only thing appropriate to the moment — praise. For the afternoon Mashburn converted 12 of 14 shots, including one three-pointer. For the weekend, Mashburn converted 26 of 31 — 83.9 percent.

"I felt like I didn't want to get Robert in foul trouble, so we started with Cedric," Sanderson said. "But Mashburn is one of the great players in the country. He's not an ordinary sophomore."

Note this: Robert Horry missed more shots (six) in the second half yesterday than Jamal Mashburn missed (five) in three games.

Horry did more than mouthin' than makin', earning a technical foul at John Pelphrey and an intentional foul for driving an elbow into Martinez's nose. He finished with 11 harmless points and a harmless scowl on his confused face.

"I don't think there is a player in the country with more potential than Jamal Mashburn," Kentucky coach Rick Pitino said. "His game keeps improving every day. The sky is the limit for him."

"Only his teammates know how good Jamal is," Woods said. Can you share the secret?

"It's scary," Woods said. "There's not any kind of shot he can't make."

Indeed. Mashburn displayed the Jamal Collection when Kentucky needed poise, precision and points most. At halftime, you see, the Wildcats appeared to be the team approaching an adrenaline shortage. Alabama, looking like the dazzling team that had dispatched Arkansas on Saturday, scored nine of the final 11 first-half points to lead, 32-29.

In the locker room several Wildcats spoke. You expect stirring words from Pitino, John Pelphrey and Woods. Talking is not Mashburn's strength. But yes-terday Mashburn talked, telling his teammates 20 minutes of vigorous work was necessary.

"I felt like we really had to pick it up, especially on defense," Mashburn said. "We've been away (from the tournament) for a while. We've waited so long to get here that we couldn't let this get away from us."

It did not get away because Kentucky got the ball to Mashburn early in the second half. Alabama led, 36-29, and truth be told, the Tide looked like the team about to roll to a 26-point victory.

But here came Mashburn slashing down the right side of the lane. Pelphrey saw him, delivered a sharp pass inside, and Mashburn laid the ball in.

A basket by Alabama's Moore followed. But now Mashburn showed the world that he does practice three-point shooting by the hundreds daily. He found a quiet spot near the key and delivered a three.

Horry's game is ruled by emotion. Seeing Mashburn's three, Horry thought a three was something he should try. So Horry tried one. And Horry missed.

And here comes Kentucky, running the way it must to win. The ball worked its way to Mashburn on the wing. Spinning twice, he pushed himself into the lane and thought about challenging two defenders. Thinking, not emotion, rules Mashburn's game. Rather than challenging Alabama's shotblockers, Mashburn teased them with a 10-foot jumper.

A basket near the glass. A basket from the perimeter. A basket in traffic. Alabama led, 38-36. But Alabama looked tired and it looked like a team that had no answer for Mashburn. There is nothing else you can ask from a player who carries 240 pounds on his tight 6-foot-8 body.

"It was just a situation where we needed to take the game to them, and my teammates got me the ball," Mashburn said. "When we came out for the second half, we said we had to attack the inside of their zone. There wasn't anything special about those shots. They're just shots I take every day in practice."

Jamal Mashburn smiled a final time. Remember, he made a promise. "And I didn't want to let the seniors down," he said. "They deserved this."

CHAPTER 49

Kentucky and Duke: As Good As It Gets

By Malcolm Moran
Special to The New York Times

Duke's Christian Laettner fires a sure 2-pointer over Deron Feldhaus (12) and John Pelphrey (34).

PHILADEPHIA, March 29, 1992 — As President Bush left his home this morning for a Sunday walk around Lafayette Park, his unsolicited question echoed the ones asked by all the others who have ever been captivated by a basketball, two hoops and the wondrous things that can happen in between.

"Did you see the ending of the Duke game?" the President asked.

How many others were asking the same question? How many others were sharing and savoring the frantic, imperfect brilliance that had driven Duke and Kentucky to the highest level of the game? How many others, beyond the 17,878 privileged witnesses inside the Spectrum on Saturday night, will one day claim they were there?

From opposite ends of the Spectrum came an overwhelming realization as soon as Duke's 104-103 overtime triumph over Kentucky in the East Regional championship game was won by Grant Hill's 75-foot-plus pass and Christian Laettner's 17-foot buzzer-beater. There was evidence all around that the final, stunning 2.1 second climax — and the passionate two and a half hours that built to the decisive basket — belonged among the most gripping moments of theater in the 54-year history of the tournament; and for that matter, in the century since James Naismith came up with a very good idea.

Driven by their belief in their skills, their ability to make quick, complex decisions and their desperate effort to extend a season, the Blue Devils and the Wildcats created a succession of remarkable plays under the most stressful circumstances. The two teams combined to make 61 percent of their shots from the field. In the final 25 minutes of the game — the second half and overtime — as each possession took on an even greater importance, the players from Duke and Kentucky defied the certainty that one team's season was about to end by shooting a combined 63.2 percent.

Laettner's final shot, a more complicated reprise of a last-second overtime shot he made to beat Connecticut and advance Duke to the 1990 Final Four, put the Blue Devils (32-2) in a national semifinal against Indiana next Saturday night. The shot was Laettner's 10th in 10 attempts from the field and his second in the last 31.5 seconds. He also made 10 of 10 foul shots, 4 of them in the final 1 minute 53 seconds. Laettner's only imperfect moment of the evening was when he intentionally stepped on Kentucky freshman Aminu Timberlake, drawing a technical foul.

Other Thrillers

But the statistics only provide part of the evidence

THE LINE-UPS

KENTUCKY (103)

	FG	FT	Pts.
Mashburn	11	3	28
Pelphrey	5	3	16
Martinez	2	0	5
Woods	9	2	21
Farmer	2	4	9
Feldhaus	2	1	5
Brown	6	3	18
Ford	0	0	0
Timberlake	0	1	1
Riddick	0	0	0
Braddy	0	0	0
Totals	**37**	**17**	**103**

DUKE (104)

	FG	FT	Pts.
Lang	2	0	4
Davis	3	7	13
Laettner	10	10	31
Hurley	6	5	22
T. Hill	6	5	19
G. Hill	5	1	11
Parks	2	0	4
Clark	0	0	0
Totals	**34**	**28**	**104**

Jamal Mashburn, who scored 28 points in this epic contest, launches a 3-point shot from the top the key.

to place this game with the most well played in tournament history. The sense of drama elevated the game among North Carolina's 1957 triple-overtime survival of Kansas and Wilt Chamberlain, and the Tar Heels' 1982 1-point victory over Georgetown and freshman Patrick Ewing on a shot by another freshman named Michael Jordan.

And North Carolina State's 1974 double-overtime, come-from-behind victory over U.C.L.A. in a national semi-final that ended the historic Bruin streak of seven national championships. And the U.C.L.A. overtime victory over Louisville one year later that led to a 10th championship in John Wooden's final season as coach.

And North Carolina State's last-second upset of Houston on Lorenzo Charles' dunk of Derek Whittenburg's airball in 1983. And Villanova's near-perfect championship game against Georgetown and Ewing in 1985, in which the Wildcats made a record 78.6 percent of their shots. Or Duke's cathartic national semi-final victory over Nevada-Las Vegas last spring.

John Pelphrey (34) and Jamal Mashburn double-team Christian Laettner.

In the final minutes, during a stop in play, the evidence could be found in the upraised eyebrows of Tim Higgins, a normally impassive official. Before Kentucky's last possession, there was the quick thinking of Duke guard Bobby Hurley.

"Bobby was saying, 'If they score, remember to call a time-out,'" Duke coach Mike Krzyzewski said. "I didn't say it, he said it."

And when exactly that happened, when a bold 13-foot, right-handed push by Sean Woods barely made it over Laettner's outstretched arm, kissed the glass and caromed into the basket, the Blue Devils were 2.1 seconds and a length of the court away from where they needed to be. All they had left was themselves, and the carefully presented conviction of their coach.

"I just said, 'We're going to win,'" Krzyzewski remembered. "Whether you completely believe it or not, you have to have the expression on your face and the words in your mouth that we're going to get a good shot to win."

Suddenly a pass and a shot cut through the noise to create a roar. Woods was on the floor, face down, motionless, a white pom-pon resting

The 1992 N.C.A.A. East Regional final against Duke was Cawood Ledford's last contest as the "Voice of the Wildcats."

on the back of his legs. Some Blue Devils piled on each other; others just wandered around the floor.

In an interview area, Kentucky coach Rick Pitino explained his decision not to place a defender against Hill's pass by erroneously saying that the play began from the sideline rather than the baseline. When he realized his mistake, Pitino apologized, thought for a moment and said, "My mind is elsewhere right now."

He asked that a question be directed toward players Richie Farmer or Jamal Mashburn. "My mind is in a total fog right now," Pitino admitted. Pitino pressed his eyes closed and held two fingers over the bridge of his nose.

Kentucky's pain was just beginning to set in. Inside the dressing room, where players sat in street clothes

and stared ahead, John Pelphry was asked if he would discuss what his team had achieved. "I'd like to," Pelphrey began to say, before the words stopped coming and he had to turn away.

Down the corridor, where the Blue Devils dressed, Hurley said, "I can't speak for any other game in the past, but this is the best game I've ever been a part of in my life."

Better than the defeat of U.N.L.V.? "What the U.N.L.V. game stands for is us beating a team that was almost unbeatable," Hurley said. "So that, on a larger scale, counted a little bit more. But this game, as far as playing the game itself, was a lot greater feeling, a lot more satisfying to me."

Krzyzewski said, "I thank God I was a part of it."

CHAPTER 50

The 1992-93 Wildcats won 30 games and lost 4. Their trip to the Final Four was their first since 1984.

4th Big Easy Puts UK
in New Orleans

BY MARK COOMES
Special to The Courier-Journal

CHARLOTTE, March 27, 1993 — It's Final. Kentucky is one of the Four. After nine long seasons on the outside looking in, the University of Kentucky is once again a member of the most exclusive club in college basketball: the Final Four.

The Wildcats didn't wait for an invitation. They kicked down the door and barged through the N.C.A.A. Tournament in four resounding routs that ended with yesterday's 106-81 blowout of No. 11 Florida State in the Southeast Regional final.

"It is an unbelievable feeling," Kentucky coach Rick Pitino said. It raised to a new plateau a team whose

season started with great promise (a No. 1 ranking by *Sports Illustrated*), great talent (a No. 1 recruiting class) and great inexperience (three freshmen and a junior-college transfer projected among the top eight players).

It all added up to one great question: Could the talented youngsters sustain or even exceed the run of success started by four departed seniors, The Unforgettables? Two signs, brandished by UK fans hoping to catch the big eyes of CBS, had the answer:

"Cats Blowout Seminoles"

"Cats Bound '4' Superdome"

Maybe UK should change its school song to "Blue Bayou" for a week or so. New Orleans is the next stop for the Big Blue Bandwagon, which claimed about

the New York Gauchos, the A.A.U. team Mashburn began playing for as a 12-year-old, Pitino heard a slightly less discouraging line. Noting that Mashburn would be only 17 upon graduating from high school (indeed, he won't turn 20 until Nov. 29), d'Almeida suggested that Jamal simply hadn't grown up yet.

All doubts had evaporated by the end of Mashburn's senior season. New York City's 32-team Catholic High School Athletic Association featured seven promising Division I prospects in its class of 1990, including such players as Christ the King High's Khalid Reeves and Derrick Phelps (they went to Arizona and North Carolina, respectively) and Tolentine High's Brian Reese and Adrian Autry (now at North Carolina and Syracuse, respectively). Mashburn was less celebrated, in part because of Murray, a self-described "hard-nosed Irishman who can be a pain in the ass sometimes," had shackled his star near the basket.

Says Queens, N.Y.-based high school scout Tom Konchalski, who publishes the recruiting newsletter *HSBI Report*, Mashburn had "the body of a blacksmith and the touch of a surgeon. He just didn't have the disposition to dominate. But at the end of the season Tom Murray stopped fighting him. He realized Jamal was the best ball-handler on the team and let him go out on the floor. Cardinal Hayes won the city championship, and Jamal invented a new position. You might call it 'point center.'"

By then Mashburn had already chosen Kentucky, for reasons that suggest advanced self-awareness. For a time he had flirted with Syracuse, a program that was attractive to him because of its loosey-goosey style, its tradition of signing New York city stars like Dwayne (Pearl) Washington, even its iridescent orange uniforms. "We let you be your own person," the Syracuse recruiting pitch went. But that's when it occurred to Mashburn that his own person was exactly what he didn't want to be. "I knew the kind of person I was," he says. "I'm laid-back. Let me be my own person, and I'm going to be a laid-back ballplayer."

Upon hearing that a player who had so clearly left his potential unplumbed was going to play for a coach who is known for converting the very last measure of potential into achievement, one coach in the Catholic league instantly sensed what would happen. "I said at the time it was like giving an atomic bomb to a ter-

Although it took a few years to improve UK's talent level, Pitino's emotionally-charged leadership quickly inspired his squad with a winning attitude.

rorist," says Christ the King coach Bob Oliva. "Jamal and Rick have made me a prophet."

Mashburn hadn't been named to the McDonald's or Dapper Dan high school all-star games, so it was hardly a jaded young man who came to play basketball for Kentucky. He didn't have boundless self-esteem, either. When Pitino administered a battery of psychological tests to his team that fall, Mashburn scored lowest in those categories relating to confidence. Mystified, Pitino confronted his freshman, who confessed that, no, he probably didn't have a disposition to dominate. "It's bizarre, because you see this man's a man," says his coach. "But when we got him a summer job delivering sandwiches at the Carnegie Deli in Manhattan, he hated it. If you watch him cross

A coach with many faces and reactions, Pitino personally won over each UK player and fan with his total commitment to building a dominating program, much like Rupp and Hall before him.

Pitino and the five Wildcat players who brought UK back to the top again: (left to right) Jamal Mashburn (24), Richie Farmer (32), Sean Woods (11), Deron Feldhaus (12) and John Pelphrey (34).

the street, it takes him 10 minutes."

Now the player who chose Kentucky in part because it was on probation — "I saw it as a positive, because I could just play and make my mistakes," he says — is ready to step boldly off the curb. His new assertiveness comes in part from a sense of unfinished business about the way Kentucky's season ended last March, when a fouled-out Mashburn watched Christian Laettner's buzzer shot send Duke to the Final Four. And it has been reinforced by a productive summer, which included a turn on USA Basketball's Select Team — the scout team that helped prep the Olympic Dream Team. Chris Mullin and Charles Barkley gave him diet tips and other life-style advice, leaving Mashburn with a newfound appreciation for the responsibility

of being a star. "His first year he was saying, 'It's (then senior) Reggie Hanson's team,' " says Pitino. "Last year he was saying, 'It's the seniors' team.' Now he knows it's his team."

In three years Pitino — he is "Coach Patina" in the local inflection, a felicitous pronunciation in light of the aura he has helped restore in Lexington — has healed the long-strained relations between Kentucky and New York. After a point-shaving scandal was discovered at Kentucky in 1951, a former Wildcat coach Adolph Rupp blamed the wise guys who hung around the old Madison Square Garden for corrupting his players. Turning on Manhattan district attorney Frank Hogan, who prosecuted the case, and Judge Saul Streit, who wrote a scathing opinion holding Rupp accountable for the program's sins, the Baron vowed that Kentucky would never go back to the city. And it didn't until the 1976 N.I.T., which the Wildcats won a year before Rupp's death.

So there's irony in a New Yorker's restoring the up-tempo essence of basketball on which Rupp raised several generations of Kentuckians. "One thing this program needed was a sense of basketball as entertainment," says Pitino, whose two immediate predecessors, Sutton and Joe B. Hall, insisted on squeezing only the safest shot out of each possession. "When Kentucky won in the past, the feeling was too much one of 'Oh, we escaped.' Our games aren't life and death anymore. We get the fans to put their hands up when someone shoots a three-pointer. We choreograph chaos. Our style doesn't give our players time to think negative thoughts. And we try not to give the fans time, either. Joe B. Hall was a wonderful coach and is a wonderful man. But he probably doesn't like the pregame music we play."

Among Pitino's first public utterances upon taking the job was a comment that while he loved Kentucky, it would be heaven if he could only get some good Italian food. Soon thereafter he opened a restaurant just steps from Rupp Arena, called Bravo Pitino. While many old-timers would have a hard time imagining the Baron running a joint called How 'Bout That Adolph, Pitino at least has a leavening sense of humor that neither Sutton nor Hall had. More common is grumbling that Pitino doesn't genuflect to the sacred symbols of Kentucky's past. In *Full-Court Pressure*, his autobiographical account of last season (1991-92), Pitino notes that when Mashburn verbally committed to the school, he said only that he wanted to play for the Knick's coach. "So much for the glorious Kentucky tradition," Pitino writes. Sportswriter Dave Kindred, in a review for The Lexington Herald-Leader, was on him in a New York minute: "The overriding sense of this book is that Pitino came to poor ol' good for nothin' Kentucky and by the power of his talent changed lead into gold."

In fact, Pitino has scrubbed away an awful lot of tarnish awfully quickly, and most of the faithful freely credit him for doing so. The more serious risk Pitino runs may be found in a passage from the Bible that Rupp liked to cite as his guiding principle in recruit-

ing: "I will lift up mine eyes unto the hills, whence cometh my help." Pitino is an apostle of a radically different testament. He pledges to try to sign one player a year from the New York area. Tapping into a network of contacts that only a Manhattan-born, Queens-raised, Long Island-schooled coach could have, Pitino has been good to his word, starting with Mashburn. He followed that up last year by signing 6-foot-9 Andre Riddick, a sophomore from Bishop Loughlin High in Brooklyn, and this year by getting 6-foot-6 Roderick Rhodes, a freshman from St. Anthony High in Jersey City. Yet last spring Big Blue fans saw Pitino come within a tick's tooth of the Final Four with three eastern Kentuckians, John Pelphrey, Richie Farmer and Deron Feldhaus. "Write it down," says one longtime Kentucky sportswriter. "Pitino is going to be criticized for recruiting the top prospects in the nation, especially those in the New York area, instead of going after the Pelphreys, Farmers and Feldhauses of tomorrow. That won't go down well with all those who looked at last year's team and felt as if they were back in the 1940's and 50's, with Adolph winning with teams built around good ol' white boys from the Kentucky hills."

Pitino responds just as you would expect a New Yorker to: directly but shrewdly. "We'll always have a few Kentucky players as well as a few New York players," he says. "But my feeling is, if a Kentucky player isn't good enough to play here, let him go somewhere where he can — because Kentucky kids love the game too much."

If Pitino hadn't added that last sentence, you might soon detect some of that Kentucky passion curdling into resentment in places like Pikeville and Pineville and Prestonburgh. But the coach understands that basketball is one thing that can cause the jaws of yawning cultural difference to close shut. As Mashburn says, "Basketball means just about the same thing in New York and Kentucky. It's just that back home there are lots of other things, and down here it's the only thing."

Pitino coaches the game and Mashburn plays it just as it was conceived by Rupp and achieved by Issel. And that has made the 700 miles between Lexington and Lexington Avenue, in hoops terms, a gimme. Given that tough times have been commonplace in the Commonwealth of late, there's no passing up a gimme.

CHAPTER 53

Kentucky's rally from a 31-point deficit in the final 15 minutes to defeat L.S.U. was perhaps the finest in Wildcat history.

UK Rallies in Big Blue Bayou, 99-95

BY MARK COOMES
Special to The Courier-Journal

BATON ROUGE, Feb. 15, 1994 — And folks down here think Mardi Gras is wild. None of the liquor-laced shenanigans on Bourbon Street last night were any crazier than the University of Kentucky's basketball game with Louisiana State.

In what has to be one of the greatest comebacks ever in college basketball, the Wildcats rallied from a 31-point deficit with 15 minutes to play and beat L.S.U., 99-95. Walter McCarty's three-pointer with 19 seconds left gave UK a 96-95 lead, and L.S.U. blew two scoring chances while UK hit 3 of 4 free throws to ice the improbable victory.

L.S.U. (1-9, 5-6 in the Southeastern Conference) lost its third straight, while No. 11 UK (18-5, 7-3) broke a two-game losing streak. L.S.U., leading 48-32 at the half, tried to kill whatever the Cats' comeback hopes right away. Clarence Caesar scored nine points in an 18-0 run early in the second half that put L.S.U. up, 68-37, with 16 minutes still to play.

The Tigers had scored nine straight when UK's frustration boiled over. The officials didn't see senior Travis Ford grab Caesar around the ankles as he dove for a loose ball, but no one could miss Ford subsequently sprinting over to bring the hammer down on Andre Owens in mid-lay-up. Ford was whistled for an intentional foul and benched by UK coach Rick Pitino. Owens hit both free throws and Jamie Brandon nailed a three for a five-point play that seemingly buried UK for good.

To their credit, the Cats dug their way out of the grave. Reserve guard Chris Harrison scored eight points in a 24-4 run that slashed L.S.U.'s 31-point lead to 72-61 with 9:51 left. L.S.U. freshman Ronnie Henderson answered with a five-point burst, but it wasn't enough to give the Tigers enough breathing room to make it to the finish line.

The Cats trailed, 48-32, at intermission, their biggest halftime deficit of the season. Pitino could hardly watch. In fact he didn't even stick around to see McCarty, who had been fouled out as time expired, make the second of two free throws. After McCarty missed the first, Pitino spun on his heel and marched off toward the locker room.

L.S.U.'s long-range shooting show was enough to send anyone scurrying for cover. Three-pointers fell from the sky like Mardi Gras beads on Bourbon Street in the first half. The Tigers, whose previous season high was 12 three-pointers in an entire game, hit 9 of thirteen in the first 20 minutes alone.

Henderson was 6 of 7 and had 22 points in the period. After he hit three straight threes, the Wildcats decided they'd better start guarding him a little closer. Didn't matter. Henderson swished back-to-back bombs with Jared Prickett, then Roderick Rhodes, sticking a mitt in his face. Prickett, Rhodes and the other starters saw an unusual amount of pine times in the first half. Only Ford played more than 12 minutes, as reserves scored 22 of UK's first 25 points.

Backup center Gimel Martinez led the Cats in the half with 12 points. McCarty had 11 and hit 2 of 4 three-pointers — his first threes in nine games.

THE LINE-UPS

KENTUCKY (99)

	FG	FT	Pts.
Delk	3	1	9
Harrison	3	0	8
Ford	3	2	10
Riddick	4	1	9
Rhodes	3	4	11
Brassow	5	0	14
Sheppard	0	0	0
Epps	0	0	0
Prickett	1	0	2
McCarty	9	1	23
Martinez	6	1	13
Totals	**37**	**10**	**99**

L.S.U. (95)

	FG	FT	Pts.
Brendon	3	6	13
Owens	1	2	4
Gipson	0	0	0
Henderson	12	4	36
Burns	1	0	2
Ceasar	10	8	32
Titus	1	3	5
Roubtcheako	1	1	3
Totals	**29**	**24**	**95**

Walter McCarty, who scored 23 points in this memorable contest, hit a 3-pointer with 19 seconds left to put Kentucky ahead, 96-95.

Senior Jeff Brassow's 14-points led the Wildcats in their victory over L.S.U.

CHAPTER 54

Rick Pitino and his Wildcats celebrate their 1995 S.E.C. Tournament victory over Arkansas.

UK Reels in Arkansas in Super Sequel

BY MARK COOMES
Special to The Courier-Journal

ATLANTA, March 12, 1995 — The University of Kentucky released the final installment of a spellbinding trilogy yesterday, rallying from a 19-point deficit in regulation — then from nine behind in overtime — to edge defending national champion Arkansas, 95-93, in the Southeastern Conference Tournament final.

"It's the proudest moment of my coaching life," UK's Rick Pitino said.

"It was a great college basketball game," Arkansas coach Nolan Richardson said afterward. "It's too bad there was a loser."

Make it two thumbs up for "Die Hard 3," a spine-tingling sequel from the producers of "The Greatest Game Ever Played" and "The Greatest Comeback Ever Made." The three scripts share a preposterous central plot that is beyond even Steven Spielberg's wildest hoop dreams:

• March 28, 1992: Playing against Duke, another defending national champ, UK rallied from a 12-point deficit to take a 103-102 lead with 2.1 seconds left in overtime. The Cinderella story ended shy of the Final Four when Christian Laetttner sank one of the most famous shots in N.C.A.A. history.

• February 15, 1994: Visiting UK pulled off what was instantly hailed as the Miracle of Mardi Gras, erasing a 31-point lead in 15 minutes to nip Louisiana State, 99-95.

• March 12, 1995: The Wildcats proved again that college basketball routinely provides the best theater in the wide world of sports. The thrill of victory and the agony of defeat were somehow embodied by the same team on the same day.

Scene I: Arkansas hit 14 of its first 22 shots — including six three-pointers — to take a 35-16 lead with 9:24 left in the first half. After committing 11 turnovers in 11 minutes, the Cats appeared to be on the brink of utter breakdown.

They regained their composure by concentrating on Pitino's pregame mantra: "Never celebrate when you're down. It's the type of tempo and the type of team that you can come back on."

Scene II: Led by an unlikely boy hero, freshman forward Antoine Walker, the Cats clawed back by

THE LINE-UPS

KENTUCKY (95)

	FG	FT	Pts.
Rhodes	2	5	9
McCarty	5	1	11
Riddick	0	2	2
Delk	6	2	15
Sheppard	3	0	6
Pope	4	3	12
Epps	2	3	8
Walker	9	5	23
Prickett	2	3	7
Harrison	1	0	2
Totals	**34**	**24**	**95**

ARKANSAS (93)

	FG	FT	Pts.
Thurman	7	0	17
Williamson	9	4	22
Robinson	5	3	14
McDaniel	5	3	16
Beck	4	2	10
Wilson	1	0	2
Stewart	0	0	0
Dillard	1	0	3
Rimac	3	0	9
Garrett	0	0	0
Totals	**35**	**12**	**93**

halftime, hitting 11 of their last 16 shots. Walker scored eight points in the 28-15 run, but the big play came from point guard Anthony Epps.

With Arkansas senior Corey Beck barking insults in his face, the UK sophomore drove for a short jumper, drew a foul on Beck and sank a free throw with 2.8 seconds left that pulled UK within 50-44 at the half. Epps dashed off the floor yelling over his shoulder at his stunned tormentor.

Scene III: Just 68 seconds into the second half, forward Roderick Rhodes barged into the lane and drew his third foul. He was replaced by Walker, who scored 15 points over the next 24 minutes. He finished with a career-high 23 points and the tournament m.v.p. award.

"I never dreamed he would step up the way he did," Epps said. "If it wasn't for him, we wouldn't be in here celebrating."

Rhodes, who led UK with nine points in the first half, played only four more minutes, including five fateful seconds at the end of regulation. "I had to go with the hot player," Pitino said.

Tony Delk (00) reaches for a Razorback rebound.

Scene IV: Arkansas forward Scotty Thurman, who scored 15 points in the first half, hit just 1 of 8 shots the rest of the way, placing the scoring load squarely on the broad shoulders of all-American forward Corliss Williamson. He delivered a team-high 22 points, including a fast-break dunk that staked Arkansas to a 72-60 lead, its largest of the second half.

Epp's three-pointer, triggered a 13-4 spurt that trimmed the margin to 76-73, and two Mark Pope free throws made it 80-all with 22 seconds left.

The Hogs went inside to Williamson, but his pass was swiped by Walker, who called a time-out with 5.5 seconds left. Pitino reinserted Rhodes, who had sat for nine minutes. He drove the lane and drew a two-shot foul. Barely a second remained and Arkansas decided to test Rhodes' nerves with a time-out and some sarcastically polite taunting.

It worked.

"Beck and (Dwight) Stewart tried to shake my hand; they were trying to psych me out, I guess," Rhodes said. "And I was a little tight."

Rhodes, a 78 percent foul shooter (fifth-best in the S.E.C.), missed the first shot long. The second barely grazed the rim. Williamson snared the rebound and waited for overtime.

Distraught, Rhodes returned to the bench, where he cried into a towel and waited for a second chance he would not get. "I told Rod to keep his head up," Walker said. "We'd win it for him."

Scene V: UK opened overtime by missing four of its first five shots, including two long three-pointers by leading scorer Tony Delk. Arkansas scored on its first five possessions and took a 91-82 lead with 1:39 remaining.

Over the next 80 seconds, the Hogs committed a turnover and hit just 2 of 6 free throws. The stage was now set for Kentucky's winning rally.

Walter McCarty converted a three-point play, and after two free throws by Arkansas' Clint McDaniel, Delk swished a three-pointer and Walker hit a lay-up that made it 93-92.

Seconds later, Epps stole a pass, drew a foul and stepped to the line with 19 ticks remaining. A record crowd of 30,067 at the Georgia Dome paused to wonder what might be running through Rhodes' troubled mind.

"My life," he said. "I was praying that they went in."

Epps swished both shots and put UK ahead, 94-93. But there was one last hope for Arkansas and one awful hurdle for UK. With four seconds left, the ball belonged to Thurman, the man who hit the shot that beat Duke for the national title last season and drained the jumper that nipped Kentucky, 94-92, in January. With Walk-

Freshman forward Antoine Walker (24) drives for 2 of his 23 points against Arkansas.

er crouched close to his face, college basketball's best last-second assassin leaned back and fired a 22-footer.

It banged off the rim and into the arms of Delk. Pitino then sprinted across court and into the arms of Epps. The party was postponed long enough for Delk to hit 1 of 2 free throws with 6 seconds left that gave UK its fourth straight S.E.C. Tournament title.

A puffy-eyed Rhodes stared into the heavens and gave silent thanks. He had escaped in the final reel — of Part III, at least.

University of Kentucky Basketball
All-Time Teams

1930-1945

First Team

Position	Player	Year
Guard	Ellis Johnson	1933
Guard	Mickey Rouse	1940
Center	Leroy Edwards	1935
Forward	Forest Sale	1933
Forward	Dave Lawrence	1935

Second Team

Position	Player	Year
Guard	Bernie Opper	1939
Guard	Lee Huber	1941
Center	John DeMoisey	1934
Forward	Ralph Carlisle	1937
Forward	Marvin Akers	1943

Honorable Mention

Position	Player	Year
Guard	Bill Davis	1934
Guard	Warfield Donohue	1937
Center	Jim King	1942
Forward	Ermal Allen	1942
Forward	Jack Tingle	1947

1946-1995

First Team

Position	Player	Year
Guard	Ralph Beard	1949
Guard	Kyle Macy	1980
Center	Dan Issel	1970
Forward	Jamal Mashburn	1993
Forward	Wallace Jones	1949

Second Team

Position	Player	Year
Guard	Louie Dampier	1967
Guard	Frank Ramsey	1954
Center	Alex Groza	1949
Forward	Kevin Grevey	1975
Forward	Cotton Nash	1964

Honorable Mention

Position	Player	Year
Guard	Vernon Hatton	1958
Guard	Rex Chapman	1988
Center	Bill Spivey	1951
Forward	Kenny Walker	1986
Forward	Cliff Hagan	1954

* - Jack Tingle played at UK in 1944, 1945, 1946 and 1947, thus qualifying for the 1930-45 All-Time Team.

Editor's Note: *Player listings are chronological by position with final varsity season indicated.*

	Date	Opponent	Place	Result	Score
1.	Dec. 18, 1930	Georgetown (Ky.)	Lexington, Ky.	Won	67-19
2.	Jan. 8, 1935	N.Y.U.	New York, N.Y.	Lost	22-23
3.	Jan 5, 1937	Notre Dame	Louisville, Ky	Lost	28-41
4.	Dec. 29, 1937	Pittsburgh	New Orleans, La.	Won	29-40
5.	Feb. 14, 1938	Marquette	Lexington, Ky.	Won	35-33
6.	March 20, 1942	Illinois	New Orleans, La.	Won	46-44
7.	Jan. 4, 1943	Ft. Knox	Lexington, Ky.	Won	64-30
8.	Jan. 23, 1943	Notre Dame	Louisville, Ky.	Won	60-55
9.	Dec. 30, 1943	St. John's	New York, N.Y.	Won	44-38
10.	March 16, 1946	Arizona	New York, N.Y.	Won	77-53
11.	March 18, 1946	West Virginia	New York, N.Y.	Won	59-51
12.	March 20, 1946	Rhode Island	New York, N.Y.	Won	46-45
13.	March 24, 1947	Utah	New York, N.Y.	Lost	45-49
14.	March 18, 1948	Columbia	New York, N.Y.	Won	76-53
15.	March 20, 1948	Holy Cross	New York, N.Y.	Won	60-52
16.	March 23, 1948	Baylor	New York, N.Y.	Won	58-42
17.	March 27, 1948	Louisville	New York, N.Y.	Won	91-57
18.	March 31, 1948	Phillips Oilers	New York, N.Y.	Lost	49-53
19.	August 13, 1948	France	London, England	Won	65-21
20.	March 21, 1949	Villanova	New York, N.Y.	Won	85-72
21.	March 22, 1949	Illinois	New York, N.Y.	Won	76-47
22.	March 26, 1949	Oklahoma A&M	Seattle, Wash.	Won	46-36
23.	March 14, 1950	C.C.N.Y.	New York, N.Y.	Lost	50-89
24.	Dec. 1, 1950	West Texas	Lexington, Ky.	Won	73-43
25.	Dec. 16, 1950	Kansas	Lexington, Ky.	Won	68-39
26.	March 20, 1951	Louisville	Raleigh, N.C.	Won	79-68
27.	March 22, 1951	St. John's	New York, N.Y.	Won	59-43
28.	March 24, 1951	Illinois	New York, N.Y.	Won	76-74
29.	March 27, 1951	Kansas State	Minneapolis, Minn.	Won	68-58
30.	Dec. 17, 1951	St. John's	Lexington, Ky.	Won	81-40
31.	Dec. 26, 1951	U.C.L.A.	Lexington, Ky.	Won	84-53
32.	Dec. 22, 1953	La Salle	Lexington, Ky.	Won	73-60
33.	March 9, 1954	L.S.U.	Nashville, Tenn.	Won	63-56
34.	Jan. 8, 1955	Georgia Tech	Lexington, Ky.	Lost	58-59
35.	Feb. 27, 1956	Georgia	Louisville, Ky.	Won	143-66
36.	Dec. 7, 1957	Temple	Lexington, Ky.	Won	85-83
37.	March 14, 1958	Miami (Ohio)	Lexington, Ky.	Won	94-70
38.	March 15, 1958	Notre Dame	Lexington, Ky.	Won	89-56
39.	March 21, 1958	Temple	Louisville, Ky.	Won	61-60
40.	March 22, 1958	Seattle	Louisville, Ky.	Won	84-72

University of Kentucky's
100 Greatest Basketball Games (1930-1995)

Date		Opponent	Place	Result	Score
41.	Dec. 20, 1958	West Virginia	Lexington, Ky.	Won	97-91
42.	March 13, 1959	Louisville	Evanston, Ill.	Lost	61-76
43.	Dec. 28, 1959	Ohio State	Lexington, Ky.	Won	96-93
44.	Dec. 31, 1963	Duke	New Orleans, La.	Won	81-79
45.	March 11, 1966	Dayton	Iowa City, Iowa	Won	86-79
46.	March 12, 1966	Michigan	Iowa City, Iowa	Won	84-77
47.	March 18, 1966	Duke	College Park, Md.	Won	83-79
48.	March 19, 1966	Texas Western	College Park, Md.	Lost	65-72
49.	March 6, 1967	Alabama	Lexington, Ky.	Won	110-78
50.	Jan. 15, 1968	Georgia	Lexington, Ky.	Won	104-73
51.	Jan. 18, 1969	Tennessee	Knoxville, Tenn.	Won	69-66
52.	Dec. 8, 1969	North Carolina	Louisville, Ky.	Won	94-87
53.	Feb 28, 1970	Vanderbilt	Lexington, Ky.	Won	90-86
54.	March 9, 1972	Tennessee	Knoxville, Tenn.	Won	67-66
55.	March 18, 1972	Florida State	Dayton, Ohio	Lost	54-73
56.	Dec. 9, 1974	North Carolina	Louisville, Ky.	Won	90-78
57.	March 22, 1975	Indiana	Dayton, Ohio	Won	92-90
58.	March 31, 1975	U.C.L.A.	San Diego, Calif.	Lost	85-92
59.	March 6, 1976	Alabama	Lexington, Ky.	Won	90-85
60.	March 8, 1976	Mississippi State	Lexington, Ky.	Won	94-93
61.	March 21, 1976	U.N.C.C.	New York, N.Y.	Won	71-67
62.	Nov. 27, 1976	Wisconsin	Lexington, Ky.	Won	72-64
63.	March 11, 1978	Florida State	Knoxville, Tenn	Won	85-76
64.	March 16, 1978	Miami (Ohio)	Dayton, Ohio	Won	91-69
65.	March 18, 1978	Michigan State	Dayton, Ohio	Won	52-49
66.	March 25, 1978	Arkansas	St. Louis, Mo.	Won	64-59
67.	March 27, 1978	Duke	St. Louis, Mo.	Won	94-88
68.	Dec. 9, 1978	Kansas	Lexington, Ky.	Won	67-66
69.	Dec. 30, 1978	Notre Dame	Louisville, Ky.	Won	81-76
70.	March 1, 1981	L.S.U.	Lexington, Ky.	Won	73-71
71.	March 26, 1983	Louisville	Knoxville, Tenn	Lost	68-80
72.	Nov. 26, 1983	Louisville	Lexington, Ky.	Won	65-44
73.	Jan. 22, 1984	Houston	Lexington, Ky.	Won	74-67
74.	March 10, 1984	Auburn	Nashville, Tenn.	Won	51-49
75.	March 22, 1984	Louisville	Lexington, Ky.	Won	72-67
76.	March 24, 1984	Illinois	Lexington, Ky.	Won	54-51
77.	March 31, 1984	Georgetown	Seattle, Wash.	Lost	40-53
78.	March 16, 1985	U.N.L.V.	Salt Lake City, Utah	Won	64-61
79.	March 22, 1985	St. John's	Denver, Colo.	Lost	70-86
80.	Dec. 28, 1985	Louisville	Lexington, Ky.	Won	69-64

University of Kentucky's
100 Greatest Basketball Games (1930-1995)

Date		Opponent	Place	Result	Score
81.	March 20, 1986	Alabama	Atlanta, Ga.	Won	68-63
82.	March 22, 1986	L.S.U.	Atlanta, Ga.	Lost	57-59
83.	Dec. 27, 1986	Louisville	Louisville, Ky.	Won	85-51
84.	Feb. 29, 1987	Oklahoma	Lexington, Ky.	Won	75-74
85.	Nov. 28, 1989	Ohio	Lexington, Ky.	Won	76-73
86.	Feb. 15, 1990	L.S.U.	Lexington, Ky.	Won	100-95
87.	Feb 26, 1991	Alabama	Lexington, Ky.	Won	79-73
88.	March 2, 1991	Auburn	Lexington, Ky.	Won	114-93
89.	Dec. 7, 1991	Indiana	Indianapolis, Ind.	Won	76-74
90.	March 15, 1992	Alabama	Birmingham, Ala.	Won	80-54
91.	March 28, 1992	Duke	Philadelphia, Pa.	Lost	103-104
92.	March 14, 1993	L.S.U.	Lexington, Ky.	Won	82-65
93.	March 19, 1993	Rider	Nashville, Tenn.	Won	96-52
94.	March 21, 1993	Utah	Nashville, Tenn.	Won	83-62
95.	March 25, 1993	Wake Forest	Charlotte, N.C.	Won	103-69
96.	March 27, 1993	Florida State	Charlotte, N.C.	Won	106-81
97.	April 3, 1993	Michigan	New Orleans, La.	Lost	78-81
98.	Feb. 15, 1994	L.S.U.	Baton Rouge, La.	Won	99-95
99.	March 11, 1995	Arkansas	Memphis, Tenn.	Won	90-78
100.	March 12, 1995	Florida	Memphis, Tenn.	Won	73-60

ABOUT THE PUBLISHER

ADCRAFT SPORTS MARKETING, headquartered in Louisville, Ky. with offices located in West Palm Beach, Miami and Chicago, is an innovative national sports marketing company. Utilizing video, television, publishing, promotional marketing and public relations, AdCraft continues to be at the forefront of all intercollegiate sports and selected professional sports.

AdCraft has recently released *The Nebraska Football Legacy*, a coffee-table-styled book which chronicles the storied 100-plus year history of the Nebraska Cornhusker football program, and *Hail to the Victors...Greatest Moments in Michigan Football History*, a book and video boxed gift set on the legendary University of Michigan Wolverines.

From its beginning in 1977, AdCraft has been led by Roy C. Hamlin Jr., the company's president. The publishing division is headed by Bob Roller, AdCraft's vice president.

PHOTO CREDITS

David Coyle: Front Cover (Mashburn), vii, ix, 126, 128, 130, 135, 140, 141, 147, 149, 150, 159, 161, 165, 168, 170, 174, 177, 183, 185, 186, 190, 191, 194-both, 195, 198, 199, 201, 202, 203, 204-all, 205, 206, 208, 209, 210, 212, 213

Ralph Beard Collection: 30

The Courier-Journal: Front Cover (Pitino), 27-both, 85, 90, 115, 120, 121, 136, 155, 166, 188, 189, 196, 200

The Herald-Leader: 56

Russell Rice Collection: 41, 43, 45, 46, 52, 79

Time Inc.: 77

University of Kentucky Archives: 8, 9, 11, 14, 20, 38, 42, 49, 54, 61, 68, 70, 71, 72, 74, 76-top, 78, 80, 86, 87, 89, 92, 96, 133, 134, Back Cover (both)

University of Kentucky Athletic Department: Front Cover (Macy, Hall, Fabulous Five), 1, 2, 3, 4, 5, 6, 10, 12, 13, 15-both, 16, 17, 19, 24, 25, 28-both, 34, 35, 39, 44, 48, 50, 53, 55, 57, 59, 60, 62, 63, 64, 65, 67, 75, 76-bottom, 81, 82, 83, 88, 94, 97, 98, 100, 101, 103, 104, 106, 107, 109, 112, 113, 114, 116, 117, 119, 122, 123, 124-both, 131, 132, 137, 139, 142, 143, 144, 146, 151, 154, 157, 158, 162, 171, 175, 176, 181, 184, 192, 211

Wide World Photo: 18, 22, 26, 33, 37, 40, 99, 102, 105, 152